Playing in Peoria

Also by MATTHEW STEVENSON

Letters of Transit:
Essays on Travel, History, Politics and Family Life Abroad

Mentioned in Dispatches

An April Across America

Rules of the Game:
The Best Sports Writing of Harper's Magazine
(EDITOR)

Remembering the Twentieth Century Limited

Whistle-Stopping America

Reading the Rails

Appalachia Spring

The Revolution as a Dinner Party

Biking with Bismarck

Our Man in Iran

Donald Trump's Circus Maximus and
Joe Biden's Excellent Adventure

The View from Churchill

Friends of a Kind

Playing in Peoria

From Abraham Lincoln to Warren Harding
by bicycle, train, and bus

by Matthew Mills Stevenson

Odysseus Books

PLAYING IN PEORIA

ISBN-13 (paperback): 979-8-9896654-1-9
ISBN-13 (eBook): 979-8-9896654-2-6

First edition. Manufactured in the United States.

For fulfillment information, address:
Odysseus Books c/o Pathway Book Service,
34 Production Avenue, Keene New Hampshire 03431.
Toll free: 1-800-345-6665. E-mail: pbs@pathwaybook.com

Please visit the book's website: www.odysseusbooks.com

To contact the author on any matter, such as to arrange a speaking engagement, please use: matthewstevenson@sunrise.ch.
Author website is: www.matthewmstevenson.com

Edited by Doreen Russo and David Aretha.
Cover and book design by Nanette Stevenson.
Cartography by Mapping Solutions, Anchorage, Alaska.

Library of Congress Cataloging-in-Publication Data
Stevenson, Matthew Mills, 1954–author.
Playing in Peoria / by Matthew Mills Stevenson.
p. cm. (Odysseus Books)
ISBN-13: 979-8-9896654-1-9 (cloth: alk. paper)
1. Stevenson, Matthew Mills, 1954—American History—Abraham Lincoln to Warren Harding. 2. American travels in the Midwest.
3. Presidential history 1860–1923.

---

10 9 8 7 6 5 4 3 2 1

This book is dedicated to

LAURA, AMY, MONET, ANNE-LOUISE, NANCY,

TOM, MARK, and LEE,

who joined me, from time to time, in my New York searches for

Teddy Roosevelt, Chester Arthur, and Ulysses S. Grant.

"Forgive me for pointing. . ."

And to

MARTIN MENDELSOHN, MARK MEDISH, and GREGORY FEIFER:

American history never had better guardians.

Contents

Introduction

Blame it on the bike.

For my birthday in the springtime, I received a Brompton folding bicycle, the kind that snaps to the size of a suitcase once you get the hang of the internal springs. What prompted such generosity from my family were my many complaints about how hard it is to travel with a full-sized bicycle. For years I had been traveling around nearby France (we live near the border in Switzerland) and struggling with a myriad of regulations that govern how European train companies treat or (as I insisted) mistreat cyclists. Now all I needed was a place to take it.

For my destination, I decided to travel overland—so to speak—from Chicago to New York, and to leave as soon as the airfares came down from their summer highs, in mid-September. I didn't plan to ride the entire distance, but would navigate with trains and buses, and use the Brompton for "the last kilometer," which in my case meant local transport.

I also knew I wanted to write something about America in the late nineteenth century, and I eventually decided to travel along the political roads that stretch from Abraham Lincoln to Warren Harding, a path that might connect a republic to an empire.

What dictated where I would go exactly were the books on my shelves. For several years I had been doing extensive, if varied, reading on the subject of American history between the start of the American Civil War and the turn of the twentieth century. I had books about the presidential elections of 1876 and 1880, biographies of Chester Arthur and Ulysses S. Grant, and several obscure volumes about Williams Jennings Bryan and the gold standard. My wife grew tired of my stale joke that often began our dinners: "Do you have any thoughts on bimetallism?"

By spending hours with a *National Geographic Road Atlas, Russell's Official National Motor Coach Guide* (how's that for a page-turner?), the Amtrak national timetable, and pages from the Internet, I figured out that I could land in Chicago, take the train into central Illinois, and turn east at Lincoln's Springfield. From there I could trace a line of bus and bike rides to Terre Haute (home of Eugene V. Debs), Indianapolis (home of President Benjamin Harrison), Ohio (loaded with dead presidents, including Rutherford B. Hayes), Buffalo (where William McKinley met his maker at the hands of an assassin), and finally Elmira, New York, where Mark Twain finished *Adventures of Huckleberry Finn*. From upstate New York, it would be easy to catch a train to New York City, which was home over time to the likes of Grant and Arthur.

In one sense it would be a political odyssey to the people and places that had shaped American politics in the late nineteenth century. At the same time, I decided to widen the scope of the road to include some writers as well, so I could take in Hannibal, Missouri—where Mark Twain grew up as Samuel Clemens—and Theodore Dreiser's birthplace in Indiana.

During the summer and early fall, the planning consumed many hours of my time, although never unpleasantly.

In the process, I was able to discover the dead ends before leaving (at least when I factored the bike or bus schedules into the equation).

Often I would check and recheck bus connections, hoping that if I just stared hard enough at the small print I would find a connection leaving when I wanted. But not only was I bumping up against America's car-only culture (many asked: "Why don't you just drive?"), I was also learning that even the country's few remaining public transportation options have given up on the rural United States. Greyhound is now largely an intercity bus business, and Amtrak mostly wanders the landscape to drop off congressional subsidies, not passengers.

In the end I decided to plug several gaps in my travel planning with two rental cars—one from Springfield to Terre Haute, and another from Dayton, Ohio, to Cleveland, so that I could also take in, across Ohio, such smaller towns and cities as Hamilton, Georgetown, Marion, Fremont, Oberlin, Akron, and Kent. I felt as if I were surrendering.

I cannot say now, some months later, that I loved all the travel aspects of this trip. My memory is of bus departures at 6:05 a.m. or of Amtrak trains hopelessly delayed. I did like it that the buses, for the most part, were nearly empty, and that, at the very least, I could buy coffee and food on the trains. To me the rental cars were a sealed tomb, from which my only connection with the outside world was the kind of talk radio that has Rush Limbaugh or Bill O'Reilly bemoaning how "they" killed General George Patton. Next time I will subscribe to some audiobooks.

Part of the reason that I picked a route across the Rust Belt is that I also wanted to see many of the cities that have become casualties of post-industrialization. Not since the 1980s had I been to Buffalo, Cleveland, or Binghamton, and only on fleeting visits in the 1990s had I been to Chicago or St. Louis. All have suffered since factory America closed its doors or shifted its production to Mexico or Asia, and I wanted to see, especially on the bike, what it looks like on the ground in places like Dayton and Indianapolis.

My last good look at many of these cities actually came in the 1960s, when I was in grade school and would often travel across the heartland with my father, whose work was to sell sugar. During breaks from school, my sisters and I would join him—always by train—on trips that would begin in Cincinnati or St. Louis, and carry us west toward Denver or south to Atlanta. Mostly we took night trains between his meetings, and that meant by the time I was in high school, I knew well such cities as Detroit, Omaha, and Kansas City.

After moving to Europe in 1991 and long after American passenger trains had become a rolling bureaucracy, I found it harder to visit the cities of my railroad childhood. On this occasion, I decided that the bike would be a perfect way to navigate cities that I remembered as flat, often somber, filled with warehouses and steel mills. At least they would stand up well as the backdrop to my reading, especially if the subjects were Mark Hanna or William Dean Howells.

Did I find what I was looking for? Yes and no. I loved biking, often after dark, through Indian summer nights and across the heartland. I warmed to such out-of-the-way cities as Quincy, Illinois, and Elmira, New York, especially when the landscape could connect me to the words of the Lincoln-Douglas debates or the memoirs of Mark Twain. (Alas, Twain's Hannibal is as mythical as Jesus's Jerusalem—a place where each might have lived, but which only came alive, later, in literature.)

Odd as it may sound, I liked sleeping with a bike at the foot of my bed, knowing that at any hour I could slip on my helmet and explore outside my door. Even now, I remember vividly my midnight ride past the prison in Auburn, New York ("We'll leave the klieg lights on"), and finding the high school that novelist Kurt Vonnegut attended in Indianapolis. ("True terror," he said, "is to wake up one morning and discover that your high school class is running the country.")

The better part of the often-late travels was that I had countless hours to devote to my books. I like reading while in motion. Not just on the transatlantic flights, but on local trains and buses, I read books about Lincoln, Grant, Debs, Dreiser, or whomever, and they became my seat companions.

Mostly what I loved in my travels were my many meetings, arranged over the weeks and months preceding my departure. I met writers and radio journalists, a former US senator, professors and historians, not to mention a panoply of friends and acquaintances. I taped some conversations on my handheld digital recorder. With others I simply took notes or listened, and later wrote down my impressions. And part of the trip connected me with childhood friends.

My boyhood friend Rob Koch steered me in the direction of the infamous Haymarket Square. In Chagrin Falls,

Ohio, I had lunch with a teacher from my high school who taught a memorable course, Topics in Alienation, that required the reading of *Portnoy's Complaint* and, if memory serves, a lot of Kafka. In the early 1970s, everyone was alienated from something.

Nearly every conversation ended with me wanting to go farther down the road or to yet another book that I needed to read.

Only later did I realize that the America I was looking for was long out of print. It vanished in the late 1960s, about the time I stopped riding trains with my father, or in the 1980s, when the republic of letters turned into a complex, concrete web that links airports and air-conditioned malls with suburban office spaces and interstate highways.

In present-day America, someone on a folding bike with a fistful of bus tickets might well be a wandering monk of the thirteenth century, trying to walk across Flanders with a mule. Most of the rail and bus stations that I passed through had the feel of halfway houses with dim lighting, broken vending machines, and garbled announcements about connections in the underworld.

Only in my reading, snatched over coffee in Indianapolis or on the train in Cleveland, did I find the country I was looking for, but then most of what I read was written fifty or a hundred years ago. Twain wrote his *Autobiography of Mark Twain* in the early 1900s; Dreiser finished his *A Hoosier Holiday* in 1916.

At least the trip worked as an exercise in memory, although most evenings my legs were more tired than my mind. In Indiana, I was reminded of Robert Kennedy's 1968 primary victory in the presidential election. Until I got to Kent and its state university, I had forgotten the internal anger over the Vietnam War, and across Ohio I recalled the parade of presidents who had formed the core of my junior and senior high school classes in American history.

In that sense, my travels felt like an endless browse through a used bookstore or a library, where I could not only remove books from the shelves but look around and see where Ernest Hemingway grew up or William McKinley had died. I know so-called enhanced books (on things like Kindles and iPads) allow video to be embedded into the text. Here I preferred to make my own illustrations of the mind, so that my reading would come alive, or, later on, I would be able to remember the places that I had marked in many passages.

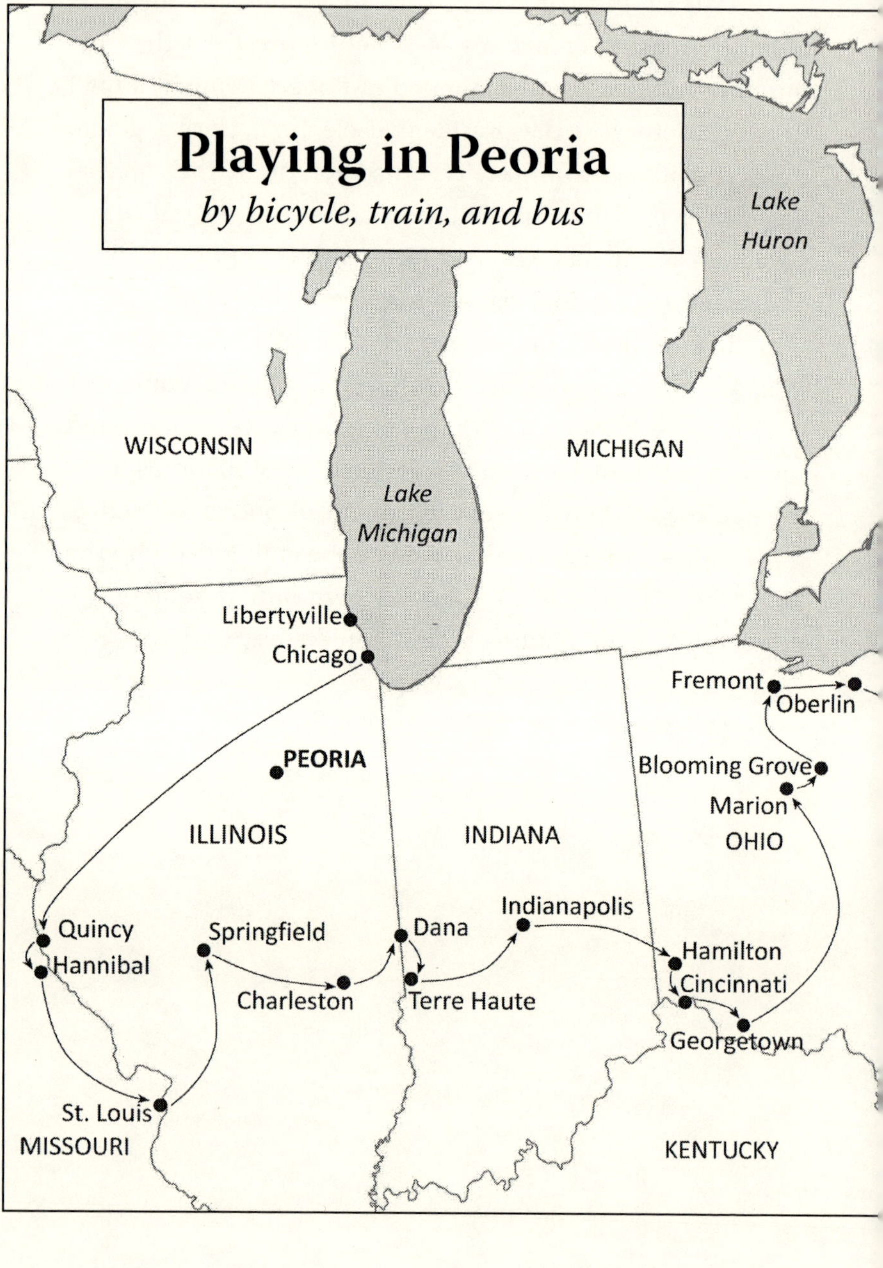

Playing in Peoria
by bicycle, train, and bus
Lake Huron
WISCONSIN
MICHIGAN
Lake Michigan
Libertyville
Chicago
Fremont
Oberlin
PEORIA
Blooming Grove
Marion
ILLINOIS
INDIANA
OHIO
Indianapolis
Quincy
Springfield
Dana
Hamilton
Hannibal
Cincinnati
Charleston
Terre Haute
Georgetown
St. Louis
MISSOURI
KENTUCKY

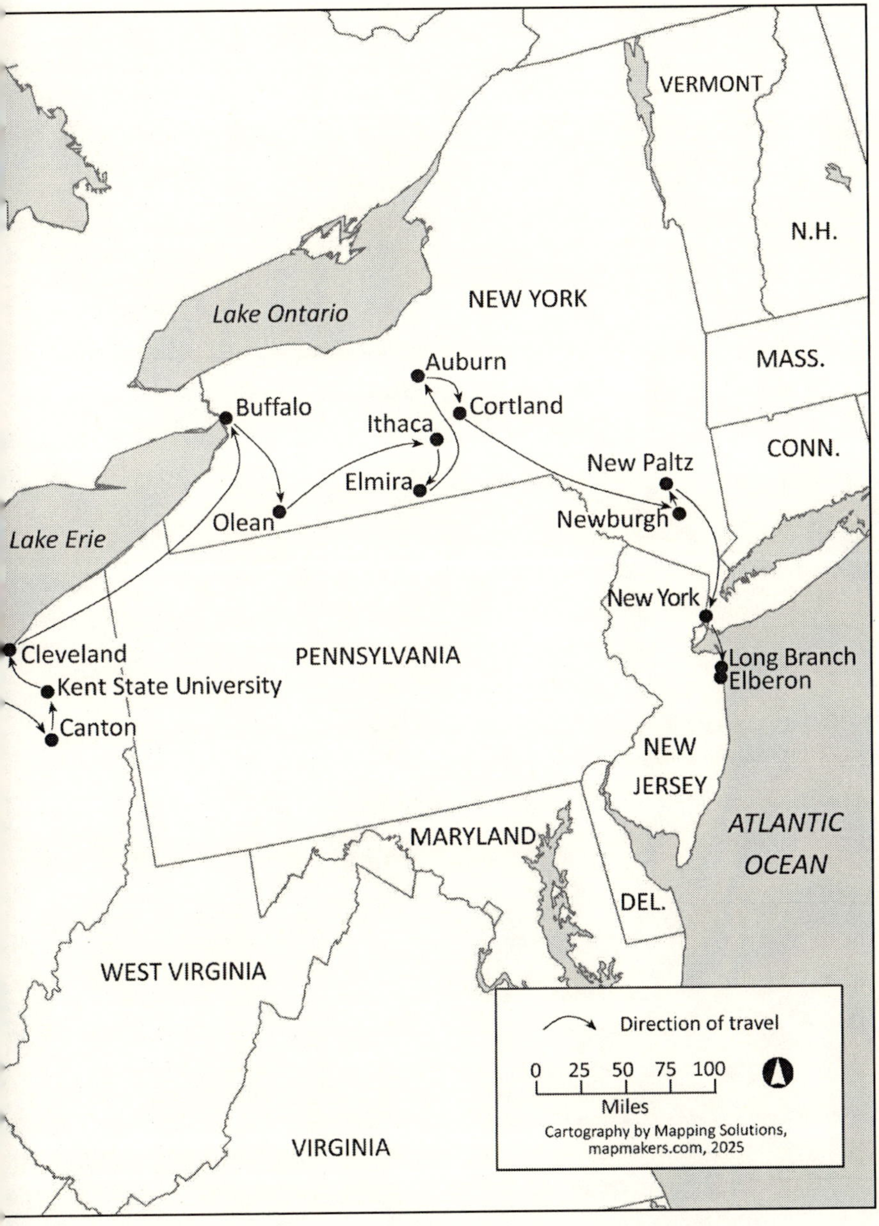
VERMONT
N.H.
MASS.
CONN.
NEW YORK
Lake Ontario
Auburn
Cortland
Buffalo
Ithaca
New Paltz
Elmira
Olean
Newburgh
Lake Erie
New York
Cleveland
PENNSYLVANIA
Long Branch
Elberon
Kent State University
Canton
NEW JERSEY
ATLANTIC OCEAN
MARYLAND
DEL.
WEST VIRGINIA
VIRGINIA
Direction of travel
0 25 50 75 100
Miles
Cartography by Mapping Solutions, mapmakers.com, 2025

"I find America so cheerful, and so full of swagger and self-satisfaction, that I hardly know it."

—Henry Adams

"I wasn't on the high road between Binghamton and Elmira at all but in some happy land that hadn't anything to do with motoring—a land of youth and affection."

—Theodore Dreiser

"You have to see it, hear it, smell it, taste it, or, you forget it."

—William Dean Howells

"Ever bike? Now that's something that makes life worth living!"

—Jack London

Playing in Peoria

Chicago, Illinois: Bike-in-a-Box

Before leaving home in Geneva, I packed everything I needed into two small bags—one like a briefcase that fit under the handlebars and the other a small pack that nestled on the bicycle's aft rack. Since the briefcase had my computer, Kindle, many wires, maps, pens, and books, my few extra clothes were in the rear pack, and they amounted to what a cowboy might have wrapped in a red bandana. I had changes of socks and underwear, some drip-dry undershirts, and a rain jacket, and I figured that I could wash clothes when I stopped to see friends or in the motel at night.

The bike and one bag I fitted into a cardboard box that I swaddled in packing tape, labeled extensively, and checked onto flights that went to Chicago's O'Hare by way of Amsterdam. I had chosen KLM for my outbound flight, on the hope that the Dutch might treat a bicycle in transit better than, say, the French, and, later, when I unwrapped the box in an airport parking lot, I found that everything had survived the flight in good order—save for one cable that had disconnected amid all the vibrations.

For the eight-hour flight, I was consigned to the middle seat of a crowded row, which, to use the English expression, allowed little room to swing a cat. Next to me was one of the few endlessly chatty Frenchmen I have ever met. Normally the traveling French nod to their seatmates and carry on with *Le Monde* or some magazine story about the failed marriages of the French president. But this one, who now lived near Chicago, had somehow absorbed the chatty American monologue, and for about an hour he talked nonstop about growing up in Lyon, working for Michelin, how his sister managed to buy a house, and transatlantic environmentalism (Europe prefers to clean water, while the US does better at improving air). I nodded for about an hour and then, with no place to turn, retreated into the in-flight movies.

For my airplane book, I had a short biography, *Hemingway Lives! Why Reading Ernest Hemingway Matters Today* by Clancy Sigal. Although my friend Gene Schulman in Geneva had given me a bound copy, I had downloaded the e-book to my Kindle, to save on weight and space. As it turned out, I could not have managed to turn pages in my cramped seat, but I could hold up the Kindle to the light and read the book, which was of interest to me because in Chicago I wanted to visit the house in suburban Oak Park where Hemingway was born and grew up.

Hemingway proved a more companionable seatmate than my Michelin man, and I spent the last four hours of the flight following Hemingway around the world. Sigal introduces him this way:

> This chest-thumping Hemingway is real enough. But there's another quieter side to him too: bookish, bespectacled (due to hereditary bad eyes), generous to young writers, a literary explorer armed only with a #2 pencil and a Royal Corona #3 typewriter, who risked his life and mind trailblazing uncharted territory that should have been marked, as on medieval maps, "Here Be Dragons." After publication of his first novel, *The Sun Also Rises,* a reviewer wrote in the *Atlantic* that Hemingway "writes as if he had never read anybody's writing, as if he had fashioned the art of writing himself."

Rob Koch was there to meet me at O'Hare. He came on his own bike, when he heard I was bringing the Brompton. For Homeland Security reasons he was forced to leave his bike in a distant parking lot, so that instead of unpacking my cardboard box in the terminal, we dragged it on a shuttle bus that left us near some rental car agencies.

There I unwrapped the box and, in a few minutes, unfolded the frame and attached the travel bags. In no time we were headed east on Higgins Boulevard, which was so congested with traffic and construction that after a while we retreated to the sidewalk. In about forty minutes, we found his house on North Sayre Avenue, in a neighborhood called Harwood Heights. Rob said as we weaved through back alleys and side streets: "We don't have to worry about crime. Our neighbors are all police and firemen."

Although I am ten years older than Rob, we had grown up together outside New York City, on Long Island. Our parents had been best of friends, and we spent many Thanksgivings and Christmases together. His father had taught me how to sail and play chess. In summers I had sailed with him on the waters of Long Island Sound, to places like Block Island and Martha's Vineyard (then just another island in New England, now a playground for presidents).

From Rob's mother, Mardo, I learned about books and laughter. Not only did she read incessantly and critically, but many afternoons when I got home from school, she was in our kitchen, having a glass of wine with my mother. I didn't always join the conversation, but often I did, and then I would listen to Mardo spin through the headlines or neighborhood gossip as if she were a cast member of *Saturday Night Live*.

For the weekend in Chicago, Rob and I had mapped out an itinerary with the car and bikes. On Saturday, I wanted to visit the grave site where his father was buried, but also the Chicago suburb of Libertyville, which was near where both his parents had grown up and the home of Adlai Stevenson II, the Illinois governor who ran for president twice in the 1950s. While prowling around the Internet, I had discovered that his house was now a center of democracy and a museum, and a letter I had written to the curator was answered by the governor's son, Adlai Stevenson III (himself a former US senator), encouraging me to visit the house. On Sunday, we planned a long bike ride across Chicago—from Hemingway's and Frank Lloyd Wright's Oak Park to the South Side, where we planned to wander through the now defunct stockyards to the University of Chicago. And if the schedule worked out, we would see the senator and his wife, Nancy, for drinks one evening.

Locking my bike to a fence in the backyard, I met for the first time Rob's wife, Donna, whom I liked immediately. For each it was a second marriage, and, feeling a bit like one of Rob's older brothers, I was pleased that he had made such a good match. Donna worked for a nearby multinational company and spent much of her free time with her extended Chicago family, which included two daughters from her first marriage. She spoke effortlessly about many Chicago neighborhoods, as siblings and cousins lived in many of them, and answered all of my questions about the Daley family (the mayor's line, that is) and possible museums to visit. She wasn't going to tour with us on the bikes, but she liked the idea that

I would be spending time with Rob (whom I don't see much anymore), and, in between, she put together some of the best meals I had on the trip. (As I first entered the kitchen, he said: "We don't eat food that's been in boxes.") That first night we grilled steaks and vegetables in the backyard and lingered over a California wine until I said: "I have to go to bed. Where I came from, it's six in the morning."

Barrington:
Lester Always Hated Being Cold

DESPITE STAYING AWAKE UNTIL 11 P.M., I was up early with jet lag, and as the sun was out and warm, I took a spin on the bike around the neighborhood, stopping at a sports store to buy a water bottle and bike lock.

Harwood Heights, at least around North Sayre, is rows of brick houses, many with adjacent driveways and nearly all with well-tended lawns. Between the houses to the rear are many alleys with garages, basketball hoops, and the greetings that take place among neighbors in a small town. The larger boulevards that cut through the neighborhood are lined with supermarkets, drugstores, and small businesses. Some blocks north of their house was the Kennedy Expressway (I-90) that appeared sunk into a concrete canyon and funneled the traffic roar of what sounded like medieval dragons.

To get to Libertyville, Rob and I used his car. We had talked about loading the bikes on a commuter train, but that would have involved several train changes, and where we wanted to go—first to Barrington, Illinois, and then to the Stevenson Center—would have meant a long ride on busy suburban arteries. Had I been on my own, I might have tried it, as I had printed out the route from MapQuest. He preferred the car, and I deferred to his local knowledge.

Before heading to his father's grave site, Rob wanted to show me the house where his father had grown up. Rob had been there occasionally, but he didn't have the street address committed to memory. He knew roughly where the house was, and, in searching around Barrington, he talked about his father's memories of childhood, such as that the house had backed onto a large woods or that later a busy road was built near the home.

It took us more than an hour to translate these fragments of memory into a street and finally a house where, by chance, new owners had just moved in. Only one other family had lived in the house since it was built in the 1930s, and the interior layout was similar to what Rob remembered hearing from his father, who left the house to fight in World War II, and later to attend Harvard and, for a legal degree, Yale. Late in his life, he suffered from depression and dementia, and as we rode from the house where he grew up to the cemetery where he is buried, I told Rob amusing stories about our overlapping childhoods, and how much I had liked and admired his father, who was never happier than when we played chess after Thanksgiving dinner.

On our way to the cemetery, Rob stopped the car near the center of Barrington and explained that the famed mobster Lester Joseph Gillis (aka George "Baby Face" Nelson) had died in a shoot-out that took place near North Side Park. In 1934—about the time the Koch family was moving to Barrington—Nelson and his wife, together with some accomplices, had fought with agents of the Federal Bureau of Investigation and exchanged hundreds of shots—seventeen of which hit Nelson. Still, he managed to escape Barrington alive and was driven to Wilmette, another Chicago suburb near Lake Michigan, where he died that evening. His mob dumped his body in front of a cemetery in Skokie, Illinois. It was wrapped in a blanket that famously had a Native American design. Later, his wife, Helen Gillis, who for a while was sought as public enemy number one for her role in the shoot-out (she drove the car), said: "Lester always hated being cold."

It was because of Rob's mother, Mardo, that I came to admire Adlai Stevenson, whom she had known when she was growing up in Lake Forest, a town near Libertyville also in the north Chicago suburbs. Her father, Albert Brace Pattou—whom I knew only by the austere name General Pattou—had served with distinction in World War II. Growing up outside Chicago, Mardo had known the Stevenson family almost as neighbors, and when I graduated from college, she gave me John Bartlow Martin's exhaustive two-volume biography of Adlai Stevenson, with the kind inscription: "Adlai would have given his shirt for someone like you."

In 1976 I read the book as if one of revelation. I had known about Adlai Stevenson for his presidential campaigns in the 1950s, but never really had any of the details. Both my parents admired him, and in the house where I grew up, it was easy to pull open a cluttered drawer and find a "Stevenson for President" button. (I am not aware of any family connections.) So the biography that Mardo gave me was, in effect, my introduction to Adlai Stevenson, and still I never tire of reading about his eloquence, courage, or wit (as Illinois governor, in vetoing a bill that would have mandated cats on leashes, he famously wrote: "It is in the nature of cats to do a certain amount of unescorted roaming.").

Rob and I found the Stevenson farm (as it was often called) at the end of a long stone driveway. The local town signs spoke more of Mettawa than Libertyville, which may have been the name in the 1930s when he bought the tract of land that backs up to the Des Plaines River. I am sure the house was then in the country. Now it is still rural, although suburban encroachments are close by.

We knew from the Stevenson Center (Rob had called them) that no one was working that day at the house or the museum, which is located in one of the barn outbuildings. Nevertheless, Rob had been told that we were welcome to stroll the grounds and look at the exhibits, which would be left open. We parked the car in front of the house—almost as if weekend guests—and spent an hour peeking in the windows of the house (which is surprisingly modern in design for one built in the late 1930s) and going through the museum, which shows with pictures and posters the life and times (1900–65) of Adlai E. Stevenson II (who in the family is referred to as "the governor" or "the gov").

Stevenson lost the presidency twice in elections against Dwight Eisenhower. Each time my own father was bitterly disappointed, as he had little time for "Ike" either as a president or a general. He would say: "Nobody can beat five stars [Eisenhower's rank as general] after a war." Of his defeats, the governor would say that he was "too old to cry, but it hurt too much to laugh."

Lincoln Park: The *Black Book* of the Adlai E. Stevensons

It was not until the next evening, Sunday, that I met Adlai E. Stevenson III and his wife, Nancy, at their Chicago home in Lincoln Park. Rob was tired from our day on the bikes, and begged off from the evening appointment. He gave me directions that involved the L (Chicago's aboveground trains) to Western (a stop on the Blue Line) and a bike ride across Western Armitage Avenue, which in the twilight looked capable of hosting the World Pothole Association's annual meeting. I bumped along the avenue, which included a bridge across the North Chicago River (think of Brooklyn's Gowanus Canal, more than the Seine crossing Paris), until I found North Fremont and the right cross streets. Near Lincoln Park, cutting through a neighborhood of elegant brownstone townhouses, I had other, and more favorable, reasons to be reminded of Brooklyn.

I had agonized over how to dress for the drinks that evening with a former senator, but since my only choice was one of two shirts in my bike bag, my angst was theoretical. Fortunately, he and Nancy were dressed casually, and they didn't seem to mind receiving a guest who came up the stairs of their brownstone carrying the folded skeleton of a bicycle and wearing a glowing reflective vest.

I sat on the sofa near the windows overlooking North Fremont Street, and they were in easy chairs across from me.

Because I was thirsty from the bike riding that day, I drank beer and nibbled hard on their cheese and crackers.

I liked Adlai and Nancy immediately. To establish some bona fides after my letter, I had mailed them a copy of my book, and, in turn, Adlai had for me a signed copy of his own book, *The Black Book of Senator Adlai E. Stevenson, 1930, Governor Adlai E. Stevenson, 1900–1965, Vice President Adlai E. Stevenson, 1835–1914*. Part family memoir, part clipping file for speeches, the book tells the story of four Stevenson generations in American politics with quotes, anecdotes, reminiscences, and backroom stories. For example, Adlai III—hereafter the senator—writes of an early moment in his political career: "An old ward committeeman once told me, 'I'll give you a million dollars' worth of free advice. Don't change your name.'"

We exchanged family stories. It wasn't really a fair exchange, as I was telling stories about raising four children in the Swiss countryside ("When we got to Geneva, school still met on Saturday mornings . . ."), while they told me about, among other things, how it was a Stevenson family relative, Jesse Fell, who persuaded Abraham Lincoln to run for president in 1860. (In response, Lincoln mailed to Fell his biography, almost his CV, in which he writes: "There is not much of it, for the reason, I suppose, that there is not much of me." He also wrote: "I was losing interest in politics, when the repeal of the Missouri Compromise aroused me again.")

As Adlai III explained, Fell was an Illinois lawyer and politician who also played a key role in organizing the Lincoln-Douglas debates. He was the ancestor whom the governor most admired, although the person who brought the Stevenson family to prominence was Adlai E. Stevenson I, who served as Grover Cleveland's vice president from 1893 to 1897. (*The Black Book* marks him as a man of spartan habits, almost a bike rider, and quotes one press report: "Mr. Stevenson never rides in a carriage of his own, but goes to the Capitol and returns from it generally on foot.") He might have succeeded Cleveland as president, although in 1896 the Democrats nominated William Jennings Bryan, who delivered his "cross of gold speech" at the convention. In 1900, however, Bryan—running again—asked Adlai Stevenson I to be his running mate, although this time they lost to William McKinley and Theodore Roosevelt.

Neither *The Black Book* nor the senator had much to say about Adlai II's father, Lewis Stevenson, although he was elected secretary of state in Illinois in 1914, when his son Adlai II was fourteen years old. Adlai II spent his childhood in Bloomington, Illinois, a city that is two hours southwest of Chicago. There his father owned the local newspaper, the *Pantagraph*, which provided sufficient means for Adlai II to attend boarding school at Choate and later Princeton University, where he was editor of the *Daily Princetonian*.

Between high school and college, Adlai II briefly enlisted in the navy, but it was too late for him to see action in World War I, and he was discharged to attend college. He did, in 1920, hire a bicycle in France and tour the battlefields along the Western Front, then little changed from the war years, when the poet Siegfried Sassoon could write:

> *I see them in foul dug-outs, gnawed by rats,*
> *And in the ruined trenches, lashed with rain,*
> *Dreaming of things they did will balls and bats*
> *Bank-holidays, and picture shows, and spats,*
> *And going to the office in the train.*

Adlai II graduated from Princeton in 1922 and law school at Northwestern in 1926. Although he went to work for a leading Chicago firm, he might best be described in the late 1920s and early 1930s as a restless lawyer. Around age thirty, he began to get involved with the Chicago Council on Foreign Relations (in which relatives of Rob's mother were also active) and to give speeches on foreign affairs that drew attention to his eloquence. He married Ellen Borden in 1927, and Adlai III was born in 1930.

Adlai II wanted more than corporate law and a country club life, and in 1933 he accepted a job in President Franklin Roosevelt's New Deal administration, where he worked on and off until the end of World War II—at first in the AAA (Agricultural Adjustment Administration) and later in the State Department. His first run for public office was in 1948, when he was elected governor of Illinois.

While we were talking—in all I must have been there for about three hours, or at least until I had finished off their pretzels—I asked the senator which biography of his father did he like the most. I had mentioned favorably John Bartlow Martin's two-volume effort, but he dismissed it as the "work of a journalist" and implied that much of the book, at least the second volume *Adlai Stevenson and the World*, came simply from the files (less so than from the man). The book he prefers is Porter McKeever's *Adlai Stevenson: His Life and Legacy*, which was in my parents' library when they died. I had saved it—I told the Stevensons—but what I didn't add was that it was, for the moment, packed away in boxes with many of their other personal effects. Without it at hand, I read Herbert Muller's *Adlai Stevenson: A Study in Values*, a serious book that is more faithful to his political idealism than, say, to his humor. He writes:

> What most plainly gives his whole political career its basic consistency was his moral courage. Even his hesitancies were linked with this. In the words of Archibald MacLeish, he had "the courage of his doubts," and was not only willing to consider all possible alternatives but unwilling not to consider them.

Adlai Stevenson II served two terms as governor of Illinois, and ran for president in 1952 and 1956. He would have run in 1960, when John F. Kennedy was nominated, but preferred to be drafted at the convention, not to actively campaign, which he never did that year. According to his son, during the campaign, in exchange for Adlai's support, Kennedy spoke to him about becoming secretary of state in a Kennedy administration—if Jack won the election. Instead, Kennedy appointed Dean Rusk to be a placeholder secretary of state—Kennedy fancied keeping the job for himself—and appointed Stevenson as US ambassador to the United Nations, a position he kept until he died in summer 1965.

The senator said his father was never happy in the UN job, feeling that his more rightful place was at State. Nevertheless, he achieved more lasting acclaim than did Rusk when, during the showdown with the Russians in the 1962 Cuban Missile Crisis, Stevenson said to Russian Ambassador Valerian Zorin before the UN Security Council: "You are in the courtroom of world opinion. You have denied they exist, and I want to know if I understood you correctly. I am prepared to wait for my answer until hell freezes over." Rusk was also saddled with the legacy of the Vietnam War, which never touched Stevenson.

As much as I wanted simply to ask the Stevensons, What was Adlai II really like? it's impossible, during such a social evening, to be so blunt. But the questions I did ask—about his relationship with the Kennedys (he liked them), Mayor Daley (he worked in the budget office when Adlai was governor), and Lyndon Johnson (Stevenson got then Congressman Lyndon Johnson a commission in the navy in World War II)—all touched on his personality, and I was pleased with how direct and forthcoming the senator was about his father.

On the question of whether Adlai II was "an intellectual," his son scoffed ever so slightly, pointing me toward a passage in *The Black Book* ("The press dubbed him the 'egghead,' but he was a pragmatic internationalist, a hard-boiled egghead") and adding that, despite his eloquence as a writer and speaker, he wasn't much of a reader. On this point, Muller writes: "He [Adlai II] had an active, alert mind, but not a particularly original or acute one; he was never far ahead of his time."

Both *The Black Book* and the conversation made it clear that Adlai II and Adlai III enjoyed a warm and enduring relationship with the Daley clan. (Like the political Stevensons, the Daleys all seem to have the same name and do the same things.) Richard J. Daley, sometimes called Boss Daley and the founder of the dynasty, worked well with Adlai II when they were together in Springfield, Illinois, and both were protégés (of a kind) of the then Chicago political boss Jacob Arvey. Later, in the 1960s and '70s, when Adlai III was beginning his political career, the Daleys were as supportive of the son as they were of his father.

I asked about the Stevensons' dealings with the Kennedys, and the senator repeated the story (told in some biographies) about candidate Kennedy in 1960 traveling to Libertyville and offering Adlai II the position of secretary of state—in so many guarded words. No doubt Stevenson heard one thing and Kennedy implied another. Nevertheless, it speaks well for both men that they got along as well as they did. Stevenson could have resented Kennedy for being a lightweight senator, and Kennedy could have held a grudge for Stevenson's last-minute attempt in Los Angeles to get the 1960 Democratic nomination. Instead, both of them, professional politicians (in the best sense of the word), looked past these differences and held each other in esteem. In fact, Adlai III said his father regretted turning over the selection of the vice presidential nominee to the convention in 1956, when he would have preferred giving the nomination to Senator Kennedy.

One of the bonds formed in the evening was over travel, in particular, the Stevenson habit (something shared by their family and mine) of seeing the world as it is on the ground, not just relying on printed accounts. As a young married couple in the 1950s, Adlai III and Nancy often traveled with the governor, or occasionally they went in his place, as they did—to my admiration—to Khartoum. (I checked in *The Black Book* and found this passage: "In 1957, in the torrid summer heat of Omdurman near Khartoum in the Sudan, Nancy and I pondered the site where in 1898 Anglo Egyptian forces used artillery and maxim guns to slaughter thirteen thousand lightly armed Sudanese, losing forty-eight British troops.")

Similarly, Adlai II went everywhere, not just as a presidential candidate but before and afterward as well: across Latin America and Asia, and to many places in between, including many countries in Africa, where he supported the liberal internationalism of the independence movement in the late 1950s. During the late days of World War II, he went overland to Moscow, by way of Turkey and Iran. When I first read about him in the 1970s, I took inspiration from his travels, and admired that he admitted to liking sightseeing—something that also gives me pleasure.[1] Muller writes "that on his travels he was often too much impressed by the French and British colonial officials who entertained him. Still, his visit to Indochina had given him some second thoughts about 'our gallant allies.'" (Few American politicians went to Vietnam in the 1950s.) Elsewhere in Asia his travels fueled additional skepticism, as Muller writes: "He saw more clearly the folly of our preaching capitalism to these wretchedly poor peoples, demanding that they be anti-Communist, and acting as if America would be hurt by their neutrality."

1: When I asked Adlai III by e-mail if this was true, he replied: "Adlai II did not 'sightsee.' As mentioned in *The Black Book,* he explored the world from on the ground, its favelas and markets as well as monuments and ministries. It was lifelong, though fame would bring demands from the heads of state, and a commission by the Eisenhower Administration. Explorations included meetings, banquets, etc., with the high and mighty. I remember Liberia vividly from a trip to Africa we shared in 1957; banquet with the president, imported wines and lobsters, with gossip across the banquet table about who had slept with whom the night before. American rubber ruled and so it went—not sightseeing but exploring at all levels and places."

City Hall:
"Chicago Ain't Ready for Reform"

As the evening wore on, we spoke less of the father's elections and more of Adlai III's political career that began in 1964, when Mayor Daley supported his at-large candidacy to the Illinois House of Representatives. Later he was the Illinois state treasurer, and in 1970 he was appointed to succeed Senator Everett Dirksen, who died in office. (*The Black Book* has Dirksen's famous observation: "A billion here, a billion there, pretty soon you're talking about real money.")

Prior to politics, Adlai III had served as a marine corps tank commander during and after the Korean War and worked on his father's campaigns and as a lawyer. He spoke a lot about his efforts in office to level the playing fields of American politics and decrease the influence of money in elections. He served on the so-called McGovern-Fraser Commission after the raucous 1968 boss-controlled Democratic convention spilled violently into the streets of Chicago. Later he writes: "Our efforts to make the democratic process more democratic made it more plutocratic." He continues: "Politics had become tactics, money and imagery," in the same vein that *The Black Book* has a quotation from alderman and political boss Paddy Bauler, who liked to say in his smoke-filled saloon: "Chicago ain't ready for reform."

In the 1980s, Adlai III ran twice for governor, losing both times. By his own admission he was a lackluster campaigner, and he even includes in *The Black Book* this description of his political style:

> He [Adlai III] makes people drowsy. His hair is thinning. He has all the oratorical fire of an algebra teacher. His clothes look like something he bought from the coroner's office. When he feels good, he looks like he has a virus. We need more politicians who make the blood run tepid.

The second time he ran for governor it was as an independent candidate, after allies of Lyndon LaRouche grabbed the Democratic nominations for lieutenant governor and Illinois secretary of state, and Adlai III refused to share the ticket with them.[2] Had he not stood on his principles, he might well have won the governorship. As it was, he got 40 percent of the popular vote, as a third-party candidate.

We talked a lot about his more recent, post-political career, as an investment banker in China. Now past eighty, he no longer felt he could travel there as widely as he had before, but he still spoke with affection about Shanghai and some of the other Chinese cities. (I put in a good word for Beijing, which may be the capital of a repressive government, but it shines on a bicycle.) He despaired the condescending manner in which the US government criticizes China's human rights policies. Later in *The Black Book,* I found a passage in response to these charges, in which "the Chinese cite the US homicide, incarceration and capital punishment record, the

2: LaRouche was a self-proclaimed Marxist and occasional candidate for president with his US Labor Party who later came out for the gold standard and Ronald Reagan's Star Wars initiative. In 1984 he also denounced the Democratic nominee Walter Mondale as a Soviet agent and called the Beatles "a product shaped according to British Psychological Warfare Division specifications."

execution of juveniles, the proliferation of offenses related to drugs, mental disease and guns."

To get from the Stevenson's brownstone to Rob's house, I found myself around 9 p.m. heading south on LaSalle Street, which has a bike lane away from the traffic and which took me down to the Loop. Away from traffic, I peeked into the windows at the old Marshall Field's department store (now owned by Macy's) and picked up North Milwaukee Avenue for the ride home.

Along Milwaukee I did six of the twelve miles to Harwood Heights. It had a bike lane but its paint has worn thin, and cars routinely cut me off to make right turns or park outside convenience stores selling beer. At California I decided to bail onto the Blue Line, which involved folding up my bike and carrying it upstairs to the platform. In the half-light netherworld, I waited about ten minutes for a train to Norwood Park. There I reassembled my bike and rode home, getting lost in the back alleys where I hoped that none of the neighborhood police would mistake me for a burglar.

Oak Park: Frank Lloyd Wright Figures the Angles

THE NEXT MORNING ROB AND I WERE OFF early on the bikes. The night before we had mapped out our route, first to Hemingway's Oak Park, which is due south of Harwood Heights, and then to Chicago's South Side, where we wanted to find Mayor Richard J. Daley's ward and President Barack Obama's South Side house, near the University of Chicago. On the way, Rob said he could also take us along Forest Avenue, where many Frank Lloyd Wright houses were built.

To get to Oak Park, Rob and I (using bikes and bus) headed down North Harlem Avenue, one of the main arteries in western Chicago. It reminded me of boulevards in Brooklyn, where my wife and I lived in the 1980s. Most of the neighborhoods through which Rob and I passed had small businesses (furniture stores, tire shops, etc.) lining the avenue. The few residents out early on a Sunday morning were well dressed, clearly heading to church. Off the boulevard were blocks of row houses, less affluent than Harwood Heights, but still well kept.

To find Wright's studio on Forest Avenue, we turned left on Chicago Avenue, and entered the world apart that is Oak Park. It has the feel of a 1920s suburb that the city later engulfed. Rob said the commercial street of Oak Park was along South Boulevard, where the commuter trains and metro stopped. We were north of there, in a residential district with large, post-Victorian houses. Wright may have kept

Oak Park on the map, but his houses are not the only showcases in the prosperous neighborhood.

We stopped in front of Wright's studio a little before 9 a.m. It was still closed, but crowds, even a bike tour, were beginning to form outside. We weighed locking the bikes to a fence railing and going inside, but I confess I was not in the mood for the $18 Wright studio tour. Instead, Rob and I took several rides on our bikes up and down Forest Avenue, which is a living showroom for his architecture.

Wright lived on the corner, in his massive house and studio. As the demand for his work increased, he designed a number of other houses in that distinctive Wright style, which can be seen along Forest Avenue. Some look like prairie chapels, and others have the appearance of suburban office buildings (complete with enclosed balconies and flagpoles). Some Wright houses are elegant and some are over the top. Nearly all are too large for their suburban lots and now have the muscular look that comes with many McMansions, especially when they are squeezed into traditional neighborhoods.

I felt sorry for the people living in these Wright houses. They had to endure streams of tourists on their front lawns and what looks like a life inside an arts-and-crafts project, with narrow stained-glassed windows instead of skylights. If I had to choose between a Wright home, with all its angular distinctiveness, or a nearby Victorian house with wraparound porches, I might live in the Victorian and look at Wright's handiwork from my deck.

At the end of Forest Avenue, I came across a small monument in Wright's honor. It was so nondescript that it could well have been a fire hydrant, had it not had a bronze portrait of Wright and some details of his life (he was born in 1867 and died in 1959). I took a picture of the monument and tried to remember what I could about Wright's life, besides his fondness for his clients' wives (he once wrote "I am a house divided against itself by circumstances I cannot control") and later the heinous Wisconsin murder (by ax and fire, and at the hand of a deranged chef) in his "love bungalow" of his girlfriend, her children, and some associates in 1914—a story that has often been told in fiction and nonfiction. That loss did not prevent Wright from rebuilding his nest at Taliesin (part family home, part studio, part hippie commune) and stocking the elegant ponds with wives, lovers, and other architectural flourishes. (His winter quarters, of the same name and persuasions, were in Scottsdale, Arizona.)

The scope of Wright's works—from the Imperial Hotel in Tokyo and New York's Guggenheim Museum to hundreds of residential houses—spans some 400 buildings, but even his Romeo and Juliet Windmill, with its distinctive angles, is recognizable as coming from his drafting table. Such was his influence on American architecture that when in the 1980s my wife and I moved into a Brooklyn brownstone (built in Flatbush around 1908), the selling agent impressed us by explaining that Wright's "school" had "influenced" the paneling in our dining room. But the more I tried to remember the details of Wright's life and work, the more I thought about one of my professors at Bucknell University, Gerry Eager, and how much I admired him and loved his courses on nineteenth and twentieth-century art.

As a senior in college, I had no business taking two art history courses. I was majoring in political science and in love with American history (although not of the academic kind).

As a sophomore, I had endured my required two semesters of "art in the dark," the survey course with H. W. Janson's mammoth *History of Art* as the illuminated manuscript or at least the required reading. Why was I back for two more semesters of art history? Part of the reason, I am sure, was that I had spent my junior year in Europe, and that involved many art museums. I must also have heard that Gerry Eager was a great professor, and at that time in my education, I was on the lookout for memorable teachers more than for important or required courses.

I never saw Gerry Eager after graduation in 1976, and I read in the alumni magazine that he died a few years ago. In my mind, he was tall and thin (a bit like Abraham Lincoln), although more athletic and with sandy blond hair and aviator glasses. His two-semester course began with the classical French painter Jacques-Louis David (yes, with Marat dead in his tub) and ended in the next century with Andy Warhol's soup cans and Jasper Johns's flags. Between our last class and graduation, he took a few students down the Susquehanna River on his homemade raft, as close as I ever got to either Thomas Eakins (Gerry loved his rowers) or Huck and Jim adrift on the Mississippi. ("You feel mighty free and easy and comfortable on a raft.")

Somewhere around the turn of the century, Gerry squeezed in Frank Lloyd Wright and showed slide after slide of his houses (especially that one with the waterfall). What made Gerry Eager a great professor and man, however, wasn't his book learning (although it was substantial) but his irreverence in the face of greatness. He would throw Picasso up on the screen and say, "Well, I know you think this is a nun falling down stairs . . .," or he would say of Édouard Manet's

Le Déjeuner sur l'herbe: "It looks like they are getting ready for dessert."

For me his wit brought art off of Mount Olympus and down to the level of humanity, where in front of a painting or a sculpture, or even one of Frank Lloyd Wright's totem houses, it was okay to laugh or remain unimpressed. What a relief. Until his courses, I went through European museums, or along Forest Avenues, convinced I was only looking at genius.

Oak Park: Ernest Hemingway Cuts His Curls

LITERALLY AROUND THE CORNER from Frank Lloyd Wright's Forest Avenue is the house where Ernest Hemingway was born and grew up (and, yes, was done up by his mother Grace with curls and dresses). And down the street from his boyhood home was the Ernest Hemingway Museum (now the two have combined).

Rob and I had no trouble finding either. The trouble was getting inside. The house was closed, exceptionally, for repairs, and the museum did not open until 1 p.m. While we were standing in front of the museum, a staff member kindly came out and invited us to attend a nondenominational church service taking place inside. We thanked him, but explained we were more interested in Hemingway the game hunter than Hemingway the churchgoer.

Unlike Forest Avenue, there wasn't much to see about Hemingway from the street. The house where he was born is a small Victorian, with elegant lines and a stately front parlor (that I could see through the parlor windows). Upstairs, I am sure, is the small bedroom where young Ernest dreamed about the wider world. But I never got there. The best we could muster in Oak Park was morning coffee. Hem probably would have preferred an eye-opener.

At least I saw the house from the outside, and that morning, up at 4 a.m. with jet lag, I had finished Clancy Sigal's *Hemingway Lives!* It is a short book, with wide margins and big type, and only 139 pages. So an easy read, but mostly that is because Sigal is so enthusiastic about the life and writing of Ernest Hemingway and, as the subtitle says, "why it matters."

Right at the beginning, Sigal compares Hemingway to Theodore Roosevelt, writing: "T.R. was Hemingway before there was a Hemingway." He dismisses Hemingway's childhood dresses as period pieces—"In fact, dressing a boy in girls' clothes up to a certain age was common in Victorian families"—although he does say that Ernest's mother had a tense relationship with her rebellious son ("Over time it became increasingly hard for Grace to deal with a growing, active son who would never, ever be like his sister, nor did she ever truly get why Ernest had to rebel against her all his life"). Nor does Sigal have much good to say about the leafy sidewalks of Oak Park:

> The Oak Park suburb he was born into was one of many American all-white "sundown towns," so called because there were signs posted at many city limits reading, typically, "Nigger, Don't Let the Sun Go Down On You Here." Oak Park may have been more genteelly racist, keeping out "undesirable elements" like Negroes. Reflexive anti-Semitism in the little town was so common that the American writer, Kenneth Fearing, an Oak Park boy of Hemingway's time, felt it best to keep his Jewish heritage a secret.

Nevertheless, Hemingway did not linger in Oak Park, graduating from high school in 1917 and immediately getting a newspaper job on the *Kansas City Star*. He was only on staff there long enough to digest the house style ("It was a fine morning . . .") before he headed for the Italian front of World

War I, where Hemingway would be grievously wounded as an ambulance driver. Sigal recounts: "Six days before his nineteenth birthday, outside the bombed-out village of Fossalta di Piave in the northern Italian Alpines, in the midst of heavy combat between the teenage soldiers of Italy's Fourth Army and the attacking Austria-Hungarians, while Ernest was handing out goodies to the troops, he and several other soldiers were hit by a fourteen pound explosive shell from an enemy Minenwerfer, or trench mortar." Recovering from his wounds in Italy, Hemingway wrote *A Farewell to Arms.*

Sigal attributes much of the anger in Hemingway to his experiences in the trenches. He writes: "Drinking was his medicine to blur the pain of war wounds, multiple illnesses, his rage at critics—'lice' and 'camp-following eunuchs of literature' are some of his milder defamatory terms—and an amazing number of 'accidents' by land, sea, and air." It sets up the dichotomy in Hemingway. At once a war hater—"Never think that war, no matter how necessary, nor how justified, is not a crime. Ask the infantry and the dead"—but on the other hand, as a writer, someone drawn to violence, war, hunting, boxing, and revolution. He said in a letter to F. Scott Fitzgerald: "If something in life hurts you in life, use it in your writing." A character in a Hemingway novel says:

> I was always embarrassed by the words sacred, glorious, and sacrifice, and the expression in vain. This is the worst justification of war. We hear it too often spoken today, and indeed all wars, that fighting must continue for the sakes of the dead.

Nevertheless, Hemingway spent the last twenty years of his life in proximity to some war or struggle.

What are my own feelings about Hemingway, and why did I want to see his house? Much of it has to do with Hemingway being a fixture in my life from a young age. I am sure in the fifth or sixth grade—at Buckley Country Day School on Long Island—I read *The Old Man and the Sea*, and through high school I read many of his short stories (and given that it was for homework, I place the emphasis on the word "short"). He was waiting for me in college as well, when I took several courses on American literature. In the 1960s, Hemingway was a tough guy; by the time I got to college in the 1970s he was an existentialist. Maybe soon he will be a laureate of transgender studies, as Sigal writes: "Hemingway had enough erotic energy, when writing, to embrace both men and women. It's what makes him modern."

Only after college, when I began to travel, did I start to see Hemingway in a new light, as someone who had an excellent command of descriptive English. Writing a magazine article in Florida in 1982, I read *To Have and Have Not*, perhaps the best novel ever set in the Florida Keys (where I went to his house in Key West, the one with fifty cats). In Mexico about the same time, I carried *Death in the Afternoon* to a bullfight and later, back in my hotel, found that Hemingway had an almost clinical understanding of what happened in the ring.

In the Italian Lakes in the 1990s, I rediscovered *A Farewell to Arms* (it helps not having to write a book report for the eighth grade afterward) and admired it on many levels, but especially as a love story and war novel. When I went to Spain in 2005, I reread *For Whom the Bell Tolls* and let Hemingway guide me around the battlefronts of the Spanish Civil War. At no time did he disappoint. On other occasions, he might have been a blowhard bully, an egoist, and much else besides, but when he was writing, as he might have said of himself, he was good.

Perhaps the most enduring bond I formed with Hemingway and his writing came in the Hürtgen Forest, a wild no-man's-land on the Belgian-German border. From September to December 1944, it became one of the most expensive pieces of real estate that Americans ever acquired, as the US Army paid in blood in the amount 33,000 casualties. (At Gettysburg, Union casualties were about 23,000.) Nor was the battle in the Hürtgen Forest even a victory, which is why so few today have ever heard about it. The fight there only ended when the Germans launched the Battle of the Bulge to the south, and each side broke off the engagement in the dark and bloody woods to the north.

Until I went to the Hürtgen Forest with my son Henry in 2008, I had no idea that Hemingway had been there as a correspondent or that he had written a novel about the battle (*Across the River and Into the Trees*). In high school, Henry was interested in the TV miniseries *Band of Brothers*, and we went for a weekend to see where they fought in the Bulge.

Before heading to Bastogne, however, we drove north into the Hürtgen Forest, which is little changed from when the American army—fresh from victories in Normandy and Paris—thought it could end the war with a big push into Germany. Instead, the bumbling US high command fed division after division into thick forests laced with ravines and cul-de-sacs. For the Americans, it wasn't so much a battlefield as a meat grinder, and one of the few correspondents to cover it was Ernest Hemingway.

I had not known of his connection to the battle until Henry and I stopped at some local museums and saw his picture and writings in the cabinets. By then, he was forty-five years old, and could well have spent his time fishing in Cuba or Key West. Instead he went forward with the men attacking into the forested void, as he wrote:

> Over three cold, wet, miserable months, the Hürtgen became the U.S. army's longest-ever battle. I know about this disaster because I joined one of its lead elements, the Fourth Infantry Division, after they returned from Europe, decimated and shell-shocked, and I had a chance to talk to its survivors. At one point the Fourth's 22nd Regiment suffered eighty percent casualties; some battle companies took nearly two hundred percent casualties—that is, every soldier had to be replaced twice over.

Across the River and Into the Trees isn't one of Hemingway's best novels, although it was his last, published after his death, a suicide, in July 1961. The title is a perfect description of the Hürtgen (which he also called "Passchendaele with tree bursts"), although I think he took the title from the last words of Thomas "Stonewall" Jackson, who said as he was dying: "Let us cross over the river, and rest under the shade of the trees."

Reading Sigal and standing in front of Hemingway's house in Oak Park reminded me of my 2008 travels in the Hürtgen with Henry. We had come up from Geneva on the train and had rented a small car, and, like the Americans in 1944, we were feeling our way cautiously through a bleak landscape of isolated farms and small, hillside villages. While we were there, it even began to snow, and we got lost in the woods, looking for this marker or that crossroads. Maybe in going to the Hürtgen, we were also looking for Hemingway? Sigal writes:

> After the war the poet John Ciardi, himself a veteran, saluted: "What counts, as I see it, is the way in which the GIs of World War II lived and died with Hemingway dialogue in their mouths. . . . Their language was not out of Hemingway but out of themselves."

South Side: Bubbling in the Back of the Yards

From Oak Park, it would have taken Rob and me at least an hour to ride to the South Side of Chicago, to the neighborhood where the new Comiskey Park (once US Cellular Park, now Guaranteed Rate Field) stands. Instead of powering along something like Lake Street into the Loop and riding south on Wabash Avenue, we hopped on the metro in Oak Park, changed trains downtown, and got off at the 35th Street stop, where we crossed under an expressway and rode around the contours of the baseball stadium.

As much as I like baseball, I hate most of the stadiums built in the last thirty years, which are constructed with public money for the enrichment of private owners. Under that formula, Guaranteed Rate Field, home to the Chicago White Sox, played the familiar game. Always, the justification of public money allocated to private teams is that keeping the franchise is "good for the local economy." But a short bike ride around the ballpark makes it clear that however good a deal the stadium financial package was for the White Sox owners (actually it was a home run), not much has trickled down from the sweetheart contracts into the nearby neighborhoods, which look as they did when Mayor Richard J. Daley lived on one of the nearby side streets.

The new stadium cost $189 million and opened in 1991. One hundred percent of the financing for the construction came from the city, which paid for it by increasing the hotel tax by 2 percent. ("Visit Chicago, and pay for our stadium.") In exchange, the White Sox pay the city nominal rent for the use of the stadium (about $1.5 million per year, with some adjustments), but the team keeps the proceeds of ticket sales, television revenue, sky box income, hot dog sales, and souvenirs. *Forbes* magazine estimates that the White Sox annual revenue is about $227 million (the figures, however, are not public), which makes the $1.5 to $2 million in rental expense the city earns comparable to the salary for a bullpen catcher. That is the bad news. The good news, for fans, is that the team won the World Series in 1906, 1917, and 2005, and bleacher seats cost $28.

From Guaranteed Rate Field, Rob and I rode west to South Lowe Avenue, where Hiz Honor Mayor Daley lived at number 3536. We had not written down the street number, so it took us a few minutes to find the exact house, which stands out on the street—this part of Chicago is known as Bridgeport—because at some point it was renovated with brick, as if to turn it into a bunker.

Down and across the street there is a firehouse, but otherwise nothing marks the house of Chicago's political boss from 1955 until his death in 1976; his son, Richard M. Daley, ran Chicago as mayor from 1989 until 2011. Father Daley had, at times, an unfortunate way of speaking (he once said "the police are not here to create disorder, they're here to preserve disorder"), but he ran the Cook County Democratic Party machine, and thus much of Illinois, as though it were an evening game of pinochle.

In the 1960 presidential election, Daley almost surely delivered some graveyard votes for John Kennedy, who would have lost the presidency had he lost Illinois. The statewide margin in Illinois was 8,858 votes. Kennedy, however, carried Daley's Cook County by a margin of 318,736 votes. Just four years earlier, Republican Dwight Eisenhower received 2,623,327 statewide votes (1,293,223 in Cook County) while favorite son Adlai Stevenson II's total was only 1,775,682 (of which 977,821 were from around Chicago). In four years, the Democrats in Cook County picked up 401,522 votes, despite running a candidate who was a Catholic senator from New England and not a popular former governor of Illinois.

That Mayor Richard J. Daley had warmly supported both Adlai Stevensons made me think better of him, although the low moment of his political career came during the 1968 Democratic convention held in Chicago. That year Senator Eugene McCarthy had challenged President Lyndon Johnson and driven him from the race, while Senator Robert Kennedy had won in Indiana and California, before his assassination in June. The convention featured the candidate of the political establishment, Vice President Hubert Humphrey, versus McCarthy and, at the last minute, Senator George McGovern (as a stand-in for Robert Kennedy).

While the convention was playing out in the International Amphitheatre along the lake, protestors against the Vietnam War took to the streets of downtown Chicago, where the police brutally suppressed their rallies. Against the backdrop of tear gas in the air and beaten students in the streets, Senator Abraham Ribicoff from Connecticut placed the name of Senator McGovern in nomination, adding: "And, with George McGovern as President of the United States, we wouldn't have to have Gestapo tactics in the streets of Chicago!" With that, national TV cameras showed Mayor Daley on his feet, shouting at Ribicoff.

In some versions of the story, he was yelling, "Fuck you, you Jew son of a bitch." I have watched the replays on YouTube and find it impossible to hear or lip-read what Daley is shouting. But the split TV screens, showing the so-called police riot in Chicago together with the boss-controlled convention inside the hall (Humphrey had only run in a few primaries and was Johnson's choice to succeed him), ended whatever chance the Democrats had to win in 1968. It looked like the party of either anarchy or oligopoly, and Richard Nixon won with the support of conservative Democrats while third-party candidate George Wallace denied Humphrey the traditional Democratic base in the South.

From the Daley house on South Lowe Avenue, we rode our bikes south toward Greenwood and the University of Chicago, but Rob made a detour so that I could see what is left of the Chicago stockyards, once the world's largest meatpacking district that had its gate at South Halsted Street and 41st Street, on the South Side. It was a short ride from South Lowe, and we found it without trouble. While there were once acres of cattle and slaughterhouses here, connected with numerous rail lines, there is now a ceremonial gate to the stockyards and a monument to the fire that in 1910 killed twenty-one firemen. The stockyards burned again in 1934, and the flames could be seen in nearby Indiana.

Plaques around the entrance to what is now a corporate park and trucking center tell some of the stockyards' story: that the site covered 375 acres; that it could accommodate daily 75,000 hogs, 21,000 heads of cattle, and 22,000 sheep; and that between 1865 and 1900, some 400 million animals were slaughtered in "the Yards." In the first year of operation alone, it received 1,286,326 hogs. Such was the waste that the stockyards dumped into the Chicago River's South Branch that it became known as "Bubbly Creek," and today it continues to bubble.

After World War II, with the development of refrigerator trucking, it made more sense to slaughter cattle where they were raised than to ship them to a railhead in Chicago or perhaps Omaha. "The Yards" closed in the 1950s and '60s, so I never saw them in operation. As a boy, traveling with my father to the West in 1967, I did see the Omaha stockyards, then among the biggest in the United States, and the site of the doomed cattle was enough—at least for a few meals—to have me swear off meat.

The only dicey part of my rides through Chicago came when we toured around Back of the Yards, the immigrant neighborhoods to the south and west of the stockyards. It was a sunny afternoon, and we were heading—but not very directly—toward the area around the University of Chicago. We got careless with our directions, and ventured down streets that were littered with entrails of wrecked cars and the broken glass of the previous night's street party.

Slums like these used to abound in New York, the American city I know best. Those desperate slums, in places like the South Bronx and East New York, are largely gone. Even Bushwick in Brooklyn, scene of the rioting in summer 1977, has become (more or less) upscale, with demand soaring in the city for housing. Not so in Chicago—or at least not in Back of the Yards. Here the houses are neglected, and the residents on the streets seem to go about their business with a sense of despair. That night on the news Rob and I heard that, overnight, Chicago had experienced twelve shootings, and a few of them had been here.

Eventually we found 51st Street, on which we went east, passing back under the expressway and riding to the boulevards that, farther north, define the Loop: State, Michigan, Wabash, and Prairie. Here on the other side of the elevated highway, Chicago was again elegant, an urban oasis of graceful houses, no longer a shooting gallery.

On Martin Luther King Boulevard South, I found a sign indicating that the five Marx Brothers (Groucho, Gummo, Zeppo, Chico, and Harpo) had lived nearby, probably on Calumet Avenue. (They wrote in a memoir: "We lived in Chicago for twelve years. I saw Ty Cobb play baseball many a day at White Sox Park. We lived right near there. We bought a house for $25,000. We paid a thousand down and owed the rest.")

Farther down the boulevard is a plaque noting the house of Robert S. Abbott (1868–1940), publisher of the *Chicago Defender,* still the oldest African American–owned newspaper (now online) published in the US. Among his many achievements, he helped to discover the writer Langston Hughes, who famously wrote, "What happens to a dream deferred?"

Hyde Park: Barack Obama Advances to Rezko Gardens

To ride past the Obama house, we rode east on East 48th Street until we came to South Greenwood, his street, and headed south. Rob remembered that the house was off Hyde Park Boulevard, but long before that, we picked up signs that said, in effect, "Stay out." Still, there were no barriers across the street and many people were out and about, some with their dogs, on the autumn Sunday afternoon. We kept riding on Greenwood until we got near the Obama property or, more to the point, up against the Secret Service guarding the empty house.

At this point we were well away from the house and in the company of other gawkers, all of whom had cameras and were wondering in which house the president had lived when working and living in Chicago. (Actually, nothing of the president's house is visible from South Greenwood Avenue. A row of tall trees has been planted to obscure it from public view.) In no time, however, an armed guard showed up to chase everyone away. His language wasn't exactly that of Mayor Daley's at the Democratic convention, but it had the same tone. Plus, he wore a bulletproof vest and a high-caliber pistol. Clearly it's a gun neighborhood, on both sides of the elevated highway.

No one cared when Rob and I circled around and looked at the fenced property from Hyde Park Boulevard, a busier thoroughfare. What saddened me (at least for the neighbors) is how tawdry are the barricades around the Obama house, which give it the look of a Beirut embassy. Maybe in the age of Homeland Security such protection is necessary, although I never read any more of the Obamas going to the house; they always seem to be in Hawaii or on Martha's Vineyard, and playing golf. But the slipshod nature of the ramparts spoke to the Obamas' indifference for their old neighbors. They had bought a showcase house on a prominent corner in Hyde Park near the university, then Barack Obama had been elected president and they moved on, leaving behind nasty armed guards and scattered concrete barriers (like those you might find on the edges of the Brooklyn-Queens Expressway).

Because no one was hassling us on Hyde Park Boulevard, which runs alongside the shaded Obama property, I could take my time to figure out in which quadrant lies Rezko Acres—the strip of land that Tony Rezko's wife bought the same day the Obamas purchased their house and parcel for $1.65 million.

When the house was for sale, the Obama home was attached to another lot, but the sellers demanded that the two pieces of property close at the same time. The Obamas did not have sufficient cash to buy both the large house and the adjoining lot. Coincidentally or not, Tony Rezko's wife came forward with a check for $625,000 for the adjoining parcel the same day the Obamas closed on the house for $1.65 million, allowing them to move their tokens to what feels like Marvin Gardens.

Now Tony Rezko is among the best-known felons in Illinois, but in 2005, when Senator Obama was stretching to buy his house, Rezko was a Democratic money man, a hand-holder for on-the-make politicians, including Barack Obama. Rezmar, Tony's company, had offered Obama a job out of law school, which Obama turned down. But Tony still kept close ties to the community organizer whose law firm—Davis, Miner, Barnhill & Galland—did multimillion-dollar business with one of Rezko's real estate companies.

That Obama needed help in buying a Kenwood mansion is the kind of information with which Rezko earned his living on the streets of Chicago. That Tony's wife, Rita, was ready with a $625,000 certified check for the adjoining parcel on the day the Obamas closed on their property is described in the official presidential histories as happenstance.

For anyone in Chicago politics, however, it must have sounded like business as usual. Keep in mind that at the time of the purchase, Barack Obama was a US senator with presidential aspirations, not an adjunct professor of law in the nearby law school nor even the Illinois state senator in 1997 who had promoted Rezko's housing project for Cottage View Terrace (which would eventually get $14 million in public funding).

A year after the joint South Greenwood properties closed, the Obamas and the Rezkos did a second transaction. Rita Rezko sold the Obamas a ten-foot strip of her property that was next to theirs. Apparently the Obamas wanted to build a fence around their yard, or they deemed it prudent to own the additional land, perhaps to keep another house from going up next to their property. Whatever the motivation, Tony Rezko's wife sold them the strip for $104,000. Meanwhile, Tony was under investigation for a variety of corruption charges. No doubt the Rezkos deemed it prudent to help out a friend and US senator, so to speak, in his own backyard.

Even though Rezko was friends with Obama and then governor Rod Blagojevich, neither all the king's horses nor all the king's men could save Tony from the big house. Beginning in 2006, just after the strip deal, he was charged with some forty counts of corruption and later convicted on sixteen. Many of the charges alleged payments or dealings with local politicians, to secure sweetheart property deals or pay-to-play contracts with local government entities. He was sentenced to more than ten years in prison; much of it, when Obama was in the White House, was bizarrely served in solitary confinement (putting him beyond the reach of the tabloids). In 2015, Rezko was released to a halfway house.

Meanwhile Rezko's neighbor and friend had become president, and he only had this to say about his early benefactor: "It was a mistake to have been engaged with him [Antoin Rezko] at all in this or any other personal business dealing that would allow him, or anyone else, to believe that he had done me a favor." Had Obama been more forthcoming, he might have quoted Groucho Marx, another resident of the South Side, who said when his hand imprint was taken at Grauman's Chinese Theatre in Hollywood: "There was no need to inform us of the protocol involved. We were from Chicago and knew all about cement."

The Loop: Cooler by the Lake

From the Obama subdivision to the campus of the University of Chicago was a short ride on the bikes. I had not been there in some years and was happy to glide through the ivy-covered campus and track down some second-hand bookstores. We thought of going through the Frank Lloyd Wright house on campus—it's the Robie House—but again the cost ($18) and the waiting line (an hour) were more than we could entertain on a sunny autumn afternoon. Instead we had lunch at an outdoor café on the university's restaurant row and rode to Lakefront Park, which has a bike path back to downtown Chicago.

It might have been the ride of the day, as the wind was at our back. (I could see the steel smokestacks of Gary, Indiana, on the lake horizon.) But the ride coincided with a downpour, and we got soaked while spinning toward the Loop. A few times we thought of bailing, but from the park the metro is some distance, and neither of us was sure where it stopped south of the Loop. Instead we kept at the pedals, passing Soldier Field, the aquarium, the Art Institute, the Field Museum, and ending up in Grant Park.

Passing the new McCormick Place convention center reminded me of my friend Larry Heinemann's delightful comic novel, *Cooler by the Lake*, set in and around downtown Chicago. He has a passage that reads:

> This may have nothing to do with the story but the first McCormick Place—the city's convention center built in

> 1960—burned to the ground in January 1967, because the fire hoses couldn't reach from the hydrants to the fire, a serious design flaw the city engineers admitted later with considerable embarrassment and professional chagrin. The building was so vast and expensive that it was not insured, a distinct municipal fiscal peculiarity, seeing as how every nitwit alderman and his dipstick brother, every city lifer with any push *or* pull—including Richard J. Daley's sons—had an insurance agency and a real-estate gig or a sham law firm on the side. Daley, who, with his white bread imagination, gave the city much and took much away, always said: "Don't take cash, boy, give them your business card." So it was mighty strange that McCormick Place was not insured—even a little. And when it went up in smoke the city turned around and built another, which looked like a giant pool table with the legs cut off, but the matter of no insurance stuck in everyone's craw.

As best as I could recall, where Rob and I stopped in Grant Park was exactly where in 1968 the police had attacked the antiwar protesters (what Ribicoff called "Gestapo tactics in the streets of Chicago"). But in the downpour few people were in the park.

Within a few blocks we could have been out of the rain and on the Blue Line train, heading home to the many comforts of Harwood Heights. Instead I insisted on a last stop, at Haymarket Square, as the details of the 1886 riot and massacre have eluded me in all my formal education. I thought now, with the Haymarket Square on the outer edge of the Loop, my chance had come to retire that debt to history. I can't say that Rob—himself wet on the edges—was thrilled with the detour, but he manned up for our last excursion, and even said that we would have a convenient metro stop not far away from there.

On the surface, Haymarket Square, despite having some of the most fateful coordinates in American political geography, is a disappointment. The historic square is gone, and in its place is a typical urban crossroads with cars moving in every direction and cheap stores and bars on the edges. Imagine if Lexington or Concord were strip malls.

After a few turns around the perimeter, we found a modernistic statue—dating to 2004—that depicts where the police opened fire on the labor rally in 1886, killing seven police and wounding dozens. Underneath the monument a plaque reads: "This memorial marks the actual spot where the wagon used as the speaker's platform stood on the evening of May 4, 1886." Another plaque continues the story:

> Over the years, the site of the Haymarket bombing has become a powerful symbol for a diverse cross-section of people, ideals, and movements. Its significance touches on the issues of free speech, the right of public assembly, organized labor, the fight for the eight-hour workday, law enforcement, justice, anarchy, and the right of every human being to pursue an equitable and prosperous life. For all, it is a lesson in the rewards and consequences inherent in such human pursuits.

Yet for all this high-blown rhetoric cast in iron, nothing in the Haymarket explains what happened in 1886 when someone threw a bomb at the police and they responded with steady gunfire.

Haymarket Square: A Deadly Mystery of National Dimension

In its day, the Haymarket Massacre was more significant politically than 9/11 is today. Where you stood on the question of what happened in the Haymarket told the world everything it needed to know about your political disposition. It defined not just the labor movement in America but the outcome of several elections, and it might even today be at the headwaters of American political disputes involving land, labor, and capital.

Much as the theories about the assassination of President John Kennedy defined later generations, so did the Haymarket put its stamp on American socialists, unionism, and civil rights—even if much of the country thought the conspirators in the square got what they deserved when, after the dust settled, eight such plotters were rounded up and executed, though there was a reasonable doubt about who or what killed the police in the square. (The *St. Louis Globe-Democrat* proclaimed, "There are no good anarchists except dead anarchists.") That said, six of the seven policemen killed in the square died from so-called "friendly fire," that is, they were shot by other policemen.

In trying to understand what happened in the Haymarket, it is best to divide the events into two parts: the violence that took place in the square on May 4, 1886, and the reaction and later the trials of the accused bombers.

By many accounts, the gathering in the Haymarket on May 4 was a peaceful affair. It followed earlier gatherings on May 1, and the speakers, mounted on the wagon now shown in the sculpture, addressed many topics around the themes of industrial justice: the eight-hour day, child labor laws, equality for women, and the like. At some point, a squad of police waded into the crowd. Throughout the day, and the days before, the police had cast a suspicious eye at the proceedings. On this day, as the police moved into the crowd, a bomb was thrown in their direction. Who did it and why remains a mystery.

In response to the bomb attack, other police on guard that day around the square began firing. (The next day the *Chicago Tribune* reported: "An incessant fire was kept up for nearly two minutes, and at least 250 shots were fired.") More than 100 protestors were wounded; some were killed. Of the police advancing in the square, seven were killed and another sixty were wounded, although upon investigation, it turned out that only one man, Officer Mathias J. Degan, died from shots fired from a non–police weapon.

Nothing prepared the city or the country for what was to follow. One account the day after reads like this:

> Chicago awoke on May 5, 1886, the morning after the Haymarket bombing, gripped in hysteria and paranoia. Behind every lamppost, in every saloon where immigrants congregated, in every darkened room, lurked a shifty-eyed anarchist clutching a dagger dripping with the blood of his latest victim, a bomb in his pocket ready to be thrown. . . . What had happened the night before was seen as not just a crime, but an attack on the nation itself. Where the national security was concerned, any measure of defense was warranted.

New York's police commissioner, Theodore Roosevelt, spoke for many when he condemned the protestors and sided with the police, saying: "I believe nothing would give them greater pleasure than a chance with rifles at one of the mobs." Nevertheless, opinion in the United States divided sharply between those who saw the Haymarket as state-sponsored violence (a police riot, along the lines of Mayor Daley's Gestapo tactics in 1968) and others who believed that the nation was under attack from subversive elements.

Much as the press fingered Osama bin Laden or Lee Harvey Oswald within an hour of the attacks on 9/11 or against President Kennedy, the Chicago police were quick to round up the usual suspects. On May 5, police raided a local German-language newspaper (nativism is a big part of the Haymarket story, and Chicago, including the stockyards, ran on immigrant labor) and arrested eight conspirators, charging them with having bomb-making equipment and being responsible for the Haymarket bombing.

When it turned out that only six of the eight conspirators were anywhere near the Haymarket when the bomb went off, the judge in the trial against the eight advanced the novel legal theory (worthy of some in Homeland America) that:

> If the past language of the accused has been such to incite violence, they are guilty of this crime, even if they knew nothing about it and were not present when it was committed.

The account of the trial continues: "On a principle which violated the basic rules of American law, in a courtroom clotted with prejudice, the eight men were convicted of murder."

Following the conviction of the eight, there were appeals and protests, not just in Chicago, but around the United States. Lawyer Clarence Darrow, writer William Dean Howells, and labor leader Eugene V. Debs were among those who protested the verdict, which nevertheless was affirmed in various higher courts. The governor of Illinois pardoned some of the defendants, citing a lack of evidence and biased proceedings. Four of those charged and convicted went to the gallows, singing "La Marseillaise." But even that was botched, and it took a long time for several to die. Others who would have been hanged committed suicide in prison.

Debs called the eight "the first martyrs in the cause of industrial freedom." Others said it was free speech itself that had been on trial. But one thing that was never proved then or subsequently was the identity of the actual bomber. Some alleged he was an anarchist, but others believed he was an agent provocateur, lighting a match that only a government repression could put out. The *New York Times* solemnly pronounced: "In the early stages of an acute outbreak of anarchy a Gatling gun, or if the case be severe, two, is the sovereign remedy. Later on hemp, in judicious doses, has an admirable effect in preventing the spread of the disease."

To take pictures of the Haymarket monument, Rob and I took turns dodging traffic, and, leaving the memorial, we rode around the contours of the modern square, wondering if we could turn up any more plaques about the event. Alas, there were none. I wondered why there was just this drab, modern sculpture in historic Haymarket Square, until, back home, I went online and learned that, over the years, the remembrances of the Haymarket Massacre have been just as controversial as the bombing.

It turned out that the main monument in the square (dating to 1889) was a pedestaled policeman with his arm extended (something pretty close to a Nazi salute, but really just a call for law and order). In the 1950s, the building of an expressway, which destroyed much of the square, shifted the monument around so that it looked more like a sign on the freeway.

Over the years, the statue was vandalized and spray-painted, until 1969—a year after the violent Democratic convention—when Weathermen student radicals blew it up. Mayor Richard J. Daley had it repaired and returned to its pedestal with a guard posted nearby, but a year later, the Weathermen blew it up again. This time the sculpture was moved to Chicago police headquarters and, finally, to the police academy, which is off-limits to the bomb-throwing public.

In the last battle of Haymarket Square, the anarchists would seem to have won.

Galesburg:
Stuck in the Middle with Amtrak

THE NEXT MORNING, with a train to Quincy, Illinois, at 7:35 a.m., I was awake at 5:30 a.m. and out the door on my packed bicycle at 6 a.m. I took the metro Blue Line into downtown and rode the few short blocks to Union Station, which was just coming to life around 7 a.m. I checked the train on the departure board, and then tried to juggle coffee and a muffin, which is hard to do when rolling a bicycle through a terminal, even one as grand as Union Station.

Part of the reason I was traveling with a folding bike was to get around Amtrak's stringent regulations about bicycles. (In general, it is easier to travel on Amtrak with a gun than with a bike.) The rules say that not all trains take bikes (only those with baggage cars), and that those bikes must be contained in official Amtrak boxes, which are the size of flatbed trucks. An exception is made for folding bikes, provided they are enclosed in a travel bag, which I had with me. Actually, through an Internet chat room, I had learned that an $8 IKEA DIMPA plastic bag worked beautifully for carrying Bromptons, and that's what I had. Even so, the nasty Amtrak conductor ragged on me about "not bagging the bicycle in the terminal."

I bagged the bike next to the departing train. The frame of the Brompton came to gather instantly, and I slid it into my IKEA bag while other passengers stood around and stared in admiration. But the conductor wasn't through with me yet, and she took the few passengers boarding the train that morning and herded us all into one car. (The rest of the cars were empty.) Clearly the conductors on duty that morning to Quincy could not be bothered to move among the cars. I had thought I would have a window seat and space beside me for my books, maps, and coffee—the reason to ride the train. Instead, I was pointed toward an aisle seat next to an obese woman. As the train left Chicago, I furtively ate my muffin and drank my coffee, in what felt like a third-grade lockdown.

I persist in riding Amtrak trains because they are in my blood. I grew up on Long Island, and some of my fondest childhood memories are of taking the Long Island Rail Road into New York City. At age six, I made my first train trip with my father—we went to Philadelphia, Reading, and Tamaqua in Pennsylvania—and I have never looked back, except to spot an approaching engine.

My bedside table is crammed with railroad timetables, and my computer has enough railroad maps for me to staff a dispatcher's tower. I first rode Amtrak when it began in 1971, and while I have taken it to all corners of the United States, I ride sullenly and under protest. Yes, it has tracks, engines, sleepers, and dining cars, but for the most part I think of it as being much like a Russian bus company—cramped, not always very clean, late, and run by conductors who sound like wardens.

If the choice is between Amtrak and a car, I will take Amtrak. If the choice is a train anywhere else in the world or Amtrak, I will go anywhere else, which may explain why I have lived in train-happy Europe for the last thirty years. Bikes are easily wheeled on to most European trains, and, except in Germany, conductors are silent, and indifferent to where you sit.

The one thing Amtrak does well is Wi-Fi, and I did appreciate, squeezed into my seat, that I could connect my computer and catch up on e-mail as the train left the station and stopped at such little used Illinois stations as Naperville, Plano, and Mendota. Not until Kewanee did I get the seats to myself, and finally I could spread out the newspaper, unfold my maps, and look out the window. By then the train was empty, and not even my nemesis conductor could insist that I be squeezed together with another passenger.

Central Illinois is mostly open farmland. I wished I could have stopped in Galesburg, which had the look of an interesting railroad town. Many freight companies come through Galesburg, including the Burlington Northern Santa Fe, and I have read somewhere that the town is building a National Railroad Hall of Fame. But other than Casey Jones, who would be inducted into such a hall? Leland Stanford of the Southern Pacific? Alexander Cassatt, the president of the Pennsylvania who built the original Penn Station on New York's West 33rd Street? James J. Hill of the Northern Pacific? It struck me that the museum could find itself long on robber barons.

Amtrak pulled into Quincy—the last stop—just after noon. As I had suspected from Google Maps, the Quincy station is no longer downtown but outside the center of the small city. A few cars and families greeted the train. The station, while quaint, has a rundown look, and I didn't see any place to pick up a map or brochure about the town. Fortunately, I had the bike to get into Quincy, but even so it took me about twenty minutes to ride into the downtown area.

At one point I stopped to overlook the Mississippi River—it was a murky brown and the current appeared dead—and then tackled some serious hills before I found Quincy's center, which unfolded around Washington Park.

Quincy: Biking with the Ghosts of Lincoln and Douglas

In truth, I wasn't headed to Quincy, but farther south on the Mississippi, to see where Mark Twain (then Samuel Clemens) had grown up in Hannibal, Missouri. Quincy, about twenty-five miles from Hannibal, was the closest stop on the train, and to get to Hannibal, I figured I might be able to catch a bus or, if there wasn't one, ride my bike. My concern about bike riding was the road, which on the map looked busy (and in my mind this means trucks).

Only when I got to Quincy did I learn that it was one of the locations where in 1858 Abraham Lincoln and Stephen A. Douglas had their famous debates. While slowly biking around the contours of Washington Park, I found a bronze statue showing Lincoln on his feet, speaking, while Douglas sits close by, his arms folded. The date on the statue is October 13, 1858, and it was at Quincy where Lincoln raised the stakes in the senatorial election, saying that slavery was "a moral, a social, and political wrong." (Douglas's view was that it was not a moral issue and that the states "can exist forever divided into free and slave states.")

Behind the statue, much to my delight, I discovered what is called the Lincoln-Douglas Debate Interpretive Center and thought, "Now that's a museum that was made for me." Even better, when I tried the front door it was open. The woman at the back, behind a counter, didn't even mind that I came in with a bicycle. All she wanted to know, for her record keeping, was where I was from. At the beginning of the trip, I would answer this question by saying "Switzerland." Later, to cut down on the conversations that followed, I would reply "New York." Finally, when all I wanted from the clerk was a nod, I would say "New Jersey." No one ever followed up that location by saying, "Now isn't that something?" Everywhere I went during my travels, the one question I always got was, "Where are you folks from?"

Once I had reviewed Swiss history with the center's volunteer, I was free to look around the museum, which turned out to be the best I would find on the Lincoln-Douglas debates. (The museums in Springfield and Charleston lack the clarity of the Quincy presentations.) In various cabinets were excerpts from the debates, displays on how the candidates traveled (by train, boat, and horse), and where they stayed in Quincy. For example, Lincoln spent time before the debate at Orville Browning's elegant house in town, but afterward, in a state of nervous collapse from speaking, he was taken—almost carried—to the Farmer's Home Hotel, where his supporters gave him a "rum sweat." According to the museum exhibit, "he was covered with blankets, and the vapors of the rum induced a profuse sweat and a period of restful sleep."

What interested me the most in the museum was a series of charts that explained how the vote divided in the Illinois election of 1858. Keep in mind: until 1913, state legislatures chose a state's US senators, so only indirectly is it possible to reconstruct the votes cast either for Lincoln or Douglas. What we have are the votes for state legislators, who, in turn, will vote (along party lines mostly) for a US senator.

Lincoln lost the 1858 senatorial election to Douglas. In the voting, Douglas (or more precisely candidates pledged to Douglas by the Democratic party) won forty of the seventy-five seats in the House of Representatives, and fourteen of the twenty-five seats in the Illinois Senate. When they voted to elect a federal senator, the vote exactly followed party lines, with fifty-four votes cast for Douglas and forty-four for Lincoln. But of the 366,983 popular votes cast, the Republicans—the party of Lincoln that had moved on from the Whigs—won 190,468 while Douglas's Democrats only received 166,374.

The reason Lincoln did not win was because not every seat in Illinois was up for reelection in 1858 and because the southern part of the state (more rural, Southern in outlook, Democratic) held a disproportionate number of seats in the state legislature. Lincoln won the upstate districts and Chicago, but lost the southern half of the state. In 1858, the population of Chicago was probably less than 100,000. A hundred years later, Mayor Daley could have found that number of votes in a few graveyards.

Even in 1858, there were voting irregularities around the state. In one of the closer contests, it was alleged that the Democrats had paid some moonshiners from "over the hills" to vote with them. It was the kind of story that was told early and often in Illinois politics, but rather than get angry or demand a recount, Lincoln, as was his wont, turned the episode into one of his stock stories—the kind he would tell in the White House, during what otherwise were thought to be important meetings of state. (Civil War generals, in particular, were always complaining that instead of talking tactics in the White House, Lincoln had spent the time telling jokes.)

Not surprisingly, Stevenson's *The Black Book* quotes one such Lincoln story, which could easily have been told about his lost 1858 election, although here he reversed the offending party. He would say:

> I remember from boyhood some rather disreputable fellows whom we never saw from one year to the next, except on election day. They had to come over the hills about twenty miles to vote, and they always did—and they always voted Republican. Somebody finally asked them if twenty miles wasn't an awful long way to come just to cast their ballots, and one of them answered, "We don't mind. The fact is, it's about the only money we make all year."

Lincoln had another quality that infuriated some of his listeners. He had a habit of laughing hard at his own jokes, which no doubt encouraged him to tell more. (I know the feeling.)

Hannibal, Missouri: Crop-Dusting to the Mississippi

I LIKED QUINCY. Many of the buildings looked historic, and from parts of the downtown I could see the Mississippi River. For some reason, the city reminded me of Bangor, Maine (where my wife was born), but, as I would later tell her, "without all the charm."

Many Quincy storefronts downtown were vacant, and a lot of the warehouses on the edge of town looked abandoned. Farmers from nearby communities were about, picking up or dropping off supplies, but overall the business district seemed to be in a recession.

With subsidies from the state, the city has set up Lincoln-Douglas commemorative plaques around town, and I followed some in Washington Park, until it was time to turn my sights to lunch and Hannibal, Missouri. I had asked in the interpretive center if there was a nearby luncheonette, and the curator had pointed me around the corner to a deli, but it was closed.

On the way south out of town, I stopped at a tourist office, and again only got vague directions about a lunch place "down the road some, and then to your left." In my saddlebag, I did have an apple and water, but I left Quincy without finding a sandwich, even though it was a twenty-five-mile ride to Mark Twain's hometown.

Usually in my rides across America there are places to eat. This time I found nothing. Highway 57 is two lanes of high-speed blacktop, but without gas stations or even many buildings. Nor did it even have shoulders on the side of the road, which meant any time I heard an eighteen-wheel truck bearing down on me, I stopped and dragged my bike into the fields. About the only commercial business I did pass was the Chelsea Adult Superstore ("Where fun and fantasy meet"), but at that point in the ride I hadn't worked up an appetite for lace underwear.

The ride to Hannibal took almost two hours, and toward the end I got lost when I decided to quit Highway 57 and take smaller roads closer to the Mississippi. They showed up on my map as quaint county roads, the kind that are usually ideal for the bike. This time I found myself on unpaved routes amidst the cornfields, like those in Alfred Hitchcock's *North by Northwest* where Cary Grant is almost done in by a crop-dusting plane.

The only way for me to ride across the Mississippi to get into Hannibal was to use a bridge on Interstate 72 and stick to the shoulder. On the Missouri side, I had to sweat up a long grade (I felt a bit like the rum Lincoln) to Palmyra Road, from where it was a long descent into Hannibal. I followed the signs for Tom Sawyer's fence, Becky Thatcher's house, and the Mark Twain cave complex, and soon I was on Main Street, which made me homesick for Quincy's dilapidated elegance.

Somewhere in my mind, I must have known that Hannibal would not be an excerpt from *Adventures of Huckleberry Finn*. I must have read somewhere that it was an off-ramp of RV America. Still I wasn't prepared, especially after crop-dusting, for MarkTwainWorld, with its gift shops, bars, motels, and Connecticut Yankee antique stores. To get my bearings, I rode around Hannibal, only stopping to wonder if Tom Sawyer bought his fence at Walmart ("they came to jeer, but remained to whitewash"). If Sam Clemens isn't turning in his grave, at least he is chuckling about his one-man show, "Personal Recollections of the Civil War," since he missed most of the war in California.

After the long ride, I was hot, tired, and in need of lunch. Instead of spending time in Mark Twain's boyhood home—not far from the statue of Tom and Huck—I sat down at a table on the main street and ordered a club sandwich and lemonade. Twain resigned from the human race when he wrote (between 1904 and 1909) his bitter *Letters from the Earth* ("His heaven is like himself: strange, interesting, astonishing, grotesque. I give you my word, it has not a single feature in it that he actually values"). I might have followed his path to self-imposed exile ("More men go to church than want to"), except that a second lemonade restored my faith in humanity.

Hannibal: Sammy Clemens Learns Long Talk

Every few years I reread *Huck Finn* or *The Adventures of Tom Sawyer,* although of late I have taken to listening to them on tape. From the novels, I have a clear image in my mind of Hannibal. For that reason, to imagine Tom, I didn't need to pay admission to the "cave complex" or, to recall some of the dialogue between Huck and Jim on the raft, take a ride on an "authentic" paddle-wheel steamer. ("Jim he couldn't see no sense in the most of it, but he allowed we was white folks and knowed better than him.") But I did want to know more about the young Sam Clemens, which led me to pick up, at a side street shop, an old book (1952) by Dixon Wecter entitled *Sam Clemens of Hannibal,* which I read on the bus to St. Louis and later mailed to myself at home.

Usually Wecter calls him Sam, not Mark or Mark Twain, and the stories he tells about the young Clemens growing up beside the Mississippi River have none of the droll wit that infects *Tom Sawyer* or *Huck Finn* with their charms. (Tom: "A robber is more high-toned than what a pirate is—as a general thing. In most countries they're awful high up in the nobility—dukes and such.") Still, Wecter separates the fact from the fiction, and, best of all to me, he explains how Twain got his storytelling skill from his mother, his ear for dialogue from the family's slaves, and his sense of adventure from the other boys in Hannibal who spent their winters chopping holes in river ice and their summers exploring the caves. Of

Twain's literary inspiration from slaves, Wecter writes: "But more typical of daily life was the Negro in his docile, easy-going, cheerful moods—friend and comrade of all children, with much time and boundless inclination to go fishing or hunting wild turkeys or blackberrying over the hills, and even when Sam was too young for such rambles, to entertain him and his brother and sisters with woodlore, African superstitions, song, and stories."

Like a character in a Twain novel, the father of Sam Clemens was well meaning but a hopeless dreamer, who moved his family to Hannibal in 1839. He believed his fortune would be made when an ancestor died and he came into property in far-off Kentucky (where earlier members of the Clemens clan had lived and invested in land). A neighbor describes the father as "never a practical man, but an energetic dreamer . . . courteous, well-educated . . . a good conversationalist." He never found his jackpot on the banks of the Mississippi, and he died when Twain was eleven, leaving the boy to be raised by his mother. Wecter writes: "But no doubt the shock of his father's death and the guilty secret of the post-mortem upon which he had spied, had stirred profounder emotional depths within this lad of eleven years than any promise to be a better boy, and its implicit renunciation of freedom."

While a conventional mother and homemaker who scrubbed her children for Sunday school and made them say prayers before bed, Jane Clemens was also a town gossip and an hysteric, prone to superstitions, sightings of ghosts, and a litany of wives' tales. (Tom had nothing on her in believing that dead cats were a cure for warts.) Wecter writes that Sam got from his mother a "Kentucky hill-woman's fascination with direful dreams and the catalogue of human woes—

such a tale of deathbeds, funeral notices, disasters, prodigal sons, and the plight of orphans as makes up a typical letter she wrote her 'dear children' a few years after their dispersal, about old Hannibal neighbors. 'This is a world of trouble,' she concludes. 'This is a gloomy evening I have written of the troubles of your old friends.'"

It was also from his mother, I am sure, that Sam acquired his sense of showmanship, his ability to tell a story on stage (an important part of the Twain legend), and his dulcet voice. Wecter writes: "His most striking mannerism was the soft-spoken drawl borrowed from his mother, which she called 'Sammy's long talk.'" After Twain became famous, Annie Laurie Hawkins (known to the world as Becky Thatcher) remembered her famous friend: "As children we considered Mark Twain humorous, not that what he said or the stories he told were particularly so, but he possessed a drawling, appealing voice." That was his mother speaking.

Twain called some of his novels "a hymn to boyhood," but, like most, he chose to idealize his growing up and, by extension, his hometown. Not everything in Hannibal was as carefree as Tom's summer vacations along the river.

The young Sam saw slaves sold "down the river" to markets in New Orleans, and in an instant some of his friends died of consumption or while playing on the icy Mississippi. His family struggled for money, especially after his father died, and a lot of Sam's younger years were spent as a printer's assistant (the wages were "uncashable promises"), wearing ill-fitting, hand-me-down clothes ("his shirts gave me the uncomfortable sense of living in a circus tent"). Nevertheless, he preferred to remember his hometown (much like the tourist board does today) in idealized images. Wecter writes:

> Hannibal forever remained his symbol of security in days when disasters and frustrations were closing in upon him . . . Mark did not dwell so exclusively upon the serenity and beauty of his idyl as to neglect the dangers and terrors it also held for a boy—drownings, corpses, ghosts, African superstitions, mobs, feuds, and manifold shapes of disaster and violent death that seem to lurk at every bend of road and river—even though in the end they are placated and transcended.

Wecter concludes, as other critics have: "All his days he wrote fiction under the cloak of autobiography, and autobiography with the trappings of fiction."

Well documented elsewhere is that the prototypes for many celebrated Twain characters roamed the streets of Hannibal when Sam was growing up. For example, Jimmy Finn was the town drunkard, and his son was a free spirit who was the envy of the other boys consigned to school during the week and church sermons on Sunday. Wecter describes the original articles: "Like Huck Finn, whose image Mark Twain repeatedly identified with him, Tom [Sawyer] was ill-fed, an outrageous wreck of rags, dirty, ignorant, cheerful, carefree, and altogether enviable, being 'the only really independent person—boy or man—in the community.'"

The way out of Hannibal for the young Clemens wasn't a raft but his storytelling, for which he first took to the stage, as a teenager, when a traveling showman on the river needed a straight man to answer the question: "Were you ever in the mesmeric state?" At age fifteen, Sam played the game to perfection, and became the talk of the town. In his *Autobiography*, however, he adds: "When the magician's engagement closed there was but one person in the village who did not believe in mesmerism and I was the one." For most of his adult life, however, Twain held America in a mesmeric state, as he took Hannibal and the Mississippi on endless tours across the country.

The boyhood of Sam Clemens ended around 1853, when he was eighteen and left for a series of jobs as a printer, journalist, sketch writer, and riverboat hand on the Mississippi. (In 1858 he was working the river as a cub pilot during the Lincoln-Douglas debate that took place in Quincy.)

Although as an adult Twain was never far from Hannibal, at least in his imagination, he only came back once to the town—in 1892, by which time he was a national celebrity, in part because of his stories set on the river. (*Tom Sawyer* was published in 1876, and *Huckleberry Finn* in 1884.)

On his return Twain stood for pictures near his boyhood house—that which since then has been moved, repainted, enlarged, gift-shopped, and rechristened as the Mark Twain Boyhood Home & Museum—and he remembered, somewhat somberly, his lost companions of youth: "I should like to call back Will Bowen and John Garth and the others, and live the life, and be as we were, and make holiday until 15, then all drown together."

As I did on this trip, Twain also spent a lot of time with friends from his childhood, catching up on what happened to those they had known together. He reported that Tom Sawyer's cave was being quarried for cement and that Tom Blankenship (aka Tom Sawyer) was working as a justice of the peace in Montana. About Hannibal he said: "These things may have been true. They may not have been true. But they were interesting. That is the main requirement in a village like that." Twain later wrote of the visit: "I went home to dream and was not disappointed."

St. Louis: The Old Man . . . the Old Miss

When I was done touring around Hannibal, I had to catch the bus to St. Louis, which is about two hours south of Twain Land. My problem was that no one along Main Street had any idea where the bus stopped. The waitress at the restaurant thought it skipped Hannibal altogether, while a woman in the bookshop said it probably stopped "somewhere out on 61," referring to a route on my map. Cutting it close to the departure, I was in something of a panic until a man said unequivocally that the bus stopped at the Hardee's on Route 61 and that I could get there by taking Broadway from the end of Main Street "up over the hill."

I decided that my best bet was to follow his advice, and, as directed, I followed Broadway and started counting traffic lights (three were mentioned in the directions). I had about thirty minutes to get out to Route 61, but I had not counted on the hills between Main Street and Hardee's. No sooner would I climb up one hill than there was another, although the newer part of Hannibal had few cars and wide streets. What it did not have, however, was prosperity, and I despair whenever I think about Hannibal's forlorn commercial district.

Rum sweating up the hills, I passed a Methodist church, a muffler center, a job training center, some bars, and general services buildings. Mostly what I rode along, however, was a main street of broken dreams, with many empty storefronts and none of the perky optimism that I had seen down the hill in Twain's fictional Hannibal. That is a Potemkin village of happy campers and Becky Thatcher look-alikes. Up here, although I was only a mile removed from the wax figures, Hannibal could well have been the poster child of faded rust belt dreams. Few people were on the sidewalks, and the post office looked as though the last letter sent from there might have come from Twain himself ("It is at our mother's knee that we acquire our highest and noblest and purest ideals but there is seldom any money in them").

I found the Hardee's with about ten minutes to spare before the bus departed. It was at a crossroads on Route 61, and the teenagers flipping burgers said the bus was usually late. Hungry from my ride, I bought a chicken sandwich that came with a drink the size of corn silo. I was thirsty so I didn't mind the indulgence, and, besides, everyone else in Hardee's was enjoying the same silage.

When the Burlington Trailways bus arrived, the driver casually loaded my bike (in its bag, although on the buses that was unnecessary) into the underneath storage locker, and I bought a ticket that cost $42 (more than the train ride from Chicago). The bus waited while some passengers fueled up inside the Hardee's (for much of the ride, french fries were in the air), and then it joined the procession of traffic that followed 61 south until we picked up Interstate 64 and drove into downtown St. Louis. (The suburb of Ferguson had been in the news, but I didn't see it.) I had dinner arranged for 8 p.m., but still had time, in the late afternoon sunshine, to explore downtown St. Louis, where I had not been since 1981.

I wish now that I stayed longer in St. Louis. I loved the city and would have been happy going to a baseball game or the art museum. I should also have made time to visit Hardscrabble, the cabin where Ulysses S. Grant lived in the 1850s when, no longer in the army, he eked out a living by cutting trees for firewood and selling the cords around St. Louis. (When a friend recognized the former army officer of the Mexican War on the sidewalk and said, "Great God, Grant, what are you doing?" the future general and president answered: "I am solving the problem of poverty.") But when I was mapping out my route across Illinois, I only saw St. Louis as a place to visit my brother-in-law's mother (she lives in Clayton) and catch the morning train to Springfield, Illinois. By the time I figured out that St. Louis held, at least for me, many attractions, I was booked in and out on the last Trailways bus and the first Amtrak train.

Like many American cities, St. Louis has turned its rail stations into hotels, shopping centers, and fast-food outlets—the elegant St. Louis Union Station Hotel is a Hilton—so I arrived at the Gateway Multimodal Transportation Center, the college phrase for yet another dreary bus station.

I knew I could turn left on Market Street and ride west for eight miles, and I would get to Clayton—or close. Instead, with a little time before my dinner, I turned right out of the transportation center and rode toward the Gateway Arch. Although it was six in the evening, rush-hour traffic appeared over, and I felt as though I had the city to myself, which made it easy to pull over at one point and photograph a curbside statue of Ulysses S. Grant, although he was without his wheelbarrow and cordwood.

On my way to the Arch, I made a little detour when I saw Busch Stadium, not expecting to find it downtown. I had assumed that the baseball Cardinals played in a suburb, as many teams do. But this ballpark is a short walk from the Arch and many local office buildings, and is surrounded by sports bars and parking (my only complaint, as open lots are a killer for graceful cities). I sensed, too, that the playing field at Busch Stadium is set below ground level, as the upper decks do not tower over the surrounding blocks.

Best of all, the new Busch Stadium, which cost $365 million and opened in 2006, was built with team money (the city only kicked in a $45 million term loan), and it allows the Cardinals to pay, on average, $31 million in city and state taxes. No wonder the Cardinals have won eleven World Series and compete for the championship most years. They play baseball while the White Sox play politics.

I didn't bike down to the river, but stood in a park outside the old courthouse that overlooks the Arch and the Mississippi. The setting sun glistened on the Arch, although at that moment my only inspiration came from Clark Griswold (Chevy Chase) in *National Lampoon's Vacation*. As Clark is driving the family west, passing over the river ("That's the Mississippi. The mighty Mississip. The old Miss . . . The old man . . ."), he looks up and says to his children in the backseat: "Do you see that, kids? That's the St. Louis Arch. The gateway to the West. It's over six hundred feet tall, and there's an elevator all the way to the top." His son Rusty asks, "Dad, can we go up on it?" to which Griswold responds, perhaps on behalf of the Universal Association of Beleaguered Vacationing Fathers (UABVF): "Nope."

Gateway Arch Park, while attractive to look at, had the feel of a world's fairground after the tents have folded. A few people were strolling about, but not many, and the rest of the waterfront—at least across the river—had an industrial feel.

As a city, St. Louis faces inland to the west, not east to the river, especially now that the steamboats and ferries are gone.

Later, when I read Theodore Dreiser's *A Hoosier Holiday* (his 1914 drive across the Midwest was similar to mine a hundred years later), I was reminded of St. Louis and its waterfront when I came upon a passage in which Dreiser despairs over how American cities—unlike those in Europe—shun elegant waterfront development: He writes:

> Today blocks and blocks of the most interesting property in the city is devoted to dead-alive stores, warehouses and tenements. It would be an easy matter and a profitable one for the city to condemn sufficient property to make a splendid drive along this river and give the city a real air. . . . The mere thought of trading the old houses for a wonderful scene which would add beauty and life to the city is too much of a stretch of the imagination for St. Louisians to accomplish. It can't be done . . . American cities are not given to imagination outside the walks of trade.

Leaving the Arch, I fell into conversation with two St. Louis policemen who were also on bicycles and amused at the appearance of my folding bike, wondering if maybe I had escaped from the circus. Not prepared for humorous cops, I responded seriously by asking them the best way to get to Clayton. They gave me directions to Forest Park Avenue, indicating that eventually I could pick up a bike path in the park.

My evening bike ride across St. Louis was among the nicest of my travels. The weather was ideal, and the streets were empty. I liked it that in downtown St. Louis many beaux arts office buildings have been converted to residential lofts, and all the restaurants on my route looked inviting. As the amusing cops had predicted, I did find Forest Park Avenue, where Market Street turns, and after going past Saint Louis University, I found the bike path that runs along one of the country's great city parks.

Because it was getting dark, I didn't wander into Forest Park, but rode along its edges. On my right were grand St. Louis houses. On my left was the park, which includes an art and a history museum. There were lakes, running paths, soft lawns, and even a municipal golf course, all of which looked inviting.

At the end of the park, I entered the campus of Washington University, which I had never seen, but which impressed me for its immaculate campus. I know, never judge a college by its quadrangle, but Washington's is as elegant as Harvard's Yard. Just before 8 p.m., I rolled into the suburban small city of Clayton in time for dinner with my brother-in-law's mother, who, when she saw my folding bike, exclaimed (a bit like the St. Louis cops): "I don't believe it."

The *Texas Eagle* to Springfield, Illinois: Lackluster

My dinner out in Clayton with Roxie Frank was elegant beyond words, and the lively conversation—she's ebullient, kind, and warm—bounced among the various members of our shared families. So much did we have to say to each other that I didn't even order from the menu, but let the restaurant owner pick for me, and I drank wine as though it was the water I had missed on the ride from Quincy. And it felt good to be a long way from the Hannibal Hardee's.

The next morning, my Amtrak train to Springfield left early (7:55 a.m.), so I wanted to be up at 6 a.m. and out the door by 6:30 a.m. for the ride into St. Louis. Nevertheless, Roxie insisted on serving me a full breakfast (scrambled eggs, bagels, juice, and coffee), and right until I carried the folding bike into the elevator in her building, we were sharing family stories and laughing (which doesn't come easily for me at six in the morning).

Just as I had wandered on my ride out to Clayton, I loved heading back into St. Louis. The sun was coming up, this time through the Arch, and a light mist lay on the grass in Forest Park. I took an interior road this time, and went by the art museum (where the ever-generous Roxie had donated money for a new gallery).

Past the art museum, I got a little lost when I strayed from the paved paths. For a few minutes, I worried about missing my train as I wandered up a steep hill in the woods near the Children's Hospital. Eventually I straightened myself out and found a long descent that brought me to Market Street, the converted Union Station (stunning in the morning light), and the insipid transportation center.

It was an hour's bike ride, but, in the end, I didn't need to rum sweat it, as my Amtrak train (the *Texas Eagle* coming from Los Angeles) was more than an hour late. That delay gave me time to drink some transportation center coffee and read the St. Louis newspapers (by that point, no longer singing the praises of "dead anarchists" but boosting the St. Louis Cardinals).

Part of the fun that Amtrak takes away from train travel is that it herds passengers like sheep, and in St. Louis the railroad doesn't allow travelers to wait on the platforms (or where they choose). Instead, before the train arrives, travelers are lined up in a linoleum hallway, as if everyone boarding the *Eagle* were an errant second grader.

Coming overnight from Texas, the train had the feel of a flophouse, with passengers sprawled across seats asleep or snoring in the corners. I left my bagged bike on the luggage rack (the conductor wasn't very happy to see it) and found a seat upstairs in the double-decker car. Alas the reading lights were out, so I shifted into the club car, which had swivel chairs and floor-to-ceiling windows, both of which I liked.

The lackluster *Eagle* crept between St. Louis and Alton, but picked up speed through the farmland of southern Illinois. I kept thinking of the districts that had voted for Stephen A. Douglas and got a good look at many towns, as, in many communities, we were running on tracks that bisected the main street. My seatmate in the club car was a high school history teacher, and she warmed to the story of my Midwest wanderings and liked it that I was headed to Springfield in search of Lincoln.

Springfield: Trailing Behind Lincoln

THE TRAIN ARRIVED IN SPRINGFIELD a little before noon, and I pieced together the Brompton next to a Lincoln Trail sign that identified this station on Jefferson Street as where the president's funeral train had arrived in May 1865, after he was assassinated. The plaque reads, in part: "The long procession moved east down Jefferson through the throngs of mourners and packed city streets."

Lincoln is buried north of downtown Springfield, in Oak Ridge Cemetery, but I rode west, to get my bearings in the city and find my room for the night, which was in a bed-and-breakfast on the other side of the capital.

Springfield has to be among the most unimpressive state capitals in the country. The architecture around the capitol is a bland mix of 1960s office functionality mixed into streets with vacant lots (for parking) and small row houses. (The poet Vachel Lindsay lived in one of the frame houses, which is still standing.) Clearly the business of running Illinois is done in Chicago, where I am sure the governor now has an office, and mostly what happens in Springfield are meetings of the legislature. Nor are there the office buildings of lobbyists on the fringe. Beyond the downtown core are neighborhoods of track suburban houses that probably were built in the 1950s.

Aside from state government, the big business in Springfield is Lincoln, with Lincoln Trail signs everywhere pointing out his law offices, train stations, library, museum, and home. Without the martyred Lincoln, Springfield might well be Pierre, South Dakota.

In less than an hour of bike riding, I had dropped off my bags in the room and been up and down Springfield several times. Instead of heading straight for the Lincoln home, I decided to book an afternoon tour and eat lunch ahead of time, remembering my meal fiasco on the road to Hannibal.

It was a late summer day, with clear sunshine, and I rode slowly along many streets to pick a restaurant, finally settling on a microbrewery that was catty-corner to the Lincoln visitor center. (Did Abe say to Mary, "Ma, shall we head over to the micro and grab some wings?") It had tables set up outside and, clearly, mugs of cold beer, but the sandwich I ordered came on a platter that could have easily fed a family of four.

Mounded all around the plate were jumbo french fries, and had I been a crocodile (they save their prey), I would have dragged the sandwich back to my lair and worked on it for days. As it was, I ate half of what was served, drank the beer, and understood better why some Americans were entering what they call the "super obese" category. On the train, an obese man near me had occupied both seats and had struggled going up and down the narrow stairs. At the time I wondered if he weighed four hundred pounds, and at lunch I wondered why everyone at the restaurant didn't weigh the same, including me.

After lunch, I watched the visitor center movie about Lincoln and joined my 2 p.m. tour of the house, which is located in a small national park of preserved wooden Springfield houses. The Lincoln home, at the center, is where there is the most activity, with a steady stream of visitors coming and going. As in Williamsburg, Virginia, many of the nearby houses are open, and they show early American kitchens, print shops, and the like.

The problem with many historic house tours is that they focus more on the china and draperies than on the politics of those who had lived there. This tour was no exception. My guide spoke about how Mrs. Lincoln persuaded Abe to buy the Greek revival home in 1844 and how they had renovated it in 1856 (he was a wealthy lawyer and could afford his wife's taste in fine carpeting and furniture).

I spent most of the time inside looking at the back parlor, where some of Lincoln's law books are on a table and there are newspapers near a rocking chair. My sense of Lincoln is that he had three pastimes besides politics and his legal work, his children, his newspapers, and his cats, and back here he could indulge all three. The room felt unchanged from Lincoln's time.

From my reading, I knew that when Adlai Stevenson II was Illinois governor and living in Springfield (the mansion is on East Jackson Street, which is nearby), he would occasionally, when facing a hard decision, walk over to the Lincoln home and sit for a while in Abe's chair. I liked the association and know Lincoln would have approved.

From the Lincoln home, I biked to his law offices. They were closed, for some reason, so I read the plaques outside and went a little farther north to the complex that is the Lincoln library and museum, both of which depressed me.

I am sure I went to Springfield thinking that I would find Lincoln as he appears in literature: witty, wry, outspoken, humane, literate, and compassionate. In my mind, I find it easy to imagine him writing a letter (so often have I seen his script) or laughing at his own jokes. In the museum, however, Lincoln is reduced to a wax figure—chopping wood on the frontier, debating Douglas, or emancipating the slaves, as though his life, instead of belonging to the ages, now belongs to Disney.

I am sure the museum was laid out with schoolchildren in mind, and maybe they take away some lessons about frontier life or a law office in the 1840s. But the embalmed Lincoln who has to work the tourist trade struck me as little different from Mark Twain's duke and dauphin, playing the Royal Nonesuch in tents along the Mississippi. In the museum it helps to believe in mesmerism.

My mood did not change dramatically in the Lincoln Presidential Library, which was across the street. My ticket seemed to work for both places. At least no one stopped me at the front door. Inside, I was hoping to find an exhibition on Lincoln's own writing—he wrote as well, if not better, than most presidents—or about the books of his life, of which there are thousands (well, enough to fill this large library).

Instead, I walked into a branch of a not-very-successful public library, the kind that has some outdated copies of *Smithsonian* magazine in the lobby and the *Encyclopedia Britannica* on a far wall. Here, Lincoln is the greeter of a trade association, the front man for a guild of authors whose job it is to write obscure tracts, along the lines of: *The Lincoln Hypothesis: A Modern-Day Abolitionist Investigates the Possible Connection Between Joseph Smith, the Book of Mormon, and Abraham Lincoln.*

Feeling like the young Sam Clemens trapped in Sunday school, I didn't think I could just turn and leave, so I looked at a temporary art exhibition (something like "Abraham Lincoln and the Image of the Frontier") and watched as two authors set up their books for a reading that evening.

For a moment, I considered coming back for the event, but I feared getting trapped among Lincoln professionals ("I'm interested in his reaction to the Kansas-Nebraska Act. . ."). I sat for a while at a long table—clearly the scholars were all upstairs in the closed stacks—and glanced at some brochures, but all I could think about was how little Lincoln himself would have liked his own library.

Lincoln's only formal schooling was part of one year in the fourth grade. For his reading, which ranged from Shakespeare to legal texts, he used books the way he used rafts on the Ohio River, as vessels to guide him along life's swift currents. I am sure he read with a pencil in his hand (something that doesn't thrill librarians), and for his legal cases and speeches, he was always hunting up compelling passages or precedents. He also likely used books to recall the eloquence that he must have sensed was in his mother (she died when he was nine), and to escape the oppression of his father (who treated Abe as an indentured servant).

I doubt he ever purchased valuable bound volumes or obscure European texts, in the sense that Thomas Jefferson did. Books were to be consumed, not collected. Lincoln was content with some basic works (the classics, novels, poetry, plays, the Bible—if you want more, there is a journal article called "What Abraham Lincoln Read"). On most nights, his books probably were stacked up next to his rocking chair, in a messy pile that infuriated Mary Todd, and never locked away in glass cabinets. Were the presidential library true to its patron's habits of mind, it would look less like a federal office building and more like a secondhand bookstore.

Springfield: Abraham Lincoln's Farewell Address

WHAT SAVED MY AFTERNOON in Springfield were two things: I retreated, as I often do when feeling glum, to a railroad station, and, to cheer myself up, I bought a book, Roy Morris Jr.'s *The Long Pursuit,* about the entangled lives of Lincoln and Stephen A. Douglas.

In following the Lincoln trail signs around Springfield, I had learned the city had preserved three railroad stations in his honor, and they struck me as perfect destinations for an afternoon bike ride.

My first stop was at Springfield's Union Station, which served several lines, although principally the Illinois Central, which connected Chicago to the Gulf of Mexico. It was on its tracks, east of here, that Steve Goodman wrote in 1970:

Riding on the City of New Orleans
Illinois Central Monday morning rail
Fifteen cars and fifteen restless riders
Three conductors and twenty-five sacks of mail . . .
Good morning, America, how are you?
Say, don't you know me? I'm your native son.

No longer in railroad service, Union Station is now the visitors' welcome center for the presidential library. The interior is beautifully restored, but I grow mournful whenever I am in stations without trains. (Think of a church absent of faith.) I didn't linger but looked at some of the railroad maps and picked up a Lincoln Trail brochure, and rode to the Great Western Depot, from which, in February 1861, Lincoln departed for his presidency.

Although the small station is well marked at 8th and Jackson, and even has a flagpole, it took me a few turns through the neighborhood until I pulled up in front of it. Because it was after 4 p.m., I could not go inside. I didn't mind, as what interested me most were the words Lincoln spoke to his townspeople and neighbors outside, before leaving on the special train to Washington.

Lincoln didn't know it that day—although he may have sensed it in that brooding Lincolnian way—but he was leaving Springfield for the last time. (His next visit would come on the funeral train.) The night before he left, he composed a short speech to say goodbye. I had not known the text until, straddling the bike, I read the words that are printed outside the station. (There is also a facsimile of his handwritten version, which may have been written later that morning on the train. Lincoln, a lawyer, liked to keep copies of his speeches and publish them.)

Lincoln's "Farewell Address," as it is now called, comes from the hand that is distinctly Lincoln's. No one else could have written it, and the structure of the language anticipates both his first and second inaugural addresses, but also that at Gettysburg. (Like Jefferson, Lincoln was his own speechwriter. By contrast, Obama traveled with four on duty and more back at the White House.) I am not sure whether Lincoln delivered it from the rear of the train, before it departed, or at the side of the track—the plaque only speaks of "this site"—but what he said was this:

> My friends, no one, not in my situation, can appreciate my feeling of sadness at this parting. To this place, and the kindness of these people, I owe every thing. Here I have lived a quarter of a century, and have passed from a young to an old man. Here my children have been born, and one is buried. I now leave, not knowing when, or whether ever, I may return, with a task before me greater than that which rested upon Washington. Without the assistance of that Divine Being, who ever attended him, I cannot succeed. With that assistance I cannot fail. Let us confidently hope that all will yet be well. To his care commending you, as I hope in your prayers you will commend me, I bid you an affectionate farewell.

Compare this spare eloquence to what a modern politician might say, upon leaving his hometown. C-SPAN probably had to block out an afternoon when Bill Clinton departed from Little Rock for Washington.

New Salem: Lincoln's Stephen A. Douglas Obsession

I did not finish Roy Morris's book in Springfield. All I did was start it, on a shaded bench near Lincoln's house next to a plaque that shows a picture of the president-elect, in 1860, on the front steps of his home. Around him are dozens of supporters, who clearly are coming and going from the house as if it were theirs. In the black-and-white picture, Lincoln towers over a group of schoolchildren, who look like his flock.

Although there are dozens of Lincoln biographies on sale in Springfield, I chose Morris's because I had read his account of the 1876 election, *Fraud of the Century*, and it was the reason that I wanted to see the house of Rutherford B. Hayes in Fremont, Ohio, on this trip. I also chose *The Long Pursuit*, about Lincoln and Douglas, because of the stop in Quincy at the interpretive debate center and because I have long believed—alas without knowing that much about them—that the Lincoln-Douglas debates represent the high-water mark in American political discourse.

The thesis of the Morris book, which I read in the opening pages on the Springfield bench, is that it is possible to understand Lincoln's politics as an angry response to Douglas, his political philosophy, and his allies in the Congress. Morris writes: "When Lincoln's law partner, William Herndon, remarked famously that Lincoln's ambition was 'a little engine that knew no rest,' he might have added that it was the portly, combative figure of Stephen Douglas who stoked the engine."

Lincoln knew of or knew Douglas for much of his adult life. Sometimes they got along, as competitors can; other times not. But beginning in the early 1850s, Lincoln's political career can be read as the antithesis of everything Douglas believed.

Morris begins the book outlining the early lives of each man. Obviously, Lincoln's story is better known, although here it bears repeating, if only in summary:

Lincoln was born in 1809, the son of Thomas Lincoln (the Lincolns were English settlers who ended up in Kentucky, by way of Virginia) and Nancy Hanks, whose portraits make her look like a replica of her son. She was even tall and brooding. As a child and young man, Lincoln moved around southern Indiana and Illinois with his uncharitable father and his stepmother, Sarah Bush Lincoln, who always believed that Abe could "make something of himself" and who transformed Thomas's log cabins into homes where at least Abe could read books by the fire.

When freed from his father's service, Lincoln read law and moved to New Salem, a community just outside Springfield, where, among other pursuits, he managed a store and departed for a brief stint as a soldier in the Black Hawk War. In New Salem, Lincoln started becoming active in state politics, running for a term in the legislature (it met in Vandalia, not yet in Springfield), where he came across another rising political figure, Stephen Douglas.

The Little Giant, as Douglas was later known, started his route to politics in Brandon, Vermont, north of Rutland (it's a misconception that he was from the South), and went west, in the spirit of the times, at age twenty (1833), first working as a teacher and reading law. He was soon appointed to a succession of political jobs around Illinois, serving before age twenty-seven as secretary of state and on the state supreme court.

Like Lincoln after his years in New Salem, Douglas settled in Springfield where he briefly dated Mary Todd, who, subsequently, married Lincoln. Is it any wonder that the two would remain rivals?

Douglas was elected to the US House of Representatives in 1843, and in 1846 to the US Senate, the same year that Abraham Lincoln began serving his only term in the US Congress. But by then they were serving different masters and worshiping different political gods.

Lincoln started out in politics as a Whig and idealized Kentucky Senator Henry Clay, who was well known to Mary Todd's family in Lexington. Lincoln only became a Republican in the late 1850s, when the big top blew off the tent of the all-inclusive Whig Party. (After a while, it didn't take a firm stand on anything, including slavery.)

By contrast, Douglas was a Democrat, and as a senator was influential in various Democratic administrations that hoped to paper over the slavery issue by letting the states decide what was best for each of them. Not everyone bought into Douglas's compromises, including the editor of a Chicago newspaper, who wrote that Douglas was "the most servile tool that has crawled in the slime and scum of slavery at the foot of the slave power."

While Douglas's political career was on the rise and his house in Washington, DC, a center of Democratic power (Morris writes it was "nicknamed 'Mount Julep' for the copious amounts of whiskey, brandy, cognac, and champagne that were said to be quaffed by the senator and his brain trust"), Lincoln's career effectively ended after one term in Congress, because of his opposition to James K. Polk's expansionist war in Mexico. Taking the defeat philosophically, as he did many things in his life, Lincoln echoed the sentiments of a fellow Whig who said: "I opposed one war, and it ruined me. From now on I am for war, pestilence, and famine."

From now on, Lincoln would be the successful lawyer in Springfield, the father of four small boys, and husband to a social-climbing wife, Mary Todd, but not an up-and-coming politician. He made money riding the circuit, took on ever-more prominent cases, played with his cats, and read in the rocking chair.

What changed things for Lincoln was the Compromise of 1850 and later the Kansas-Nebraska Act, both of which he viewed as attempts, by Democrats such as Douglas, to end the Missouri Compromise and, worse, to push slavery into the new territories of the West.

It was the debates over "Bloody Kansas," whether Kansas should enter the Union as a free or slave state, that ended Lincoln's political retirement, and he channeled much of his anger, and often his eloquence and wit, toward opposing Stephen Douglas. Those jibes came easily; Morris describes an incident early in their careers when a local newspaper published letters lampooning Douglas's vanity. Everyone assumed that Lincoln had written the satires, although he denied it, saying: "We have adopted it as part of our policy here, to never speak of Douglas at all. Isn't that the best mode of treating so small a matter?"

The presidential campaign of 1856, in which both Douglas and Lincoln were active as surrogate campaigners for their parties, brought out many of the issues that would be argued, again, in the 1858 debates and the presidential election of 1860, in which Lincoln ran, again, against Douglas.

The election of 1856 was the first to feature a Republican national candidate, John C. Frémont, and he ran and lost against James Buchanan, who, some were saying, was a Douglas puppet.

The abolitionist editor Horace Greeley said this about Douglas: "His is a bulldog mentality, a combination of the swineherd and the Caliban. He can blackguard his betters like a fish-selling harridan. He can run through the whole diapason of political falsehood with unrivaled skill, from the delicate note of suggested prevarication down to the double-bass of unmitigated lying."

Douglas earned such a reputation for his fierce defense of Southern politics (the doctrine was "popular sovereignty" and it meant to let the states decide) and his acid tongue in the Senate. He called senators Salmon Chase and Charles Sumner "pure, unadulterated representatives of Abolitionism, Free Soilism, Niggerism in the Congress of the United States." In response, Sumner said: "As for Douglas, he was 'the squire of slavery, its very Sancho Panza, ready to do all its humiliating offices.'"

The 1856 election proved especially bitter. Republicans talked about "Free Soil, Free Speech, Free Men, Frémont," while the Democratic press (in this case the *Richmond Enquirer*) said all the Republicans wanted was "free niggers, free women, free land, and Frémont."

A third-party candidate in the election, former president Millard Fillmore, ran on the principle that "Americans must rule America," and Buchanan won because Frémont took more abuse than any one candidate could refute. Morris writes: "Charges of rampant womanizing (more or less true) were joined by charges that Frémont was a secret Catholic (more or less false). Virginia governor Henry Wise mercilessly characterized the Republican candidate as 'a Frenchman's bastard (whose] mother was a strumpet in a Richmond brothel.'"

None of these issues had been settled by the time Illinois had to choose its US senator in 1858, and the newly formed Republican party nominated Lincoln to stand against Douglas. Intellectually, Lincoln opposed the doctrine of popular sovereignty more than he opposed the practice of slavery. He wasn't running in 1858 to eliminate slavery from the South. He just did not want it to spread into the territories or become an option for Northern states that might choose to adopt the practice. (New York's financial houses were dependent on cotton and, by extension, slavery.) Lincoln said: "I now do no more than oppose the *extension* of slavery."

Emotionally, however, Lincoln was also in the race to take down his nemesis Stephen Douglas, who was not only mean-spirited and wrong on the extension of slavery and the Constitution, but often drunk. As the Whigs liked to say about Franklin Pierce, a joke no doubt that Lincoln repeated, Douglas was "the hero of many a well-fought bottle."

One of the best appreciations I have read about the Lincoln-Douglas debates appears in Neil Postman's *Amusing Ourselves to Death: Public Discourse in the Age of Show Business*. Postman was a professor at New York University who wrote books about American decadence—the decline of literacy, the malevolence of television, and the cult of celebrity.

About the Lincoln-Douglas debates, Postman marveled that an audience could listen to two men talk politics for seven hours and that the candidates could speak in sentences that later fit so neatly on the printed page. He calls the language used "pure print" (that Lincoln and Douglas wrote themselves) and believes it would impossible for two modern politicians, dependent on speech writers and Fox News moderators, to approach either man's eloquence (whatever the merits of what they were saying). Here is Postman's summary of the debate structure:

> The first of seven famous debates between Abraham Lincoln and Stephen A. Douglas took place on August 21, 1858, in Ottawa, Illinois. Their arrangement provided that Douglas would speak first, for one hour; Lincoln would take an hour and a half to reply; Douglas, a half hour to rebut Lincoln's reply. This debate was considerably shorter than those to which the two men were accustomed. In fact, they had tangled several times before, and all of their encounters had been much lengthier and more exhausting. For example, on October 16, 1854, in Peoria, Illinois, Douglas delivered a three-hour address to which Lincoln, by agreement, was to respond. When Lincoln's turn came, he reminded the audience that it was already 5 p.m., tht he would probably require as much time as Douglas and that Douglas was still scheduled for a rebuttal. He proposed, therefore, that the audience go home, have dinner, and return refreshed for four more hours of talk. The audience amiably agreed, and matters proceeded as Lincoln had outlined.

Later in his book, Postman argues that, in political terms, the Age of Exposition (in which the Lincoln-Douglas debates are a fine example) gave way to the Age of Show Business, in which politics has become a form of vaudeville. "In America," he writes that "we are never denied the opportunity to amuse ourselves."

Along the Sangamon River: Abe Freezes His Feet

THAT NIGHT, BEFORE DINNER, I picked up a rental car from an agency not far from the capital. I biked over to the office, signed all the papers, loaded in my bicycle, and drove off—much to my regret. The reason I went down these paved roads was because the next day, I wanted to connect a number of dots, all off the trails of buses and trains, and end up in Terre Haute, Indiana, where I had an appointment at the Eugene V. Debs Museum. If I took the bus and rode my bike across eastern Illinois, I would miss Charleston, where there was another Lincoln-Douglas debate museum, several Lincoln log cabins (although all across the Midwest they are thick on the ground), and the Indiana home in Dana of the World War II correspondent Ernie Pyle. (While he did not fit into the political world between 1860 and 1900, I have always admired his courage and writing, and wanted to make the detour if I could.) If I left Springfield early in a rental car, I could see most, if not all, of these things and still make my appointment in Terre Haute. So I rented a white sedan with bucket seats in the late afternoon, and for a test drive, of sorts, drove out of Springfield to Lincoln's New Salem, on the banks of the Sangamon River.

I knew the village would be closed. It has been preserved, so to speak, as a log cabin community, complete with the Berry-Lincoln Store, a doctor's house, a blacksmith shop, and a sawmill down by the river. I had thought maybe the settlement would be visible from the road or the parking lot, but it was locked away behind a sturdy fence (taller than Tom Sawyer's and gray instead of white).

Reading a sign, I learned that the settlement hosted a number of events—a marathon, bluegrass concerts, book readings, Scout meetings, and the like—but nothing was on that night. All I could do was console myself with a passage from Roy Morris's book, as it had prompted me, in the first place, to drive out to New Salem when a more logical person would have gone to a Springfield bar for a drink.

Morris describes Lincoln's first electoral victory, to the state assembly, when he still lived in New Salem. He had run before and lost, but this time he won, and a friend of Lincoln's explains why. Morris quotes him:

> Well, it is hard to say just why. It was because of the standing he had got in the county, and especially the prominence given him by his captaincy in the Black Hawk War—because he was a good fellow, because he told good stories, and remembered good jokes—because he was genial, kind, sympathetic, open-hearted—because when he was asked a question and gave an answer it was always characteristic, brief, pointed, *a propos,* out of the common way and manner, and yet exactly suited to the time, place and thing—because of a thousand things which cannot now be remembered or told.

I am sure the same summary could be given for his election to the presidency.

The next morning, I was up early and out the door before 7 a.m. As long as I was paying for a car, I figured I ought to make the most of it, and that meant heading for a Lincoln log cabin, on the banks of the Sangamon east of Springfield. (Clearly, if any river flowed through Lincoln's emotions and memories, it was this one.)

Before 8 a.m., I drove into the parking lot of what felt like a small state park. A groundskeeper was mowing the grass—on a riding tractor—but he paid no attention to me, as I cautiously drove around the site, wondering where I might find the Lincoln cabin. As it turned out, the answer was nowhere, as long ago it vanished in some river high water, possibly soon after the Lincolns had lived here. All I could find, as I walked around the park, was a set of wooden steps down to the fast-moving river and a plaque describing the heavy snows during a winter of discontent in 1830–31 (Lincoln was twenty-one).

According to the posted story, all the Lincolns had gotten sick while living by the river (aches and chills). In the depths of winter, they ran out of food, forcing Abraham to go in search of a neighbor who could help. On his way, he fell into the frozen river and spent two weeks in the neighbor's cabin, recuperating. The neighbor applied goose grease, skunk oil, and rabbit fat to his frozen feet, a cure no doubt Mark Twain's mother would have known.

Come spring, Abraham no longer owed his father any wages that he earned, and he departed down the river, to New Salem, where he began his adult life. His parents, Thomas and Sarah, headed east toward Charleston, where they moved onto farmland more hospitable than this dark tract of the Sangamon. From here, Lincoln's hard years were over. He remained close, emotionally anyway, to his stepmother, but never reconciled with his father, and it has been written that one reason Lincoln so opposed slavery was how his father treated him, as an indentured servant, growing up. (He said later: "I always thought that the man who made the corn should eat the corn.")

Bement, Illinois: The Deal with the Debates

East of the park is Decatur, Illinois, and I stopped there and went in search of breakfast. I parked the car near some Looking for Lincoln signs (he had attended an Anti-Nebraska Editors Convention here in 1856 that issued a proclamation favoring the restoration of the Missouri Compromise) and walked around the town until I found a breakfast diner.

Decatur interested me because it is the headquarters of Archer Daniels Midland, a grain conglomerate, with which my father did business in the 1970s. The headquarters is still in a nondescript brick building in the center of town, as if engaged in shoe repair, not a company with a market capitalization of $28 billion.

Although I sat at the diner counter, clearly I was "from away," and I chatted generally with the waitress and cook about Springfield and being out on the Lincoln Trail. At that hour, it sounded simpler than going into the "madman from Switzerland with a folding bike" story.

After breakfast, although I was heading southeast to Charleston, Illinois, I detoured east to a small cottage museum in the railroad town of Bement. There, in the Bryant Cottage, which is still standing, Lincoln and Douglas had met to agree to the terms of their seven senatorial campaign debates. The brief meeting took place on July 29, 1858, and the house belonged to a Douglas ally.

Part of the reason each candidate was eager to debate the other was because debating was something they had done together since 1839. By the same token, the Adlai Stevensons' ancestor Jesse Fell had been encouraging Douglas and Lincoln to debate going back to 1854, when Lincoln decided to reenter politics as a result of the Kansas-Nebraska Act. Finally, both Lincoln and Douglas realized that a series of debates on such national questions as popular sovereignty was bound to generate national press and enhance both men's chances for their party's nomination in 1860.

They agreed to seven debates, one in each of the congressional districts, but the majority were to be held in the central part of the state, where the election would be decided. As the sitting senator, Douglas entered the race as the favorite. Still, he understood his opponent, saying to the journalist and politician John W. Forney:

> He is the strong man of his party,—full of wit, facts, dates,—and the best stump speaker, with his droll ways and dry jokes, in the West. He is as honest as he is shrewd; and if I beat him my victory will be hardly won.

There wasn't much to do at the Byrant Cottage but pick up a leaflet, look around the small living room, take a picture of the wood stove, and thank the volunteer on duty for her time. I did this, and drove south on a county road to Highway 36, where I went east to Camargo and south on Route 130 directly to Charleston, where the fifth Lincoln-Douglas debate was held.

Charleston: Lincoln and Douglas Debate Manifest Destiny

Charleston is one of the few places on the drive where I was unable to pick up any Looking for Lincoln signs. I circled slowly around the main square, its Gothic pile of a town hall in the center. When I didn't see any Lincoln directions, I parked and went inside.

A guard screening visitors explained that the debate museum is slightly out of town, at the Charleston fairground, which, he said, was "just across the tracks on 316." I did find the log cabin museum, which out in front has a Lincoln and Douglas statue (in mid-debate), but it took a few extra turns as, again, there was no sign and the building is tucked away inside the fairground. At least when Lincoln and Douglas showed up for one of the debates, they were paraded through the town to the arranged stage and serenaded with marching bands. And when Lincoln got to Charleston, he had the further good fortune to meet his stepmother, Sarah Bush Lincoln, who was living in Charleston with her daughter. (Lincoln's father died in 1851.) It is one of the last visits they would have.

No one was working inside the debate museum, but the door was open, and signs explained how individual visitors or school groups could go around the large open room. Fortunately, at one of my stops I had picked up Allen C. Guelzo's *Lincoln and Douglas: The Debates That Defined America,* although I only read it after I got home.

Appropriately for a Lincoln scholar, Guelzo is a professor of history at Gettysburg College, and his account of the debates is one of the few still in print. His thesis is that the wily Lincoln, a grand master of politics and thinking many moves ahead, used the debates to burst the bubble on popular sovereignty and thus eliminated Douglas as an effective candidate in 1860. Guelzo writes: "Douglas saw the real issue of 1858 as the sinister designs of lunatic-pious abolitionists, who wanted to disturb the racial status quo, thwart the will of the people, and plunge the whole country into pointless conflict. For Douglas, the agitation was the problem, and slavery merely the occasion; for Lincoln, slavery was the problem, and containment the best solution."

For anyone interested in the evolution of Lincoln's thinking on the slave question, the 1858 debates offer a clear diagram of his transition from thinking only that slavery must be excluded from the territories to the Lincoln of the Emancipation Proclamation, for whom it was a moral wrong. But that doesn't mean that the debating Lincoln always exhibited the moral clarity of the Lincoln seated in the Washington, DC, memorial. Yes, speaking in Charleston, he did articulate the themes that a "house divided against itself cannot stand," for which he is justly famous. Less often quoted, but still on the record, is something else he said during the Charleston debate, which is:

> I am not nor ever have been in favor of bringing about in any way, the social and political equality of the white and black races. I am not, nor ever have been in favor of making voters of the Negroes, or jurors, or qualifying them to hold office, or having them to marry with white people.

Douglas might have been the more ambitious of the two politicians (Guelzo quotes this observation: "He was a perfect 'steam engine in breeches,'" and "to see him threading the glittering crowd with a pleasant smile or a kind word for every body, one would have taken him for a trained courtier"). But on the slavery question, Lincoln moved cautiously, although I believe that without the debates he might never have made the leap of faith to call for its elimination.

Not everything about the debates, however, lived up to Neil Postman's romantic notions that they were a visitation of Periclean Athens on rural Illinois. Not even Lincoln and Douglas could come up with original material, so much of what they said was repetitious, and in long sections of the debates, each was reading from a prepared script. Often the candidates were exhausted, and allegedly Douglas was sometimes drunk (at least when they reconvened after dinner).

Even the appearance of the debates was often comical. Guelzo writes: "Lincoln towered over Douglas by a foot, and even that foot seemed exaggerated, since Douglas's stumpy legs and paunchy torso made him look like Humpty Dumpty in a toupee, while Lincoln's height was entirely in his legs and gave audiences the impression of a scarecrow come to life." He says Lincoln, when seated on a plank waiting his turn to speak, "more nearly resembled 'the skeleton of some greyhound' than a US senator."

The gotcha moments were few and far between. Lincoln had one at Quincy, when he said: "The real issue in this controversy—the one pressing upon every mind—is the sentiment on the part of one class that looks upon the institution of slavery as a wrong, and of another class that does not look upon it as a wrong." But the Douglas in the debates wasn't the intemperate Douglas on occasion in the Senate, and he was on strong ground in arguing that the framers of the Constitution wanted the slave question left to the states. It only mentions slavery once, in outlawing the slave trade in 1808. On the rest, it is silent, which by definition means it is a state question.[3]

The most useful exhibit in the small Charleston museum was a poster that summarizes the key positions in each debate. Like a school kid working on a book report ("Lincoln was a great man because. . ."), I jotted into my notebook the highlights of each debate, as follows:

- In Ottawa, Lincoln said that the United States could not be half free and half slave while Douglas argued that the people should decide or a state legislature should decide, and that slavery was not a federal question.
- In Freeport, Lincoln posed the now-famous Freeport question—"Can the people of the United States Territory, in any lawful way, against the wishes of any citizen of the United States, exclude slavery from its limits prior to the formation of a State Constitution?"—in which he tried to trap Douglas into choosing between the Kansas-Nebraska Act of 1854 (which allowed his popular sovereignty) and the Supreme Court's *Dred Scott* decision, which said that, legally, states could not prohibit slavery in the territories. The crafty Douglas parried Lincoln, saying, in effect, that both the Nebraska law and the Supreme Court were right. (He said: "Hence, no

3: The Tenth Amendment reads: "The powers not delegated to the United States by the Constitution, nor prohibited by it to the States, are reserved to the States respectively, or to the people."

matter what the decision of the Supreme Court may be on that abstract question, still the right of the people to make a Slave Territory or a Free Territory is perfect and complete under the Nebraska bill. I hope Mr. Lincoln deems my answer satisfactory on that point.")

- At Jonesboro, in southern Illinois, Lincoln said that according to his reading of the Constitution, "the federal government wanted to exclude slavery from the territories." Douglas responded by saying that the Constitution very much tolerate a "house divided."
- At Charleston, Douglas questioned Lincoln's "all or nothing approach" to the slavery question, saying it would lead to civil war. Lincoln countered by saying that if Douglas won the election, slavery would be extended not just to the territories, but all over the United States.
- In Galesburg, Douglas held forth that the founding fathers wanted each state to decide the slavery question for themselves. Lincoln said that slavery was the only question that threatened the entire Union.
- In Quincy, Douglas argued that it was everyone's duty to follow the Constitution, and that without it, there would only be mob rule. Lincoln raised the stakes here, saying that slavery was a moral wrong and wrong for the whole nation.
- In Alton, which is near St. Louis and was the location of the last debate, Douglas beat the drum for popular sovereignty and said Lincoln's house divided speech threatened the Union more than did the slave question. Lincoln came back, quoting his hero Henry Clay, and argued that it was wrong to exclude the Negro from the

Declaration of Independence. (He said: "That is the real issue in the nation—the Declaration").

Much of the debates can be understood as an extended legal argument—how the country should interpret the Missouri Compromise (banning slavery in the territories), the Compromise of 1850 (reopening the question of slavery in the West), the Kansas-Nebraska Act of 1854 (promulgating popular sovereignty to decide slavery), and the Supreme Court's *Dred Scott* decision (1857), which said that not even popular sovereignty could exclude the rights of slaveholders anywhere in the United States.

Lincoln and Douglas disagreed on all these issues. After Douglas played a key legislative role, first, in the Compromise of 1850 and then with the Kansas-Nebraska Act in 1854, Lincoln got back into politics and eventually ran for the Senate in 1858. And without the debates, Lincoln might never have come to his "moral" view regarding slavery, which he first articulated in Quincy.

Guelzo concludes that "both Jefferson and Lincoln understood these rights [those of the Negro] to be natural rights, something akin to the natural law that the moral philosophers of the nineteenth century saw giving an underlying order to the moral and natural worlds. They were unalienable, because they were hardwired into human nature by their Creator, and self-evident, so that even the most superficial self-inspection would reveal an unforced longing for them in everyone."

Douglas won the election, but he never made Lincoln's leap of faith.

Lincoln's Log Cabin: Sold for Spare Parts

In front of the Charleston debate museum, I had a picnic sitting on a bench next to the Lincoln-Douglas statue. It was the only company I could find. I do not think either man would have minded breaking bread with the other. Yes, they were rivals, first for the hand of Mary Todd (who married Lincoln), and later for the Senate in Illinois and the presidency. Much of Lincoln's political career, as Roy Morris argues, can be viewed as a rage against Douglas and his views. Nevertheless, they had to coexist in the small worlds of Springfield and Illinois politics, and I am sure many nights on the campaign trail they found themselves waiting on the same train platform or staying in the same backwater hotel.

In 1859, Lincoln personally asked Douglas if he could help secure a place for Lincoln's son Robert at Harvard College, and Douglas wrote to the university president, James Walker, whom he knew. (Robert went to Harvard.) In 1860 and 1861, after Douglas lost the presidency to Lincoln, he was vigorous in his support of Lincoln, as president-elect, and about preserving the Union. No doubt the course of the Civil War would have been different had Douglas not died in June 1861, just as the serious fighting was beginning.

The farm of Thomas and Sarah Lincoln is located about nine miles south of Charleston, and I debated whether it was, as the Michelin guide might say, "worth a detour." It turned out it was not, but on my map it appeared only as "Lincoln

Log Cabin Site," and I thought Abraham had lived there with his parents. He never did.

Driving south from the fairground, I saw a small sign pointing to the grave site of Thomas Lincoln, Lincoln's father. Given the complexity of their relationship, I did think that was worth a detour, and I turned off on East Lincoln Highway and followed signs to the cemetery, which was about a mile or so on the right.

Near where I parked the car on the side of the road there was a Looking for Lincoln sign (it cheered me that I was back on track), and it implied that successful lawyer Lincoln had been generous, in the 1840s when riding the legal circuit, in helping out his parents with money and stopping by to visit. But the gravestone suggested otherwise. It looked to me like something that posterity had tried to clean up, and then added a wrought iron fence to as protection from pilgrims, who in the nineteenth century had a habit of carrying away everything Lincoln, including some of his log cabins.

From Morris I had the story that on Lincoln's to-do list, before he departed Springfield for his presidency, was a visit to his stepmother in Charleston where he would have another stone cut for his father's grave. (Apparently there was only a rock there.) Morris reports that while he saw Sarah in Charleston, he did nothing about the headstone, further indication that Abraham never reconciled himself to his father's stern parenting. Guelzo writes that Thomas said "the boy 'was a constant and . . . stubborn reader,' but the only appreciation Thomas Lincoln showed was 'to slash him for neglecting his work by reading.'" Clearly he didn't want his own son going to Harvard.

I did drive on to the Lincoln Log Cabin State Historic Site, but quickly decided it was a hoax. Apparently the real Lincoln cabin was sold off to speculators to be put up at the 1893 Chicago World's Fair, but was then left to rot on a side street. So what I saw was a Home Depot log cabin, which is staffed by volunteers speaking "authentic" east Kentucky dialect ("Well, we had some young 'ems up from that yonder school group . . ."). I decided against feeding any of the goats or trying my hand at churning butter. According to one of the brochures, Lincoln's parents moved here (or at least to the Charleston area) when they left the banks of the Sangamon River (where Abe's feet were frozen looking for food).

Walking around "the working, living history farm" before almost sprinting back to the car, I decided that Thomas Lincoln, however stern and gruff with his son, was a nineteenth-century hippie, someone from a proud background who preferred to live off the land, tend chickens, work as a carpenter, and build log cabins. And he would have mass-produced the latter if he had known they would fetch big prices at the 1893 World's Fair.

Dana, Indiana: Hometown of Ernie Pyle, "Thanks, Pal"

I MADE ANOTHER MISTAKE (blame it on the car) in detouring to Dana, Indiana ("Hometown of Ernie Pyle"). It was less than an hour's drive on good roads, and I didn't have to be in Terre Haute until 4:30 p.m. But then a Looking for Lincoln sign in Paris, Illinois, got me out of the car. It read: "Abraham Lincoln traveled this way as he rode the circuit of the eighth judicial district 1837–1857" (although omitted from the plaque was Morris's observation that the system was "part legal hearing, part traveling minstrel show").

By the time I arrived in Dana, I had learned two more things: that the Ernie Pyle World War II Museum was closed, and Indiana operates on Eastern Standard Time, not that of Central Standard, which rules Illinois. I had lost time idling in Paris, Illinois, so now it was 3:45 p.m., not 2:45 p.m. I would never make it in time to my 4:30 p.m. appointment at the Eugene V. Debs Museum in Terre Haute.

Before setting off on a mad dash to Terre Haute, I admired the setting of the Pyle house, which is by the railroad tracks, next to some grain elevators, near the post office, and on the edge of a pretty Indiana farm town. I peeked in the windows and walked around to a Quonset hut in the back that has some artillery and tanks. And I consoled myself with the thought that the peripatetic Pyle (1900–45, thus born around the same time as Adlai Stevenson II and Ernest

Hemingway), would not have spent much time in Dana after he enlisted in the navy in 1917.

In the 1920s and '30s, Pyle wrote a syndicated newspaper column from all corners of the United States, and he brought the same folky style to his war correspondence in World War II, first in Europe during the campaign in Italy, and finally in Okinawa, where he was killed in April 1945 during the fighting.

Pyle wrote more complex sentences than did Hemingway, although they were in the same vein and, like Ernest, he spent his war with the infantry. Outside the museum, there is an excerpt from one of his columns, written as he was leaving North Africa in 1943:

> That is our war, and we will carry it with us as we go on from one battleground to another until it is all over, leaving some of us behind on every beach, in every field. We are just beginning with the ones who lie back of us here in Tunisia. I don't know whether it was their good fortune or their misfortune to get out of it so early in the game. I guess it doesn't make any difference, once a man has gone. Medals and speeches and victories are nothing to them any more. They died and others lived and nobody knows why it is so. They died and thereby the rest of us can go on and on. When we leave here for the next shore, there is nothing we can do for the ones beneath the wooden crosses, except perhaps to pause and murmur, "Thanks, pal."

In my travels around Europe and the Pacific, I have often read collections of his columns, and every now and then they made excellent histories of various campaigns. His language is spare, direct, empathetic, and concise. He went from North Africa and Sicily, to the Italian peninsula, and finally Normandy. In Honolulu in 1987, I rented a car and drove up to the National Memorial Cemetery of the Pacific, otherwise called the Punchbowl, and tracked down his headstone, which lies unpretentiously among the war dead.

When I went to Okinawa fifteen years later, I asked my guide if we could drive to the memorial that shows where he was killed, but it turned out to be on the small island of Iejima, which is a three-hour drive from the capital, Naha. I never got there, but read later that the marker for the fallen correspondent, capturing the language of his wartime dispatches, reads: "At this spot the 77th Infantry Division lost a buddy. Ernie Pyle, 18 April 1945."

Terre Haute: Debs, Dreiser, and Bird

I HAVE NO MEMORY OF THE HURRIED DRIVE from Dana to Terre Haute. I only know that it took thirty minutes, from farmland to cityscape, and, after all of my fretting, I was only ten minutes late for my appointment, arriving at 4:40 p.m. I had tried calling from Dana to say that I was delayed, but no one had answered the phone, which I took to be a bad omen. Still, I was sure that the museum director at the home of Eugene V. Debs would have waited at least fifteen minutes to see if I would show up. But I was wrong, and the house was closed. It got me thinking that maybe I should call this book "A Brief History of Closed Museums Across the United States." Of course, I was trying to visit obscure places that are staffed with volunteers, chronically underfunded, and open limited hours. Still, it could also be that history isn't what it used to be.

I walked around the two-story white frame Debs house, now in the middle of Indiana State University, and read the inscription out front:

> Home of Eugene V. Debs: Debs (1855–1926) was leading pioneer in industrial unionism, social reformer, and peace advocate. Founded American Railway Union, 1893; cofounded American Socialist Party, 1900; and ran five times for United States presidency; declared National Historic Landmark, 1966.

Debs spent his adult life in conflict with American railroads, believing them to represent all that was evil about capitalist power. Now Terre Haute doesn't even have train service, aside from freight.

I returned to the parking lot, dropped off the rental car at the return center, and went to my hotel, which was on the main drag of Terre Haute, Highway 150, just south of the downtown and campus. I was delighted to be done with the car and back on the bike, and spent no time lingering in the room before I was back on the streets.

Terre Haute is a city of sixty thousand residents, many of whom are affiliated with Indiana State University. (The Boston Celtics basketball player Larry Bird went there.) The downtown lies east of the Wabash River but suffers from the traffic that runs in six lanes on highways 41 and 150, and off of Interstate 70, which cuts through the south of the city.

I never felt comfortable biking around Terre Haute, especially if it meant crossing a main highway. Around the old downtown area, things were quieter, especially on campus. But no matter where I went, I often heard a car revving its engine behind me. I got the feeling, despite all the students, that bicycles are a novelty in Terre Haute, and that without cars it would come to a halt.

I am still sorry that I missed my interview at the Debs home, because I was well prepared, having been to the Haymarket and read much of Ray Ginger's lengthy *Eugene V. Debs: A Biography* (it's 540 pages, which makes for a lot of Debs). I wanted to know more about him because of his work with the railroads, his many runs for the presidency, his Espionage Act conviction that Woodrow Wilson visited upon him, and the commutation of his sentence in 1921 by Warren Harding, whom Debs then visited in the

White House. (The always amiable Harding greeted the convicted labor leader by shaking his hand and saying: "Well, I have heard so damn much about you, Mr. Debs, that I am now very glad to meet you personally.") Any socialist imprisoned by Wilson and pardoned by Harding is worth getting to know better.

Terre Haute: Eugene V. Debs Rides the Rails to Prison

Born in Terre Haute, Debs left school early to work as a fireman on the railways. Ginger has this passage: "'As a locomotive fireman,' Debs wrote, 'I learned of the hardships of the rail in snow, sleet and hail, of the ceaseless danger that lurks along the iron highway, the uncertainty of employment, scant wages and altogether trying lot of the workingman, so that from my very boyhood I was made to feel the wrongs of labor.'" He survived several wrecks—once jumping from an engine during a snowstorm.

Like Lincoln, Debs was a reader and a self-starter. Ginger writes: "Every Sunday he went to his parents' home, where he and Daniel [his father] recited poetry and discussed Hugo's *Les Misérables.* Debs also studied Shakespeare, history, science, but many of his tastes were less discriminating—he reveled in mawkish doggerel, and Negro dialect jokes by the page found their way into *The Magazine.* The shelves in the second floor study [in the Debs house] held technical books on railroading, bulky reports on labor conditions by the state and Federal governments, French and German classics, together with the worst poetry being written in this country and newspaper clippings about circus freaks."

Debs married the slightly reclusive Kate Metzel, who fussed endlessly over the house. Ginger writes: "His wife did not need to be a constantly charming companion; she did need to be stable, secure, self-reliant . . . Debs was seeking a typical wife but an unusual marriage." It was more her house than his that I would have visited.

Debs's true marriage was to the industrial labor union movement, which he helped to create. At age thirty, when he was elected to the state House of Representatives, he arrived in office with a bill already drafted for workman's compensation on the railroads (it did not pass). But it was as the head of the American Railway Union that he achieved his fame. He wanted it modeled after the US Constitution, in which the affiliated unions would be considered sovereign states.

Debs traveled ceaselessly and for months at a time, organizing local trade unions or trying to get existing ones to affiliate with his American Railway Union. Ginger writes: "Everywhere he spoke the same words: *organize*; *federate*." He liked to quote Lincoln: "Liberty before property; the man before the dollar." He said: "The greatest tribute that was ever paid to me was that of the section men after the Great Northern strike. As my train pulled out of St. Paul, those men with shovels in hand and happiness fairly radiating from their faces, yet with tears in their eyes—those section men stood at attention. That tribute was more precious to me than all of the banquets in the world."

Two events radicalized Debs, turning him from a labor leader into a passionate spokesman for the working man and the underprivileged, if not a presidential candidate: the Haymarket massacre and, later, over the Pullman strike, the betrayal he felt from the Democratic administration of Grover Cleveland.

Debs had no doubt that the targets of the violence in the Haymarket were organized labor and free speech. He thought none of the eight who were convicted were guilty. Ginger writes: "His objection to the Haymarket trial was based on other factors: The irregular proceedings, a belief that the indictment was a punishment of free speech, a conviction that the employers were trying to frame eight labor leaders."

The Pullman strike—in effect Eugene V. Debs vs. George Pullman, a manufacturer of railroad sleeping cars—started in Chicago and spilled over into the rest of the country, when affiliates of Debs's union refused to move trains that had Pullman cars.

Pullman's Arcade Building is located around 111th Street on Chicago's South Side. I wish now I had included it on my riding tour with Rob. In some ways—at least according to Pullman brochures—it was a model community of housing, schools, and medical care for the workers. But one union man said: "We are born in a Pullman house, fed from the Pullman shop, taught in the Pullman school, catechized in the Pullman church, and when we die we shall be buried in the Pullman cemetery and go to the Pullman hell."

Sounding like Lincoln during one of the debates, Debs charged Pullman with violating the working man's natural and moral rights. He exhorted one crowd: "The paternalism of Pullman is the same as the self-interest of a slave-holder in his human chattels. You are striking to avert slavery and degradation." Nevertheless, the strike ended when the Cleveland administration brought an injunction against the ARU and threw Debs in jail. Debs said: "The crime of the American Railway Union was the practical exhibition of sympathy for the Pullman employees." Never again would Debs have faith in a major American political party.

The Ginger biography offers, I think, the best description of Debs's time in jail, as it captures the soul of the organizer, his optimism, cheerfulness, and courage, usually in the face of overwhelming odds. Ginger writes:

> The seven ARU chiefs wasted no time in demonstrating that they were born organizers. They elected officers for the duration of their terms, and named their new creation the Co-operative Colony of Liberty Jail. Each morning they rose at six o'clock and did an hour's military drill before breakfast. Sheriff Eckert kindly let them use his rifle for the exercises. At 7:30 they had a breakfast of a steak or chops, fried potatoes, and coffee in the Eckert's dining room. They then studied economics and history until noon from the library of two hundred volumes, which included the Utopian socialist writings of Gronlund, Bellamy, and Robert Blatchford. Debs read Victor Hugo and Eugène Sue, but he also glanced through several Fabian essays, the works of Henry George, and *Wealth Against Commonwealth.* Henry Demarest Lloyd, who had sent a complimentary copy of his classic to Debs the previous December, now did the same favor for the other prisoners. . . . Eugene Debs, while confined in McHenry County Jail, was more prominent in national affairs than he had ever been in his life.

Debs's third career, as a presidential candidate, began in 1900 and lasted until 1920, when he ran for office while in prison for sedition. His best performance was in 1912, when he received almost 6 percent of the popular vote. (The presence of Theodore Roosevelt as a third-party candidate that year made it unusual, and resulted in Wilson's election with only 42 percent of the vote.) Nevertheless, it was Debs's first try for the presidency in 1900 that marked his style as an independent candidate. Ginger writes about his special campaign train: "The *Red Special* . . . had travelled nine thousand miles and made a hundred and ninety stops. Debs had spoken to two hundred and seventy-five thousand persons in less than a month."

Nominally, Debs was the Socialist Party candidate in each of his elections, but after the first run, he never attended another Socialist Party convention, and conducted his runs as variations on his union barnstorming. He cited as his heroes, and political antecedents, not just Lincoln but, according to Ginger, Thomas Paine, Patrick Henry, John Brown, and the Haymarket martyrs. I doubt he ever read Marx or Engels, except maybe in summaries.

Debs's gift as a speaker was that he gave listeners in the crowd the impression that he was speaking with them personally and could relate to their own experiences. He had little time for theory or philosophy, and despite being a socialist, he never really questioned the existence of the capitalist system: he just wanted it to be more equitable.

Debs dressed well and rarely drank, and he mourned any time a member of the rank and file suffered a loss or an injury. Later, he directed much of his elegant fury in the direction of Theodore Roosevelt, believing him to be no friend of the working man and his government an instrument of corporate repression. He often reminded his audiences of the Roosevelt quote: "To hell with habeas corpus; we'll give 'em postmortems." And I am sure Debs took it somewhat personally when Roosevelt said: "The sentiment now animating a large proportion of our people can only be suppressed . . . by taking ten or a dozen of their leaders out, standing . . . them against a wall, and shooting them dead. I believe it will come to that."

Not only did Debs believe passionately in the rights of working men—especially the eight-hour day and workman's compensation for disability—but he hated war, going back to the jingoism of the Spanish-American War in 1898. He took the view that the war was being fought to open up new markets, on which American companies could dump the products that had been made by exploited workers. According to Ginger, in 1898 Debs told an audience of trade unionists in Indianapolis: "We are making a market over there in the Orient for the products of half-paid labor in this country; making the market by the force of arms and at the expense of the lives of a people whose only offense has been their love of freedom and self-control." Ginger adds: "Those were Debs' views in 1898. When he said exactly the same thing twenty years later, he was sent to prison."

The speech that got him sentenced to prison was given in Nimisilla Park in Canton, Ohio. Nevertheless, he did not say anything there that he had not said throughout World War I. For example, in 1914, he said: "We socialists are not wanting in genuine patriotism but we are deadly hostile to the fraudulent species which is 'the last refuge of the scoundrel' and which prompts every crook and grafter and every blood-sucking vampire to wrap his reeking carcass in the folds of the national flag that he may carry on his piracy and plunder in the name of patriotism." Ginger writes that he believed "the American government was little else than an armed guard for capitalist investments" or that "newspapers existed only on sufferance from the Federal authorities."

In Canton, Debs said, in part:

> And here let me emphasize the fact—and it cannot be repeated too often—that the working class who fight all the battles, the working class who make the supreme sacrifices, the working class who freely shed their blood and furnish the corpses, have never yet had a voice in either declaring war or making peace. It is the ruling class that invariably does both. They alone declare war and they alone make peace.

Former university professor and president Woodrow Wilson did not brook criticism, especially from men he deemed his social inferiors. He said Debs was a "traitor to his country." The trial under the Espionage Act was held in Columbus, Ohio. Debs called no defense witnesses. Instead, he asked to address the court, which he did for two hours and then again after he was sentenced. At one point he said: "I am opposing a social order in which it is possible for one man who does absolutely nothing that is useful to amass a fortune of hundreds of millions of dollars, while millions of men and women who work all the days of their lives secure barely enough for a wretched existence."

A witness to the legal proceedings, journalist Heywood Broun, wrote: "Debs made a speech to the judge and jury at Columbus after his conviction, and to me it seems one of the most beautiful and moving passages in the English language. He was for that one afternoon touched with inspiration." The judge—who called himself "a conserver of the peace and a defender of the Constitution of the United States"—wasn't listening, and gave Debs ten years, beginning in November 1918.

Going to prison did not bother Debs. He almost felt liberated, saying: "The sovereignty of my citizenship resulted in my imprisonment. The government made me a citizen of the world." There he could not vote, but still he received more than 3 percent of the vote in the 1920 presidential election.

Released in 1921, Debs only stayed a short time in the White House with Warren Harding. Then Debs hurried back to Terre Haute. Earlier in his life, when he was offered a job outside Indiana, he reflected on his home: "I can't make up my mind to leave Terre Haute. It has always been my home. I was born here and my father and mother are both buried here. No, I shall never leave Terre Haute. It shall always be home to me, even if my work will not permit staying at home as much as I should like to." He died in 1926.

Terre Haute: An American Tragedy on the Banks of the Wabash

I HAD FUN THAT NIGHT BIKING around Terre Haute on the Brompton. Once the rush hour ended, the traffic lessened, and I rode back to the campus bookstore to see if it had any books about Eugene V. Debs or Theodore Dreiser, who was also born here.

Barnes & Noble owns the college store, so it is long on sweatshirts and short on books about the industrial proletariat. The clerk looked in his computer but nodded no, saying the store had nothing about either man. I thought about making a little speech about the Debs home on campus and the Dreiser books that touch on Terre Haute, but, really, what would have been the point? I looked around the first floor, but instead of books all I saw was glassware, stuffed animals, mugs, water bottles, T-shirts, key chains, Christmas tree ornaments, ISU teddy bears, tank tops, gimme hats, decals, headbands, and shot glasses, and after that I didn't have the energy to browse the stacks.

Instead, I bought dinner from a take-out Mexican restaurant that was delicious, rode my bike across the Wabash River, and found a small brick house (now in a park) in which both the lyricist of "On the Banks of the Wabash, Far Away," Paul Dresser, and Dreiser were born (they were brothers, but Paul changed his name for show business reasons). The Indiana state song includes this verse:

Oh, the moonlight's fair tonight along the Wabash,
From the fields there comes the breath of new-mown hay.
Through the sycamores the candle lights are gleaming,
On the banks of the Wabash, far away.

To be truthful, if anyone wrote a similar song about the Wabash today, at least as it flows through Terre Haute, there might be a verse that included:

Oh, the neon's bright along the highway,
Where gas and Dunkin Donuts hold their sway
Through empty lots of parking that are eerie,
On the banks of the Wabash, I'm away.

Paul Dresser, one of Theodore's older and more successful brothers—it was a largely dysfunctional family of ten children—gets top billing at the house. The plaque reads: "Birthplace of Paul Dresser (1859—1906) Composer of Indiana State Song, 'On the Banks of the Wabash,' and other songs popular in the Gay Nineties. His famous brother, Theodore Dreiser, wrote *An American Tragedy* and other novels."

In addition to learning more about Eugene Debs, I had also come to Terre Haute because of Dreiser, whose novels—*Sister Carrie*, *The Genius*, the Cowperwood trilogy, as well as *An American Tragedy*—I read with abandon in the 1980s. My friend at the time Joseph Epstein said of the books, "There's no safety net in Dreiser," by which he meant that bad things happen to many Dreiser characters. (George Hurstwood kills himself in a gas oven in *Sister Carrie*, after saying "What's the use?" Clyde Griffiths in *An American Tragedy* gets the chair for killing his impregnated girlfriend, Roberta Alden.)

Most people I know find Dreiser's writing to be turgid, overblown, self-important, awkward, dense, and verbose—and I don't think they are wrong.

That said, I read him with pleasure as the Balzac of the streetcar industry (it's the get-rich-quick scheme of the 1910s), and because, in their seductions, bankruptcies, lusts, and corporate sleights of hand, very few of Dreiser's characters (to use the worn expression) "fail to live."

Charlie Drouet, who lures Caroline Meeber (Sister Carrie) off the path of innocence in Chicago, is my beau ideal for a sweet-talking huckster, while Eugene Witla—the egotistical writer, artist, editor, and publisher in *The "Genius"*—could be half the people I know in the world that they call "the arts." Read for their stories and low-life characters, not for their sentence structure (which can detour across many bridges), Dreiser's works sing, at least to me. As an early editor said to Dreiser when he was breaking into newspapers in the Midwest: "You know, Theodore, you have your faults, but you do know how to observe."

Aside from a Theodore Dreiser Memorial Bridge (made with industrial cement and iron) spanning the river, I found no evidence of Dreiser's life around town. There's no Dreiser Library or Dreiser Dry Cleaning, as there would be, for example, a Hemingway Liquor Store in Key West.

Dreiser went west to Chicago, and then east to New York, to make his reputation and fortune (most of which he spent), and did not look back to Terre Haute until 1916, when he wrote *A Hoosier Holiday,* a narrative about driving from New York City to Indiana. In his mind, it was a loving memoir to his native soil, but local residents read it as the literary equivalent of a drive-by shooting. He returns to Terre Haute

("Here I was entering it now for the first time since I had left it, between seven and eight years of age, exactly thirty-seven years before") and writes about the home in which he grew up: "There was gloom, no work, often no bread, or scarcely any, in the house." He continues:

> And here was I walking about, not knowing a single soul here really, intent upon finding one man perhaps who had known my father and had been kind to him; for the rest, looking up the houses in which we had lived, the first school which I had ever attended, the first church, and thinking over all the ills we had endured rather than the pleasures we had enjoyed (for of the latter I could scarcely recall any), was all with which I had to employ myself.

Clearly, Dreiser's homecoming day was different from that celebrated up the road at the state university. He must never have gone to the bookstore and bought the lyrics to the school song, which go like this:

Though the years to come may part us,
Friends and comrades true,
ISU, our Alma Mater,
here's our pledge to you.

Terre Haute: Theodore Dreiser's Broken Dreams

WANTING TO KNOW MORE about Dreiser the man, I turned to W. A. Swanberg's one-volume biography, published in 1965. Other biographies of the writer have since been published, but I had the Swanberg book thanks to his son, Jack, who read one of my books and kindly mailed his father's Dreiser biography.

W. A. Swanberg is well known for his biographies of Henry Luce and William Randolph Hearst, and his account of Dreiser's life reads like one of Theodore's novels. He begins, "Theodore Dreiser was reared in superstition, fanaticism, ignorance, poverty and humiliation," and then paints a portrait of the artist as a newspaperman, magazine writer, novelist, diplomat, investor, philanderer, and man about town in such an unpleasant light that even I—a fan of the novels—grew tired of Dreiser in the flesh.

Most biographers find some common ground with their subjects, but Swanberg finds little. He writes: "The story of Theodore's struggle with reality, so ridiculous in its externals (as he later candidly acknowledged), has all the tragedy of a wounded, confused, maladjusted boyhood." For much of his childhood, Dreiser's parents lived apart. "Among his earliest reflections was the realization of the sharp schism between his mother's way of life and his father's, the schism between the pagan and the puritan."

What allowed Dreiser to break away from his past were his high school years in Warsaw, Indiana. He had friends, and he read widely, as he writes in *A Hoosier Holiday*. Going back to Warsaw, he remembers:

> Warsaw was an idyllic town for a youth of my temperament and age to have been brought to just at that time. The public school was to me like a paradise after the stern religiosity of this other school. Education began to mean something to me.

> As I see it now, I must have been a very peculiar youth, a dreamer, for I loved to sit and dream all the while. . . . At this time I had found Dickens, Scott, Thackeray, Hawthorne, Fielding, Defoe, and a score of others, and had been reading, reading, reading, swiftly and with enjoyment. Cooper, Irving and Lew Wallace ("Ben Hur" at least) were a part of my mental pabulum. From the library I drew Dryden, Pope, Shakespeare, Herrick and a dozen other English and American poets, and brought them here.

No one can read these words and not take heart about public education.

After a year in Bloomington at Indiana University, Dreiser dropped out and worked around the United States at various newspaper jobs, living at times in Chicago (just after the Haymarket), St. Louis, Toledo, and New York. He dreamed for a while of running a small-town newspaper, but his sites were on the big-city lights.

Still in his twenties, he published *Sister Carrie*, and to favorable reviews, despite the realism of the prose and the depressing story (small-town girl finds vice in the cities). Swanberg writes that:

> The book was published November 8, 1900, and soon Dreiser's and Norris' [the publisher] spirits sank. Dreiser was ahead of his time. Carrie was widely reviewed—a tribute to Norris' efforts—but some reviews appeared as much as three or four months after publication and a majority of the critics condemned the book's "immorality," dreariness and philosophy of despair.

Dreiser had no idea that he had written a masterpiece of American literature. Swanberg notes: "He seems to have had no inkling that he was creating a revolutionary work. He wrote with a compassion for human suffering that was exclusive with him in America." It remains the best of his novels.

After *Carrie*, Dreiser's novels borrowed heavily from his own life, which in his thirties was a whirlwind of women, parties, serious work, tirades, and dreams. Swanberg says: "His writing mirrored the man—a lack of taste combined with nervousness, insecurity and his actual fear of time."

His success with women, about which he boasted to friends, was all the more remarkable in that his appearance bordered on caricature. An acquaintance Homer Croy said: "He struck me as a man training to be an ogre," yet there were no shortages of conquests, and the likes of Rita Sohlberg, Antoinette Nowak, Stephanie Platow, Cecily Haguenin, and Florence Cochrane would live on in his novels—even if they had to date streetcar magnates, like Frank Cowperwood.

A secretary said: "He had a great animal magnetism," she recalled. "You almost felt it."

Dreiser treated his first wife as a disposable dishcloth, spending many nights away with girlfriends and denying her money, but even after they separated, she felt an affection for him, as did others he treated poorly. His second wife, Helen, once had to serve breakfast to Theodore and the girl he had brought home for the night. He had a long estrangement from his best friend H. L. Mencken, whose early, favorable reviews had established Theodore's reputation. Still, Mencken could say: "Like most peasants, Dreiser is bearing money very badly. . . . True enough, he can't write, but nevertheless is a great writer, just as Whitman was."

An American Tragedy, published in 1925, brought Dreiser wealth, fame, and the success of a "great American writer," but also made him insufferable. He no longer had to chase magazine commissions—I can say, from observation, that Dreiser was a genius at negotiating fees from publications—and could devote himself to writing and women. His book *A Gallery of Women* is essentially a score sheet—*The Complete Memoirs of Jacques Casanova de Seingalt* if the Venetian had lived on 57th Street or worked from an office near Union Square. But Dreiser's 1920s trip to Russia—in the phrase of the time he would have been "a fellow traveler"—shows the fine lines between genius and gullibility.

Swanberg's description of Dreiser "looking at Russia" is, for me, a highlight of the biography, and it reads like burlesque. Now the great man, Dreiser decides to tackle a subject the size of his own ego—the Soviet Union as a beacon of paradise. After sailing for the continent (in Paris he is at a party with Hemingway, but the two don't click), he installs himself in a Kremlin-supported office near Red Square, attended by apparatchiks that Joseph Stalin has assigned to keep an eye on the left-leaning author.

Stalin only let Dreiser into Russia during a moment of weakness, when someone in the Politburo suggested some favorable press could help relations with the West. The next thing anyone knows, Dreiser is in Red Square, demanding interviews with the general secretary, better hotel accommodations, more vodka, edible food, and, most of all, that the Russians hurry up and pay him back his expenses. Meanwhile, to make the best of his wait, he takes his local secretary as a mistress.

"Dreiser sailed as an individualist," Swanberg writes, "an evolutionist, scoffing at socialism and communism but eager to see Russia and judge for himself." Slowly it must have dawned on Dreiser, sitting in his dank office off Red Square, that not all was well in Russia or with his program. Stalin declined to see him. Press minders refused his requests for interviews or travel. (Eventually they packed him off to Ukraine and the Caucasus.) In his letters home, Dreiser fumes at his hosts—"I was filled with a rage at everything Russian, such a lack of system, such inexcusable negligence. . . . I'd rather die in the United States than live here"—but still he would remind his paymasters that they were behind with the expense money.

While in Russia, he hated the bedbugs, cockroaches, food, and much more, but back home, when he put pen to paper, Swanberg writes: "He began to remember the beauties of Russia." In the book, *Dreiser Looks at Russia*, published in

1928, he sees the future working, even though that same year, Stalin began his extermination of the kulaks.

The end of Dreiser's life is forgettable. With the money from *An American Tragedy* and other books, he built a modern weekend house in Mount Kisco, a New York suburb, of Citizen Kane proportions. A friend quipped: "It looked like a warm-up for the World's Fair." When it was done and the *Evening Post* came out to interview him, the reporter wrote: "The trouble with that fellow is that he has been reading too much Theodore Dreiser."

Bloomington: Breaking Away

I DIDN'T MIND THE EARLY WAKE-UP in my hotel for the ride to Terre Haute Transit and the bus to Indianapolis. Already at 6:15 a.m., the breakfast buffet (well, donuts and coffee) was set up in a room off the lobby, and fifteen minutes later I was riding up Seventh Street toward the downtown that only reflected the isolated predawn gloom of an Edward Hopper painting. I passed a signpost that indicated this intersection (Wabash and Seventh) in 1926 was known as the "Crossroads of America." Two legs of the federal highway system met here. Since then, the traffic has moved to the interstates, leaving downtown Terre Haute off the grid.

There was only one woman at the bus station, and she was washing windows. She nodded toward where the Miller Transportation bus to Indianapolis would stop.

Because I was early, I made a little tour through the neighborhood, circling again past the Debs house (still closed) and a Larry Bird monument in front of a field house. (The plaque reads, in part: "He enrolled at Indiana State University in 1975 and earned 29 school records including the top spot on ISU's all-time scoring list. . . . Bird led the Sycamores to a near perfect 33-1 season. . . . went on to play thirteen seasons for the Boston Celtics, earning three world championships.")

The Bird statue—him making a shot—is not far from the public inscription of Max Ehrmann's "Desiderata." Ehrmann was a Terre Haute lawyer and poet, who in 1927 composed the well-known homily, coming-soon-to-a-kitchen-towel-near-you, which contains the advice:

> *With all its sham, drudgery, and broken dreams,*
> *it is still a beautiful world.*
> *Be cheerful.*
> *Strive to be happy.*

The bus driver taking us to Indianapolis must have been happy, as only three passengers lined up for the 7:35 a.m. service. I placed the bagged bike in the luggage compartment, and took a row of seats for the hourlong drive to Bloomington, a stop on the way.

Miller time started on I-70, but then switched to the back roads through Ashboro and Spencer, where preparations were being made for a catfish fishing tournament. Otherwise, the landscape was more rolling than I had expected—Indiana in my mind is a flat potato field—and prettier, dotted with many fall colors.

Part of the reason I had booked on the early bus to Indianapolis via Bloomington rather than the later direct service is that I wanted to see the university in Bloomington, at least in passing. My only other visits to Indiana University (IU) have come through watching the 1979 bicycle film *Breaking Away*, which was filmed entirely in Bloomington. The coming-of-age movie is about four teenagers—they call themselves the "cutters," after the locals who work the quarries—who are drifting after high school. Dave Stoller, one of them, is in love with his racing bicycle and all things Italian. ("*Buon giorno, papa.*" "I'm not 'papa.' I'm your god-damned father.")

In our house, the movie is a feel-good standby, both for the bike race at the end (the cutters race the IU "college boys" in the Little Five Hundred) and for all the quotes that are now embedded in our family language. ("I know I-ty food when I hear it! It's all them 'eenie' foods . . . zucchini . . . and linguine . . . and fettuccine. I want some American food, dammit! I want french fries!") Alas, I saw nothing of the movie-set town from the bus, as all we did was cruise down a side street, pick up a few passengers, and head toward Indianapolis.

Indianapolis: Copenhagenized

INDIANAPOLIS IS ANOTHER CITY with an intermodal transportation center, although at least this one is carved into the entrails of an old railroad station. I looked around the waiting room that Amtrak shares with the bus companies, and it had the atmosphere of the Heartbreak Hotel. A few people were sitting in the molded, plastic chairs. The only vending machine I saw had a hand-printed sign indicating it was "Out of Service." Only two trains a day leave the station, and the one from Washington arrives at the convenient hour of 5:20 a.m.

Across the street from the transportation center was a post office, where I mailed off to myself a box of books, papers, and maps that I had collected in Illinois. (All my Lincoln Trail maps were inside.) To find my hotel, I biked around the contours of Lucas Oil Stadium (where the football Colts play). The red brick behemoth—home for many years to quarterback Peyton Manning—cost $700 million to build, most of which came from the public troughs in Indiana (to the benefit of the Colts' owner, Jim Irsay).

The local government decided to amortize the debt by increasing the taxes on hotel rooms and rental cars (Indianapolis is a booming convention city). Incompetent financial management of the stadium debt cost the taxpayers another $45 million in 2009, and the 2012 Super Bowl, held in Indianapolis, did not produce the projected windfall (it's just a weekend, after all). At least when Irsay was arrested for DUI, he had with him $29,000 in cash, although the reports were vague about whether he planned to use some or all of it to cover part of the $250,000 annual rent that the Colts pay to use the $700 million stadium. That's $31,250 a game or about fifty cents per fan, who paid, on average in 2013, $86.32 each to see the Colts games.

I could not immediately get into my room, but the cheerful hotel staff, which wowed over the bike ("I gotta get me one of them"), stored my bags and gave me a map and directions for Indianapolis. My first stop, after circling around the Soldiers and Sailors Monument (with bronze Indian killers at the base), was a bike store, as I needed air for my tires and more lights. I ended up buying a reflective vest and spoke reflectors, as well, and then—happily kitted out—I hopped on the Cultural Trail that is a bike path encircling Indianapolis, perhaps the finest such cycle lane in any American city.

I read about the bike trail before arriving in Indianapolis, but I had no idea it was such a completely segregated path, away from the traffic and with its own streetlights and markings. I had thought maybe it was just another city bike path that has paint on the road and signs pointing to the next landmark. Instead, the path floats through downtown Indianapolis as if a Venetian canal, and during the day I rode much of the twelve miles on the main artery (other paths have now been added to the system).

Apparently, the bike trail cost $63 million to build, but what the taxpayers and private donors got for their money (as opposed to a stadium that is used about twenty days a year) is bike-enhanced urban renewal. (The verb for this effect is *Copenhagenize,* and there is now an index of the same name, to rank cities according to their bike friendliness.) At least along the bike path, Indianapolis shines, and had I stopped at each marked destination off the trail (the USS *Indianapolis* memorial, the Indianapolis Museum of Art, NCAA Hall of Champions, etc.), it might have taken me three days to make the loop.

Indianapolis: Benjamin "Kid Gloves" Harrison Gets Remarried

For my first stop of the day, I chose the Benjamin Harrison Presidential Site, located on North Delaware Street, just south of East 13th, on a street of upscale houses. Before knocking on the front door and joining a house tour led by Martha ("I am a retired first-grade teacher"), all I knew about Harrison was that the Democratic press called him "Kid Gloves" Harrison (in reference to his wealth as a corporate lawyer) and others called him the "Human Iceberg," for all the warmth he radiated on the campaign trail. I knew, as well, that his Republican presidency was a Grover Cleveland interregnum (1889–1893, between the Democrat's two terms), but beyond that I was hazy, other than that he was a Grant man.

I am under no illusion that a visit to the house of a president or a writer sheds any light on his or her work or character. I just find it useful, when later reading about a person, to visualize where they lived or worked. To learn something, I first need to see it. I was only ever able to read William Faulkner after a visit to his home in Oxford, Mississippi, and I developed an affection for the worldliness of Emily Dickinson only after I went through her house in Amherst, Massachusetts. But my system doesn't always hold together. All I learned about Alexander Hamilton when I went to his New York City house, the Grange, is that he liked to eat off fine china (there was no mention that he dallied with his neighbor's wife), and a walk around Herman Melville's house in Pittsfield, Massachusetts, will tell you nothing about him (except that Mount Greylock, visible from his writing table, does look something like a white whale).

What interested Martha most about the Harrison house was the furniture, the pictures, and the interior design. ("All the floors are oak, and the side paneling is a butternut, indigenous to Indiana.") She was less clear on Harrison's Civil War record ("the battle of Peachtree rings a bell") or his attitude toward organized labor ("Harrison was a successful lawyer who worked here in Indianapolis, on Market Street").

Clearly in the Harrison household, the pick of the litter was Benjamin's wife, Caroline, who arranged the furniture, painted fans, played the piano, raised the two children, and fed the pets, including Whiskers, a goat, and Pepper the dog. During the tour, which together with the museum lasted almost two hours, I kept waiting for Martha to upbraid me: "Now, Matthew, I want you to stop looking at the books on the shelves and listen to what I have to say about Caroline's china."

In 1833, Benjamin Harrison was born in North Bend, Ohio, outside Cincinnati, the grandson of William Henry Harrison, the Indian killer and thirty-day president. (I have always had my doubts about Tippecanoe as a great military or moral victory, but that lies outside this story.)

Harrison started his undergraduate studies at Farmers' College (where he met Caroline) but earned his degree at Miami University of Ohio. They married in 1853, the year before Benjamin set up his law practice in Indianapolis. He was a successful lawyer but took time off from his practice in 1862, at the request of Governor Oliver Morton, to organize the Seventieth Indiana Infantry Regiment, in which he started as a lieutenant and ended as a brigadier general.

The regiment's notable actions were fought, under General William T. Sherman's command, on the road from Chattanooga to Atlanta, in 1864. Upstairs at the house, in the obligatory children's room that is complete with adorable cradles and developmentally sensitive wooden toys, there were lots of books, including one about Sherman from a series on great Americans. Before the campaign for Atlanta began, someone overheard Harrison speaking to the men of his regiment, who were spellbound by his eloquence. This officer later slapped a Captain Samuel Merrill of the regiment on the back and said: "By George, Captain, that Colonel of yours will be President of the United States some day."

After the war, Harrison was content to return to his law practice—in the 1870s he prosecuted the sensational murder trial of Nancy Clem, the respectable wife of a grocer, who killed a local businessman and his wife in grisly fashion, apparently over money. Despite Harrison's summation to the jury, which took eight hours, it only found her guilty of perjury, and she served only four years in jail.

In the 1870s, as a brigadier general in Sherman's corps and a successful corporate lawyer (he tried fifteen cases before the US Supreme Court and earned $21,000 in 1874), Harrison attracted political attention. He twice tried to become governor of Indiana, losing once before getting the nomination and the second time in the general election. He was encouraged to run for Congress but demurred, preferring to boost other candidates. Still, he served legal roles in the presidential administrations of Civil War generals Grant and Hayes, and was the Indiana go-to man for the election of (General) James Garfield, who offered him a place in his cabinet. Instead, Harrison chose to serve as a US senator, which he did from 1881 to 1887. The next year the Republicans nominated Harrison on the eighth ballot, after various front-runners, including James G. Blaine and John Sherman (brother of the general), lost interest or supporters.

In Harrison's North Delaware Street house, into which he moved in 1874, Martha showed us the spot in the back parlor where Harrison accepted the nomination on July 4, 1888. When I asked about it, she scoffed at the "Human Iceberg" nickname. In turn I demurred from telling the tour group ("we're here for the Maryland football game") a common story of the 1880s, which was that they didn't let Benjamin campaign, as each hand he shook turned the greeter into a Democrat.

Instead of glad-handing, Harrison gave more than eighty speeches from his front porch, beginning the campaigning style that later William McKinley and Warren Harding were to perfect.

As president, Harrison was a trust lawyer for Grantism, and he stayed close to God, country, and the tariff, which protected industrial Republican stalwarts from overseas competition. In his inaugural address, Harrison spoke of protectionism, more money for the navy, and equal opportunity. Aside from the McKinley Tariff (1890), the other notable piece of legislation passed during his presidency was the

Sherman Antitrust Act, although at that time, it was more lip service than an attack on his former corporate clients. Less sensationally, as Martha pointed out, his was the first White House that had electricity, but such was the Harrisons' fear of the current that they only let the servants switch on and off the lights.

As president, Harrison set aside the land for national parks to be established at Yosemite, Sequoia, and the General Grant grove of sequoias, which became part of Kings Canyon. He established a national military park at Chattanooga, which included where he was quartered on Lookout Mountain. With almost missionary zeal, he believed that Indians ought to be assimilated equally into American culture, although that led to intolerance over their reservations, religion, and non-American ways, and the massacre at Wounded Knee happened during his presidency.

Abroad, Harrison saber-rattled against Chile and took control of the Samoan Islands. Generally, he let James Blaine, his secretary of state, manage the overseas portfolio, which some said later became a blueprint for the presidencies of William McKinley and Theodore Roosevelt, especially as regards the expanded navy and the brinkmanship over trade.

What cost Harrison his reelection in 1892—he lost to Cleveland—was probably his ice-cold personality, which had alienated him from other leaders in the Republican party (McKinley and Blaine) and made him few friends in government or around the country. He ran the county as a law firm, and treated even leading senators as junior associates. As well, by 1892 the country was tired of being run by bearded, Civil War generals from Ohio. And the Democrats were becoming the party of the working man, such as those in Debs's rank and file. To them Harrison looked liked another railroad lawyer sent out to bust a union.

For all that Harrison was a man in full—the president of the local YMCA, a deacon in his Presbyterian church, head of the University Club—Martha did tell a story about the end of his life that sounded more from the pages of a Dreiser novel than Harrison's own memoir, *This Country of Ours*. In the White House, Caroline Harrison came down with tuberculosis, forcing her to send for a widowed niece, Mary Dimmick, to act as her social secretary and, sometimes, as a stand-in during White House events. Mary lived two years in the White House, and helped not just the First Lady, but often worked closely with Benjamin, sorting his papers or whatever. Caroline died of her illness in 1892—the last year of the Harrison administration, which may explain too why he was isolated from his cabinet and party.

After leaving office, according to the official story, Benjamin and Mary began a passionate correspondence that ended with them getting married in 1896. He was sixty-three; she was thirty-eight. According to Martha, Benjamin's children with Caroline—Russell and Mary Harrison—deeply resented their father's second marriage to the younger woman, their first cousin at that. Mary Harrison called the match "purely one of ambition" on the part of Mary Dimmick, and broke off contact with her father, especially after Harrison and Mary had a daughter, "Baby" Elizabeth, in 1897.

When Harrison died in 1901, he left his entire estate—$400,000, which today would be $10 million—to his second wife, never having reconciled with his children. After the funeral, Martha said, they did not even stay in the home where they had grown up.[4]

No wonder on the third floor of the Harrison house, where the tour ended in a small museum with exhibition cabinets, there is a sheet of paper explaining the "Language of the Fan." Caroline Harrison loved fans, collected fans, even painted them, always with delight. The paper decodes the language a fan can express, depending on how it is held. For example, according to the rules of the game, when the fan is placed near the heart it means: "You have won my love." When it touches the right eye, the meaning is: "When may I be allowed to see you?" Left resting on the right cheek, it says: "Yes." On the left cheek, the answer is "No." Held over the left ear, it says: "I wish to get rid of you." Clearly Mary Dimmick never held her fan—or those of Caroline, if the collection came to her—over her left ear, and Benjamin Harrison, who made his fortune reading judges and juries, didn't miss the signs.

4: As a footnote to this story, in 1937 a US congressman introduced a bill that would have provided a pension for Harrison's widow, Mrs. Mary Scott Dimmick Harrison, then living on Fifth Avenue in New York. No reason was given why, having inherited her husband's estate of $400,000, she needed a government pension of $5,000 a year (the same as Mrs. Wilson received, as a widow). The bill moved along through Congress until Russell Harrison, the president's estranged son, heard about it, and he killed it in its tracks.

Indianapolis: Kurt Vonnegut's Many Banned Books

When I was done with the Harrisons, I went on the bike in search of lunch, but I struggled to find a place that would allow me to eat outside and keep an eye on the Brompton. I did, however, run across yet another Lincoln plaque on the bike trail and figured out that he had stopped in Indianapolis the same day that he had left Springfield—February 11, 1861—after delivering his "Farewell Address" at the Great Western Depot. When his special train stopped in Indianapolis later that day, he made his way to Washington and Missouri streets, and said:

> I, as already intimated, am but an accidental instrument, temporary, and to serve but for a limited time, but I appeal to you again to constantly bear in mind that with you, and not with politicians, not with Presidents, not with office-seekers, but with you, is the question: Shall the Union and shall the liberties of this country be preserved to the latest generations?

What the plaque doesn't say is that by that day, seven of the future eleven Confederate states had already seceded. While Lincoln was waiting for his inauguration day on March 4, 1861, and tending (or not) to his father's grave near Charleston, South Carolina, Mississippi, Florida, Alabama, Georgia, Louisiana, and Texas had already left the Union. It's one of my few criticisms about Lincoln—that after his election he didn't head South, perhaps with Stephen Douglas at his side, to meet face-to-face with the secessionists. Douglas would have gone, I am sure, but Lincoln refused to budge until he had power.

I finally found a Starbucks that served (shrink-wrapped) sandwiches through a speakeasy window on a small square. The day was warm and sunny, and it felt good to be outside, after trooping around the gloomy Harrison manor. At 3 p.m. I made my way over to the Kurt Vonnegut Museum and Library, where I had an interview with the director, Julia Whitehead.

When I arrived at the small, storefront museum and library, it turned out that she was otherwise engaged, so I met her associate, Chris Lafave, who was waiting for me, although also preoccupied with running the library in Julia's absence. Nevertheless, I was still able to tape an interview with him about the novelist Kurt Vonnegut, who was born in 1922 and grew up in Indianapolis, attending Shortridge High School on the north side of town.

My arrival coincided with what the library was calling "Banned Book Week," and on a table near the front window (the entire space is very small) there was a stack of books that had all been banned somewhere at some time in the United States. Needless to say, the pile was enormous, and—waiting for Chris—as I looked through the collection of banned books, it struck me that the same books could also be placed on a table for great American novels. Here was *Huck Finn*; *The Great Gatsby*; *Catch-22*; Vonnegut's *Cat's Cradle*; *The Color Purple*; *A Farewell to Arms*; *For Whom the Bell Tolls*; *Heart of Darkness*; *Native Son*; *Rabbit, Run*; Vonnegut's *Slaughterhouse-Five*; *To Kill a Mockingbird*; *The Sun Also Rises*, and many others, all of which had fallen afoul of some school board or head librarian.

To commemorate Banned Book Week at the library, a self-styled performance artist (who slept on a mattress in the front window) was seated at a desk in the window, typing on Kurt Vonnegut's typewriter (or one just like it) the entire manuscript of *Cat's Cradle.* At the end of the week, the plan was to shred, burn, or otherwise destroy the typewritten book, presumably so that others might live—at least in circulating libraries. I confess, the exact reason that he was retyping the book was never clear to me, but the old sound of electric typewriter keys striking paper did remind me of my college days, when I was first introduced to Vonnegut's novels.

I taped my interview with Chris over a cabinet in the library. Around us, on the walls of the museum, were various posters and pictures of Vonnegut and his writing life. One showed him in Dresden in 1967, on a Guggenheim Fellowship to the city where he was a prisoner in World War II. Another showed him protesting the Vietnam War while a more modern picture was taken of him on the step of his summer home, on the eastern end of Long Island, in Sagaponack. In that picture he is relaxed, wearing sneakers, and surrounded by flowering hydrangeas.

Also on the library walls were facsimiles of pages from his book manuscripts, and more than a few rejection letters. More than most best-selling writers, Vonnegut struggled to get published for the first twenty years of his career, which began after the war. Later, when he became, well, Kurt Vonnegut, I am sure he savored each earlier rejection letter, including the one that said the humor in his story "is a little too heavy-handed." Not until *Slaughterhouse-Five, or The Children's Crusade: A Duty-Dance with Death* was published in 1969 did Vonnegut become a household name. Before that, his books were published but he was second-lining.

Chris, the associate director of the memorial library, talked a lot about Vonnegut's time in Indianapolis, and little of it sounded easy. He grew up in a German American family. His father was a wealthy architect, and in the 1920s the family lived at 4401 North Illinois in a large house, one of comparable size and design to those on Frank Lloyd Wright's Forest Avenue. Then came the 1929 Depression, from which his father never recovered, and the Vonneguts struggled, as did many families.

Instead of attending private school, as did his brothers, Vonnegut went to Shortridge High School, the oldest in Indiana and located between the city and the family house. Kurt did well in high school, had friends, and wrote humor stories for the school newspaper. He also wrote articles that denounced war in general, and World War II in particular.

As Chris told the story of Kurt's academic career, he struggled with required courses, papers, deadlines, and professorial expectations that he conform, something he never did well. To keep from failing out of Cornell, he attended summer classes at Butler University (in Indianapolis and close to his house). In his sophomore year, an article in the Cornell newspaper and bad grades cost him his place at the university.

Without a student deferment and facing the draft, he enlisted in the army and did basic training at Fort Bragg. Chris told the painful story of Vonnegut coming home on leave, in 1944, and finding his mother dead, a suicide. Without time to grieve, he was shipped overseas to England, from where he was deployed, with regiments of the 106th Infantry, to a quiet sector in the Belgian lines between Luxembourg and the Hürtgen Forest. In December 1944, those same lines would be overrun in the first days of the Battle of Bulge, during which Hitler tried to cut a broad salient between English and American lines, hoping it would force the Allies to negotiate a truce.

Dresden, Germany: Slaughterhouse-Five

On the same trip that took my son Henry and me to the Hürtgen Forest, we also explored the landscape of the Battle of the Bulge, and, by chance, we were taken by our guide to a place near where Vonnegut's second battalion of the 423rd Infantry Regiment was overrun. It was outside Schönberg, near St. Vith and Malmedy, through which the German invasion stormed on December 18, 1944.

Whether the 106th Infantry Division could have held their ground and fought the Germans is a matter of intense military debate. Those sympathetic to the men on the ground—Vonnegut among them—argue that the division was too spread out along the German border to defend anything, let alone fight back. No one in the American high command, including generals Eisenhower and Bradley, had expected a German attack into the Belgian Ardennes. The divisions posted there were recuperating from earlier fights, in either Normandy or the Hürtgen, and expected to do little more than patrol a quiet frontier.

Critics of the American army in the Bulge argue that such regiments as Vonnegut's 423rd did little more than cut and run when they saw the enemy advancing across the Western Wall, and that the surrender of more than seven thousand soldiers in the first days of the battle represents one of the darkest chapters in the army's history. They accuse the division's officers, many new to combat, of lacking the habits of leadership and command, and say many men simply threw down their weapons and ran to the rear. By contrast, they point to the actions of more seasoned divisions—notably the Eighty-Second Airborne at Elsenborn Ridge—to make the point that their predicament was the same as that of the 106th, but that its desperate stand (fighting at times in the woods with bayonets) deflected the German attack to the south—a key element in the eventual Allied victory in the Bulge. (Essentially the Allies from the north and down squeezed the shoulders of the German salient, forcing it to a point that was then destroyed and rolled back.)

The lengthy subtitle of Vonnegut's *Slaughterhouse-Five* reads as follows:

> A FOURTH-GENERATION GERMAN-AMERICAN NOW LIVING IN EASY CIRCUMSTANCES ON CAPE COD [AND SMOKING TOO MUCH], WHO, AS AN AMERICAN INFANTRY SCOUT HORS DE COMBAT, AS A PRISONER OF WAR, WITNESSED THE FIRE-BOMBING OF DRESDEN, GERMANY "THE FLORENCE OF THE ELBE," A LONG TIME AGO, AND SURVIVED TO TELL THE TALE. THIS IS A NOVEL SOMEWHAT IN THE TELEGRAPHIC SCHIZOPHRENIC MANNER OF TALES OF THE PLANET TRALFAMADORE, WHERE THE FLYING SAUCERS COME FROM. PEACE.

The hero of the story is Billy Pilgrim, who, while not exactly Vonnegut's alter ego, did share with him the experience of capture in the Ardennes and later imprisonment in Dresden.

In the novel, Vonnegut describes the experience of losing a battle:

> When Billy joined the regiment, it was in the process of being destroyed by the Germans in the famous Battle of the Bulge. Billy never even got to meet the chaplain he was supposed to assist, was never even issued a steel helmet and combat boots. This was in December of 1944, during the last mighty German attack of the war. . . .
>
> They went Indian file. First came the scouts, clever, graceful, quiet. They had rifles. Next came the antitank gunner, clumsy and dense, warning Germans away with a Colt .45 automatic in one hand and a trench knife in the other.
>
> Last came Billy Pilgrim, empty-handed, bleakly ready for death. Billy was preposterous—six feet and three inches tall, with a chest and shoulders like a box of kitchen matches. . . .
>
> He could scarcely distinguish between sleep and wakefulness now, on the third day, found no important differences, either, between walking and standing still. . . .
>
> There was no undergrowth. Four inches of unmarked snow blanketed the ground. The Americans had no choice but to leave trails in the snow as unambiguous as diagrams in a book on ballroom dancing—*step, slide, rest-step, slide, rest. . . .*
>
> Through the valley flowed a Mississippi of humiliated Americans. Tens of thousands of Americans shuffled eastward, their hands clasped on top of their heads. They sighed and groaned.

After being captured, Vonnegut was sent to a prison camp in Dresden, where on the night of February 13–14, he was a witness to the firebombing of the ancient city, the story of which is told in *Slaughterhouse-Five*. (That was the name of the building in which Vonnegut was held as a prisoner. It was an old stockyard.) He writes: "One thing was clear: Absolutely everybody in the city was supposed to be dead, regardless of what they were, and that anybody that moved in it represented a flaw in the design. There were to be no moon men at all."

Chris Lafave picked up the story of Vonnegut's academics and writing career after he came home from the war. He married a girl from his high school and enrolled in anthropology at the University of Chicago, but never got his degree—they didn't like his thesis, which he rewrote several times. Finally in 1948, he accepted a public relations job at General Electric in Schenectady. He worked there for three years, while writing short stories at night. Selling one to *Collier's* magazine, he quit the corporate life in 1951, moved his growing family to Cape Cod, and there struggled as a writer through the 1950s and '60s. He sold stories and novels where he could, but nothing was a bestseller until he won the Guggenheim Fellowship in 1967, which allowed him to travel back to Dresden. (An early passage in *Slaughterhouse-Five* reads: "I really *did* go back to Dresden with Guggenheim money [God love it] in 1967. It looked a lot like Dayton, Ohio, more open spaces than Dayton has. There must be tons of human bone meal in the ground.")

Chris said that trip led to *Slaughterhouse-Five*, a bestseller, which sent his fans back to the earlier novels—

Cat's Cradle among them—that he had written before and which sold only in small numbers to a cult following, largely on college campuses.

You might think, from all my devotion to Kurt Vonnegut's story, that I am devoted to his novels. The fact is that I struggle with a lot of his writing, as, in general, I do poorly with science fiction, and in many Vonnegut stories spaceships show with the regularity of city buses. I also can't say I love his humor, for which it helps to be a college freshman. But even when I was myself a college freshman, and a hall-mate pressed several Vonneguts on me—"Matt, you like books and you like to laugh; you'll love these!"—I read *Cat's Cradle* and *God Bless You, Mr. Rosewater* but found them belabored, and the humor awkward.

My devotion to Vonnegut comes elsewhere, and at the time all I did was shake his hand. In 1980, I was working for *Harper's Magazine*, and it folded (although later it rose from the ashes). Today a print magazine folding would not merit an AP dispatch, but then it was front-page news, and on the day of the announcement the office was in turmoil.

For whatever reasons, Kurt Vonnegut showed up in the waiting room and sat there for much of the afternoon, trying to lend solidarity to the cause of *Harper's*, or magazines, or just writing in general. I didn't know him and never talked with him that day, but I did admire the stand he was taking—just by sitting there in a waiting room chair.

For that gesture, I was happy to repay him with my visit to the Battle of the Bulge, where his own words—"Shells were bursting in the treetops with terrific bangs . . . showering down knives and needles and razorblades"—became the keys that Henry and I used to understand the battle. And after Indianapolis, I was determined to get back to Dresden and find the actual Slaughterhouse-Five.

Indianapolis by Night: Potemkin Villages

ALREADY THEN I KNEW I would spend the warm evening riding around Indianapolis, and Chris kindly supplied me with some needed addresses and directions. He explained where I could find the house in which Vonnegut had grown up, which was about five miles to the north. He also told me where I could find his high school, Shortridge, and the Athenaeum Club, a *brauhaus* in Indianapolis where, in his day, Vonnegut's father would hang out. From Chris, I also got directions to the Benjamin Harrison tomb in Crown Hill Cemetery and to the city park where in 1968 Robert F. Kennedy delivered a speech to an audience of black Americans, informing them of the news that Martin Luther King Jr. had just been assassinated.

Because it was still midafternoon, I detoured on my ride back to the hotel and took in more of the Cultural Trail, stopping at the memorial of the USS *Indianapolis*, a heavy cruiser that the Japanese sank two weeks before the end of the war, on July 30, 1945, killing some 880 sailors (316 survived). It was the greatest loss of life ever suffered by the American navy, although the Shakespearean tragedy of her sinking was that it followed delivery of the atomic bomb to the island of Tinian, from which the B-29 bomber *Enola Gay* dropped it on Hiroshima.

I stopped also at the Eiteljorg Museum of American Indians and Western Art, which was a short distance from the bike path. By the time I got there, it was 4:30 p.m., and the museum was closing at 5 p.m. The guard on duty at the ticket booth, nevertheless, encouraged me to come in, and for thirty minutes (not enough time to become overwhelmed) I looked at Frederic Remington paintings and sculptures, a picture of a little boy looking up admiringly at a steam engine (why, that could be me), and an 1848 George Winter canvas showing an Indian family on the banks of the Wabash River. The caption reads: "Winter traveled west to Indiana in 1837 where he observed many members of the Miami and Potawatomi tribes living along the banks of the Wabash River. He knew that the government was forcing most of them to move out of the region. Motivated by a sense of urgency, he believed, like many of his peers, that they would cease to exist. To preserve knowledge of their ways of life, he created hundreds of sketches and paintings." The painting shows an Indian family, as if already in exile, living on a small island in the Wabash River. It might well, in terms of American Indian culture, be called *The Last Supper*.

Before the sun went down, I caught up on e-mails back at the hotel and enjoyed the luxury of my hotel room, which was only marginally smaller than Lucas Oil Stadium. I indulged in potato chips from the lobby shop and drank mineral water from the minibar. Shortly after 7:30 p.m., I roused myself from my comforts and biked into the night.

Although I stopped often to be sure I was biking in the right direction, it took less than a half hour to find the Vonnegut boyhood home on North Illinois. At first I wasn't sure I had found it—no plaque marks the spot, unfortunately—but after digging into my notebook and checking the address Chris had given me, I was sure of the location.

In *Slaughterhouse-Five,* there is a passage in which Billy Pilgrim (the alter ego of Kurt Vonnegut) goes back to the house where he grew up, which in the novel is in Dayton, Ohio. He writes of going home: "Billy drove through a scene of even greater desolation. It looked like Dresden after it was firebombed—like the surface of the moon. The house where Billy had grown up used to be somewhere in what was so empty now. This was urban renewal." That imagery could have been of Indianapolis, in the 1960s, with much racial tension. But it did not fit the house at which I was looking, which has a slate roof, numerous bedrooms, and an ample garden, and spoke to many upper-class dreams.

Because Chris had spoken of it favorably, I detoured from the Vonnegut house to the Indianapolis Museum of Art, which is south of Butler University, where Kurt struggled through his summer school. I had to ride there on a sidewalk, in near darkness, as the traffic on East 38th unnerved me. I thought of locking the bike and going into the museum, but I wasn't in the mood for a gallery spin, and in no time, I was back on the other side of East 38th Street, in search of Benjamin Harrison's tomb.

I knew he was buried in Crown Hill Cemetery, which was on my right, and I suspected that he was buried in a ménage à trois, together with Caroline and Mary Dimmick. Hard as I tried, I could not slip into the cemetery while there was still light and hunt around for the gravestones. Instead I had to poke around in the dark until I found the cemetery entrance on East 34th Street, by which time it was closed.

By that time, I had lost interest in Harrison's eternal resting place (I know, Dreiser could have gotten several chapters from the arrangements of the headstones). Instead I went east on East 34th Street, and rode directly into Kurt Vonnegut's all-American high school, Shortridge, which had illuminated columns around the entrance. As Vonnegut said, not very profoundly: "High school is closer to the core of the American experience than anything else I can think of."

It was hard to tell from the outside, but clearly some teachers inside this staid building had fired Vonnegut's imagination for discordant words and humor. It would have been nice to hear what they had said to him. About this time, the famous Chicago educator Robert Hutchins wrote: "My idea of education is to unsettle the minds of the young and inflame their intellects." With Kurt, at least from a distance, he succeeded.

In the darkness I biked around the building (there were sports facilities in the back) and continued east on 34th. I had one more stop that evening, at Martin Luther King Park around East 20th Street, where in April 1968 Robert Kennedy had to break the news to a black audience that King was dead.

While cutting through the side streets between East 34th and East 20th, I saw a number of houses that were falling down, with weeds sprouting where once there had been dreams. Sometimes there was a man or a couple, sitting on the front stoop, nursing a bottle. In other places, the house was boarded up and the yard was overgrown. These houses were less than four miles from the glittering downtown, where the NCAA has its headquarters, there are many elegant museums, and Marriott had just opened a sprawling, Soviet-sized hotel with 622 rooms.

As much as I liked downtown Indianapolis—the Cultural Trail, the bike paths along the canals—from East 20th Street I saw it as a Potemkin village, a facade of opulence to reassure the rest of America that the dream still includes a conference center, sports bars, Astroturf on the practice fields, and expense account dinners. In much of uptown Indianapolis, however, it is still 1969, which is when Vonnegut wrote: “The neighborhood reminded Billy of some of the towns he had seen in the war. The curbs and sidewalks were crushed in many places, showing where the National Guard tanks and half-tracks had been.”

Indianapolis: Robert F. Kennedy Mourns Martin Luther King Jr.

About the time that Martin Luther King Jr. was shot and killed at the Lorraine Motel in Memphis, Tennessee, on April 4, 1968, Robert Kennedy was flying to Indianapolis, to continue campaigning in the Indiana primary for the Democratic nomination.

When his plane landed, Kennedy was told that King had been shot, and as his motorcade drove toward the corner of 17th Street and Broadway, he and his aides hastily rewrote the speech that he would give to the largely black American audience that was expected in the street.

When he arrived at the rally, Kennedy mounted a flatbed truck and took a microphone in his hand. He did not read the prepared speech or even look at notes when he spoke. An historian of the event writes: "There was almost no artificial lighting, just a couple of floodlights on the platform." He also calls it "a phantasmagoric scene."

Had Kennedy been elected president in 1968 (instead, he himself was assassinated exactly two months later), his speech in Indianapolis might today be remembered for eloquence that approached Lincoln's when he gave his inaugural addresses. Instead the speech is largely forgotten, except among a few Kennedy aficionados, who keep a copy of the words in their desk to remind themselves that, someday, they need to write something about the occasion. I say that as someone who has held on to a copy of the remarks since the 1970s.

Where Kennedy gave his Indianapolis speech there is now a sidewalk plaque. On one side it reads:

> Here on the evening of April 4, 1968, Kennedy came to address a large crowd of mostly African Americans in his bid for Democratic Party nomination for president of U.S. Instead, visibly shaken, he gave an impromptu speech about the assassination of Martin Luther King, Jr. that day in Memphis, Tenn.

On the other side it says:

> Kennedy urged the crowd to follow Rev. King's lead and respond with understanding and prayer. Citing the need to avoid division, hatred, and violence, he called for love, wisdom, compassion, and justice. The speech is credited with keeping Indianapolis calm, while other cities reacted with violence.

The surrounding neighborhood, at least at night on a warm evening, feels like much of inner-city Indianapolis, at least that outside the golden triangle downtown. There is a mix of public housing projects and small row houses, most well maintained. To the north, Martin Luther King Memorial Park stretches for three city blocks. At the center is a monument, on either side of a sidewalk, that shows Robert Kennedy and King reaching out for each other—although they are being pulled in opposition directions, as if into a maelstrom. They might almost be passengers on two separate sinking ships—one for white America, the other for blacks—crying out to each other for salvation. The tragedy of the sculpture, as in their lives, is that their grasping hands fall short; neither could save the other.

Still, Kennedy did his best to breach the divide when he spoke these words:

> Ladies and Gentlemen,
>
> I have some very sad news for all of you, and that is that Martin Luther King was shot and was killed tonight in Memphis, Tennessee.
>
> Martin Luther King dedicated his life to love and to justice between fellow human beings. He died in the cause of that effort. In this difficult day, in this difficult time for the United States, it's perhaps well to ask what kind of a nation we are and what direction we want to move in. For those of you who are black—considering the evidence evidently is that there were white people who were responsible—you can be filled with bitterness, and with hatred, and a desire for revenge.
>
> We can move in that direction as a country, in greater polarization—black people amongst blacks, and white amongst whites, filled with hatred toward one another. Or we can make an effort, as Martin Luther King did, to understand, and to comprehend, and replace that violence, that stain of bloodshed that has spread across our land, with an effort to understand, compassion, and love.
>
> For those of you who are black and are tempted to fill with—be filled with hatred and mistrust of the injustice of such an act, against all white people, I would only say that I can also feel in my own heart the same kind of feeling. I had a member of my family killed, but he was killed by a white man.

But we have to make an effort in the United States. We have to make an effort to understand, to get beyond, or go beyond these rather difficult times.

My favorite poem, my—my favorite poet was Aeschylus. And he once wrote:

> *Even in our sleep, pain which cannot forget*
> *falls drop by drop upon the heart,*
> *until, in our own despair,*
> *against our will,*
> *comes wisdom*
> *through the awful grace of God.*

What we need in the United States is not division; what we need in the United States is not hatred; what we need in the United States is not violence and lawlessness, but is love, and wisdom, and compassion toward one another, and a feeling of justice toward those who still suffer within our country, whether they be white or whether they be black.

So I ask you tonight to return home, to say a prayer for the family of Martin Luther King—yeah, it's true—but more importantly to say a prayer for our own country, which all of us love—a prayer for understanding and that compassion of which I spoke.

We can do well in this country. We will have difficult times. We've had difficult times in the past, but we—and we will have difficult times in the future. It is not the end of violence; it is not the end of lawlessness; and it's not the end of disorder.

But the vast majority of white people and the vast majority of black people in this country want to live together, want to improve the quality of our life, and want justice for all human beings that abide in our land.

And let's dedicate ourselves to what the Greeks wrote so many years ago: to tame the savageness of man and make gentle the life of this world. Let us dedicate ourselves to that, and say a prayer for our country and for our people.

Thank you very much.

Indianapolis: 1968 Democratic Indiana Primary

When Martin Luther King Jr. was shot, I was fourteen years old, in the eighth grade and in my room listening on a transistor radio to a New York Rangers hockey game. A news bulletin interrupted the broadcast, and I switched to an all-news station and listened to the accounts of the assassination.

Even for someone loving middle school, as I did at the time, 1967–68 was an ugly time—with riots in many American cities, desperate fighting in Vietnam, several challengers vying for the Democratic presidential nomination following Lyndon Johnson's withdrawal, and now the King shooting. The personal connection to this domestic violence came one week later when *Life* magazine was delivered to our house, and it reported on the street violence. Living with us in her retirement, my grandmother looked at the picture of a dead teenager lying in a Newark street and recognized the boy. A substitute teacher near Newark late in her career, she put her finger on the bloody page and said: "He was in one of my classes. So was his brother."

Around this time, I had also met Robert Kennedy. He spoke to a group from the League of Women Voters, and my mother, on the board in Long Island, had taken me out of school to meet him. The event was a small gathering in a Great Neck living room, and, standing in front of the fireplace, Kennedy spoke to us for about fifteen minutes. As he was leaving for his next appointment, he stopped, shook my hand, and bantered with me for a few minutes—about missing my classes (I was) and whether I played football (I did). In those years, a visit from an Olympian god would have made less of an impression.

Because of my personal connection to Robert Kennedy, I followed the presidential primaries that spring with intensity. I would read the newspaper daily, listen to the results on the radio, and watch television specials. In traveling now to Indiana, one thing I wanted to do was refresh myself on the details of the Kennedy win in that primary, which took place in May 1968.

Even to an eighth grader that spring, it had made no sense that Kennedy—a Catholic, liberal, New York senator against the Vietnam War—should have won in hard-hatted, steelworker, agricultural Indiana. I didn't get it, but during the intervening years, I never bothered to find out how and why he had won. Just carrying the antiwar and black vote would not have been enough. On this trip I was determined to fill in the blanks.

Unfortunately, aside from the Kennedy-King memorial in the park, there are no reminders around Indianapolis about the 1968 primary. I asked in a bookshop during my rides but, again, the clerk shrugged and suggested I try online, which is what I did and where I found Ray Boomhower's *Robert F. Kennedy and the 1968 Indiana Primary*, just the book I wanted. (Is it any wonder bookshops are struggling when two big ones in Indiana have nothing on Debs, Dreiser, and Kennedy?)

A local professor of political science, Boomhower makes it clear that Indiana was a near-run thing for Kennedy, that his advisers didn't want him to run there, and that he could easily have lost to the favorite-son governor Roger Branigan, which would have ended his chances for the nomination. (Imagine the headlines: "Kennedy Loses to Little-Known Governor")

Among those with whom Kennedy consulted about the state was John Bartlow Martin, who wrote the Adlai Stevenson biographies that Mardo gave me in 1977. Martin grew up in Indianapolis on Brookside Avenue, on what he called "a mean street in a mean city." (Brookside is east of the Harrison house and south of the King park.) According to Boomhower, Martin warned Kennedy "that Indianapolis was home to the national headquarters of the American Legion and the place where Robert Welch Jr. had founded the ultraconservative John Birch Society on December 9, 1958, to fight Communist infiltration of the American government."

Nevertheless, Kennedy decided to put all his chips on the primary. "Indiana is the ballgame," he said. "This is my West Virginia." The latter reference was to the primary in 1960 that got his brother John the Democratic nomination.

Kennedy, however, came to Indiana looking like a usurper and a spoiled child. Senator Eugene McCarthy had first taken up the mantle to unseat President Lyndon Johnson (Kennedy himself had declined to run). With a liberal coalition of those who opposed the Vietnam War, McCarthy had shown well enough in New Hampshire to force Johnson to withdraw. Then, at McCarthy's moment of triumph, the Minnesota senator learned that Kennedy was now joining the race. A man of considerable wit, McCarthy said: "We woke up after the New Hampshire primary like it was Christmas Day. And when we went down to the tree, we found Bobby Kennedy had stolen our presents."

The three candidates running in Indiana that spring were Robert Kennedy, Eugene McCarthy, and Roger Branigan. The governor was in the race to attend the Democratic convention (that year in Chicago) with the delegates pledged to him. Still, he said, "I am running and I'm running to win." Branigan also had little time for Johnson, calling the president "a selfish, opinionated man of considerable mediocrity. As a matter of fact, he's rather a triumph of mediocrity."

Branigan ran an excellent campaign in a state he knew intimately while, despite help from actor Paul Newman, the McCarthy machine faltered and Kennedy brought his A game. Boomhower quotes one McCarthy aide saying: "He was overscheduled, underscheduled, lost, driven impossibly long distances, and later estimated that he wasted eighty percent of his time." Another said: "He's a terrible snob and he had decided early that the Indiana people just weren't his kind." Boomhower writes: "A reporter who covered Congress said McCarthy seemed to believe he could campaign 'by just traveling around all alone like some medieval minstrel singing his songs.'"

Despite the long odds—Indiana had steelworkers near Chicago and Southerners around Vincennes—Kennedy managed to connect with the diverse, conservative voter base. Boomhower quotes a Kennedy aide, John Douglas, saying "that probably no national candidate in modern times worked as hard as Kennedy did. He came across as authentic, direct, and straightforward—a person in whom the people could have confidence. And that's what, I think, brought Indiana around." Branigan charged Kennedy with trying to buy the victory. Kennedy shot back: "If I were trying to buy the state I wouldn't be here."

A signature Kennedy campaign moment was when he chartered a train, nicknamed the "Wabash Cannonball," to whistle-stop across rural towns in central Indiana—the Branigan heartland. According to Boomhower, a Kennedy advance man named Joe Dolan "had noted that travel by railroad offered several advantages for a candidate. 'He doesn't have to get in or out of the car. And on the plane everybody has access to him.'" Plus, the connection with Harry Truman "giving them hell" in 1948 was obvious. Boomhower adds: "Local political officials could also ride the train with the candidate and chat with him in relative comfort until the next stop, when a new set would climb aboard. And as the train traveled from town to town, Kennedy could confer with his staff about his next speech or other matters."

While campaigning, Kennedy dialed back his liberal sentiments, which frustrated some of his staffers, but he did not dilute his message, which was antiwar, greater equality for blacks, and growth based on economic justice for working men and women. That was his coalition. Of the 776,000 votes cast in the primary, Kennedy polled 42.3 percent while Branigan got 30.7 percent and McCarthy 27 percent. He won nine of the eleven congressional districts, and fifty-seven of the ninety-two counties. Boomhower quotes John Bartlow Martin on the primary results, saying: "Indiana people are not generous nor sympathetic; they are hardhearted, not warm and generous; but he must have touched something in them, pushed a button somewhere. He alone did it."

Dayton Trotwood: Going Greyhound

I DID NOT EAT DINNER until almost 11 p.m. that night. Only when I rode back into the downtown area did I find a bar serving beer and tacos, and I had several of each in the warmth of what felt like a summer evening. I sat opposite the former Indianapolis railroad station, now a Crowne Plaza hotel and office complex, which shunted Amtrak into the urinal-modern building next door. Then I was up the next morning at 5 a.m. to catch a 6:15 a.m. Greyhound bus to Dayton Trotwood, which is outside downtown Dayton.

I spilled my coffee on the ride over to the transportation center (next time, bring a thermos), which struck me, even at that early hour, as immune to time changes. It looks the same at 6 a.m. as it does at 6 p.m., which is to say dreary. I wondered if maybe I wasn't seeing the same persons still wedged into the plastic chairs. They looked headed to purgatory (with a twenty-minute rest stop in Muncie).

The ride to Dayton was all on interstates. I could not read, as the light switch above my seat was broken. (Greyhound motto: "If it has a switch, it's usually not working.") I typed e-mails on my computer, which has an illuminated keyboard, and we arrived in Dayton Trotwood just after 8 a.m.

There's no there there in Dayton Trotwood. It's a shopping center, which the Long Dog uses as a hub for some of its lines. I got off the bus, collected my bike, and stood like a zombie, wondering what to do. I had another car rented for the drive across Ohio (not even buses connect those cities, and I was heading out of town), but I needed to pick it up at the airport, about seven miles to the north. As I was preparing the bike for the ride, a middle-aged woman asked me if I knew how she could get to the car-rental agencies at the airport. We fell into conversation and, when one showed up, shared a taxi to the airport.

I never got the name of my taxi companion, but despite the early hour and the setting—a mall parking lot at dawn—we talked easily about a number of subjects, although most about her job. She worked for a state university in Indiana as a professor, and she told me about the unfairness of her position. She had more students than any professor should have and, it seemed, less pay every year. The state legislature had cut back her salary during a budget-cutting session, and now she was worried that she would not have a pension when retirement came down the road.

No combination of train, bike, and bus could have taken me across Ohio on my appointed rounds. I wanted to stop in the remote towns of Georgetown (near Cincinnati, where Ulysses S. Grant grew up), Marion (the hometown of Warren Harding), Fremont (where Rutherford B. Hayes had his mansion), and Canton (home to William McKinley and the Debs-speech park), and end up in Cleveland.

Trains in Ohio only touch the northern and southern edges, and the lines exist to connect Cleveland and Cincinnati with New York, Washington, and Chicago. There is no train, for example, that runs from Cincinnati to Dayton, Columbus, Akron, and Cleveland. Why? That would require state funding, and Ohio is broke. Amtrak keeps its federal funding by running trains to as many congressional districts as its planners can connect. Think of it as an appropriations rider, not a railroad. Even though, as I would learn, Ohio's interstates are clogged with traffic, there's no corridor train service inside the state. You can go between Cleveland and Toledo once a day, although that train departs at 3:27 a.m., which has a way of cutting down on commuters. As for the rest, go Greyhound.

The problem that I had with the bus in Ohio was that it had discontinued service to the smaller towns. I would have been happy on a bus to Marion or Fremont, but once I was there, it would have been impossible for me to keep going in the direction of Cleveland. As I have learned (the hard way), public transportation only works if it runs often (say every hour or so) and connects well into far-flung grids. In Switzerland, where I live, every city, town, and village has service from either the train or a postal bus. Usually that service runs all the time. For example, we go often to a village in the Alps, and a mountain train stops there twenty-six times a day. By comparison, Cleveland—with a population just under four hundred thousand—gets four trains a day, although three of them stop between 1:45 a.m. and 3:30 a.m. The other arrives at the civilized hour of 5:38 a.m.

Instead of heading east on mass transit, I was back in a rental car, which I drove in morning rush-hour traffic through downtown Dayton (with a drive-by salute to the Wright brothers, at least their bicycle shop) to Hamilton, Ohio. This stop was a last-minute inspiration. I had thought of going to North Bend, Ohio, where Benjamin Harrison was born and William Henry Harrison is buried. But I was losing enthusiasm for the Harrisons, at least their burial grounds.

Instead, I decided to stop in Hamilton, which is near Cincinnati (although outside its congestion) and where the nineteenth-century writer and editor William Dean Howells (whom I admire) grew up.

Hamilton, Ohio: William Dean Howells Takes Up the Writing Trade

William Dean Howells is the one who described Mark Twain as the "Lincoln of our literature." His literary career stretched from the 1850s to the 1920s, when he knew many, if not all, of the major literary figures of the time. He edited the *Atlantic Monthly,* wrote a column for *Harper's Magazine,* wrote dozens of books, plays, and poems, and shaped the work of countless other writers—from Twain to Willa Cather and Henry James. His own books are largely forgotten, except for *The Rise of Silas Lapham* and *A Hazard of New Fortunes* (a novel about hunting for real estate in New York in the 1880s!). But without Howells, I am willing to wager, we would never have had such realists in our literature as Dreiser, Hemingway, and F. Scott Fitzgerald. All are descended from his pen.

Hamilton lies along the banks of the Great Miami River, which when I saw it was brackish and still. It's a separate town from Cincinnati, but still in the orbit of the big city, which is thirty-five miles to the south. In my Internet searching, I had learned that there was an historical society in town, and that it had a brochure containing a walking tour of all the places that figured in Howells's Hamilton life ("A Boy's Town Tour"). "That ought to suit," I said to myself, and I found the historical society on a small street, located in a frame house.

The woman at the desk of the historical society responded well to my several requests. She did, indeed, have a Howells brochure and a map, but she was also happy (for $4.50) to photocopy an essay that had been written a long time ago about his boyhood in Hamilton. (One of the bonds he formed with Twain was based on their shared experience of childhoods in the West in the 1840s and '50s.) While the museum curator copied the files, I flipped through some brochures near the front door and discovered that Robert McCloskey, who wrote *Make Way for Ducklings* and other books for children, had also been born and grew up in Hamilton. (A friend of a friend knew McCloskey when he was writing about the Mallards in the Boston Public Garden and said that he filled the bathtub with ducks and would hold them aloft to draw them better in flight.)

Because Hamilton isn't very big, it didn't take long for me to find the addresses where the houses of Howells's family had stood in the mid-nineteenth century. Most of the houses are now gone, although there is a park by the river with a small, plank house that could be similar to the ones in which Howells had lived. I found a plaque that marked the place of one home. It calls Howells "the dean of American letters" and quotes from his memoir about Hamilton, *A Boy's Life*: "I still must recur to the ten or eleven years passed in Hamilton as the gladdest in all of my years." It was later said of Howells, such was his steady output of books, that he pursued "a writer's career as vigorously as any industrialist built his railroad or rolled his steel." Not surprisingly, a biographer wrote of his early years: "No one grew up in the Howells household without understanding that writing—from newspaper copy to great books—was a business."

Like Twain, Howells got into journalism though his early days spent as a printer's assistant. There is this passage in the Wecter biography of young Sam Clemens of Hannibal: "Another self-made youth, Abraham Lincoln, liked to call the printing shop 'the poor boy's college.' The phrase was not original with him. Under that caption the *Hannibal Gazette* on April 1, 1847, had observed: 'There is something in the very atmosphere of a printing office, calculated to awake the mind and inspire a thirst for knowledge.'"

By coincidence, Howells's literary break came early, when in 1860 he wrote a campaign biography of Lincoln, one of the few that Abraham ever read about himself or liked. When he became president, he appointed the young Howells as the American consul to Venice. Yes, he was officially a diplomat; but consulships were a form of literary patronage. Around the same time, Nathaniel Hawthorne was consul in Liverpool.

Howells returned from Europe in 1865, one reason it was sometimes quipped that he had "spent the Civil War in a gondola." With a personality that was self-confident and cheerful, he never minded the jab, as his time abroad acquainted him with Italy, which became a lifelong love and obsession. In 1907 he went back to Venice and wrote: "The fact is, that in the course of time one becomes skeptical of one's whole youth, and Venice had been a great part, a vital part of my youth." He also captured the dichotomy of life abroad, when he said he was "torn between two homesicknesses: the longing for America, and the desire to stay in Italy."

Always writing, Howells took a job after the war as editor of the *Atlantic Monthly,* where one day Twain came through the door, seeking a review of his book *The Innocents Abroad* (one of my favorites of all his works). They began a friendship that never wavered and lasted until Twain died in

1910. (They were an odd pair: "Howells balding, short, and stocky; Twain tall, wild-eyed, and feathery-browned.")

Howells lived and worked for much of his adult life around Boston (where the *Atlantic* had its offices), while Twain was in nearby Hartford. They saw a lot of each other. Twain valued Howells's thoughts about his writing, as perhaps no one else's, and would refer to him as "my brother." Howells said of their meetings: "smoking the last of innumerable cigars, and soothing his tense nerves with a mild hot Scotch, while we both talked and talked and talked, of everything in the heavens and on the earth, and the waters under the earth."

Twain admired Howells as a writer, saying: "In forty years [Howells's] English has been to me a continual delight and astonishment. In the sustained exhibition of certain great qualities—clearness, compression, verbal exactness, and unforced and seemingly unconscious felicity of phrasing—he is, in my belief, without his peer in the English-writing world." That Howells is no longer read with the enthusiasm that readers still bring to Twain has to do with the dated nature of his subjects, and because his literary successors—from F. Scott Fitzgerald to the contemporary Tom Wolfe—offer more modern, accessible examples of realism.

The Who's Who nature of Howells's Rolodex remains astonishing, not just for the persons he knew but for the credit they give him in developing their writing. He married Elinor Mead, from Brattleboro, Vermont. Her brother, William Mead, was an architect and later a partner in McKim, Mead, and White. Elinor was a cousin of Rutherford B. Hayes. Through Twain, Howells knew General Grant, and he was acquainted with James Garfield. Later Howells published the writing of Theodore Roosevelt and created a stir when he refused to share a platform with a young English politician and writer, Winston Churchill (too much a warmonger for Howells, who never did well with imperialism, calling the Spanish-American War "a wicked, wanton thing" or, sometimes, "the Newspaper War").

Most of Howells's friends and acquaintances were writers and are as well known as those on the banned-book table at the Vonnegut Memorial Library. For years Howells was close with Henry James. (He gave James this advice: "It doesn't so much matter what you do—but live.") James once heard Howells give a lecture at Harvard about Italy. Henry later said that "as his friend spoke, he [James] had closed his eyes and imagined a window opening out to Florence." As testament to his first-class personality, Howells remained close to James despite Twain having little time for the debonair novelist. Twain wrote: "I would rather be damned to John Bunyan's heaven than finish reading *The Bostonians*."

Howells had the supreme gift for literary friendship. In addition to Twain and James, he met Harriet Beecher Stowe (Lincoln's "little woman who wrote the book that started this great war") when she passed through Venice, Herman Melville in New York (they were not close), Brett Harte (who was eager to take in Howells's theories about literary realism), James Russell Lowell (editor of the *Atlantic*), and Oliver Wendell Holmes. As a young man, he made a pilgrimage from Ohio to Boston and met Thoreau, Emerson, and Hawthorne. He admired Tolstoy and had tea with Matthew Arnold in London.

A biographer writes: "Howells saw American literature—its authors, readers, and place in the general culture—

as a personal responsibility." Among those on his nurturing list were Stephen Crane, Edith Wharton, and Sarah Orne Jewett. It was said: "Had [Emily] Dickinson written to Howells instead of Thomas Wentworth Higginson she might well have been 'discovered' in her lifetime." During one of his trips to England, another friend wrote a letter back to the States, saying: "W. D. Howells is over here, and we have seen a great deal of him. To know him is to love him: I think he is one of the most winning personalities I have ever met . . . with such a fund of genius and strength."

Biking around Hamilton, trying to match up the addresses I had for Howells's homes with vacant lots, I thought more about his contribution to American letters (as the "dean") than of his own writing (although I like *Silas Lapham*, which is one of the few novels ever written about an American businessman that doesn't turn him into a swindler).

Howells is an important bridge (both in a literary and personal sense, as he actually knew the figures) between Hawthorne, Emerson, Melville, and Longfellow to the realist writers of the nineteenth and twentieth centuries. He said: "I have never been able to see much difference between what seemed to me Literature and what seemed to me Life." That could be a quote from Hemingway. In 1887 Howells said that fiction should "speak the dialect, the language, that most Americans know—the language of unaffected people everywhere—and we believe that even its masterpieces will find a response in all readers."

Finally, Howells (along with Twain) might have invented the modern travel guide, with his early books about Venice and Tuscany. He wrote about what he saw and heard, and what interested him, which now is commonplace but was then revolutionary. As he said to many about writing: "You have to see it, hear it, smell it, taste it, or, you forget it."

Georgetown: Grant Grows Up

WHEN I TURNED SOUTH from Dayton to Hamilton, I was also signing up for Georgetown, Ohio, the small town east of Cincinnati where Ulysses Grant grew up. Had I not taken the car, I would have gone to Columbus on the bus and then on the bike to Marion. Instead, with all that horsepower under my saddle, I decided to tack on Grant, a sidestep I came to doubt when I got stuck in traffic on Interstate 275, the beltway around Cincinnati. My only consolation was that I decided to skip his birthplace in Point Pleasant on the Ohio River, another thirty miles west.

Instead of taking an hour to drive from Hamilton to Georgetown, it took me two, as County Road 125 from the interstate was a line of slow-moving cars. Sitting under endless traffic lights, I regretted all my enthusiasm for the boyhood homes of William Dean Howells, even if he did put my travel frustrations in the proper light, when he wrote: "A nation which produced . . . Lincoln, Longfellow, Grant, Emerson, John Brown, Mrs. Stowe, Hawthorne, not to name many others eminent in art and science and finance . . . has subtly but surely done its work."

The Grant boyhood home is a short distance from the main street of Georgetown, a modest town in a rolling landscape east of Cincinnati. The door to the small house museum was locked when I arrived, but as I stood in the parking lot, wondering if maybe another stop was closed, Ellen arrived on foot to let me in and show me around the old brick house.

Grant's father had a leather tannery across the street, and the family lived here—with ample food and heat—when Grant was growing up from 1823 to 1839. The boy hated helping his father in the tannery, a messy, dirty business, at least to Grant. He could, however, break in nearly any wild horse, and all his life he was an expert rider. His mother would say: "Horses seem to understand Ulysses."

Grant left the Georgetown house to attend the US Military Academy at West Point, from which he graduated in 1843. At the end of the Civil War in 1865, he was a full general, commanding all Union armies. He served as president from 1869 to 1877. He went a long way from Georgetown, but while his parents were living, he would often come home during the course of his travels. His great trait was stubborn determination to get on with the job at hand until it was done. He refused ever to "backtrack." The one object at the home that testifies to his character is a slab of granite or stone that his father asked him to move to the back of the house. Sleight of build, even as an adult, Ulysses struggled with the massive slab until he got it in the desired place. He would spend his adult life moving similar immovable objects. (Vicksburg was just one of them.)

I confess that I have a love-hate relationship with Ulysses Grant. I admire his simplicity, his steadiness under fire in the Civil War, and his ability to draft concise English, be it in orders to his troops or with his book *Personal Memoirs*. I like Grant's determination, his refusal to take "no backward" steps, his desire to "fight it out on this line if it takes all summer." I am drawn to the traveler in Grant, and how after his presidency he literally went around the world, although I balance that intellectual curiosity with his presidential policies that made such a mess of Reconstruction—in effect canceling out the gains achieved by his men during the Civil War.

I do like Grant's relationship with Julia Dent, to whom he was married from 1848 until his death in 1885, and how they raised their children. I appreciate and admire how he provided for his family in hard times—selling firewood on the streets of St. Louis and, later, racked with cancer, writing his memoirs. I have no doubt he wrote the books himself. I like how Grant dictated the peace at Appomattox, with justice and compassion, and I think he deserves as much credit as Lincoln for saving the Union. I think that it speaks well about Grant that he was not a war lover and recoiled at the losses of his men.

On the negative side, I do not like Grant's tactics in many Civil War battles, which varied little from the later mentality that sent men "over the top" of World War I trenches. He often suffered enormous casualties in his ranks, often for negligible gains. Battles such as Shiloh, the Wilderness, and Cold Harbor ought to be filed under the word "massacre." And I have serious questions about the corruption in his presidential administration and even suspect that he, personally, had his hand in the till—or at least received "gifts" from wealthy supporters. I cannot square that such a capable man and executive, as was Grant on the battlefield, could allow his presidential administration to turn into a bucket shop. And I despise how he schemed in 1880 to wrest the Republican nomination away from his loyal ally James Garfield.

In short, I am never quite sure which Grant is before me—the modest courageous soldier who moved granite to take Chattanooga and save the Union, or the more vain Grant who drove men into the trenches of Spotsylvania or loaded his administration with placemen—and I am sure I drove out of my way to Georgetown to wrestle with my confusion.

The Mexican War:
The Making of General Grant

THE MUSEUM HAD A FEW BOOKS for sale on the life and times of U. S. Grant, but the one I added to my collection was Jean Edward Smith's *Grant,* which balances a biography of the general with a book about Grant as a man. Smith's conclusions? He writes that the greatest role model in Grant's military life was Zachary Taylor, who shunned formality on the battlefield—he dressed like a corporal, as did Grant. Smith believes that Grant's forced resignation from the army in 1854 and his subsequent years of economic struggle later made him an easy mark for confidence men, who realized his longings for security.

In the Civil War, Grant had only one interest: to pursue the enemy to its destruction. He cared less about strategic crossroads and fortified positions. In the Andrew Johnson administration—as head of the army and secretary of war—he played key roles in confronting France over Mexico, demobilizing the army, and pursuing Lincoln's goal for reconstruction. Smith credits Grant as president with keeping the peace with Spain, settling the *Alabama* claims, and, most significantly, restoring postwar prosperity by again pegging the dollar to gold, thus ending the wartime inflation. In short, Smith's Grant is the commoner made good, a triumph of democratic values at war and in peace. I didn't necessarily buy it all, but at least he writes well.

Although they later fought each other in the Civil War, Grant's roommate and best friend at West Point was James Longstreet, who served under Robert E. Lee as a Confederate general. (Lee was ahead of Grant but they knew each other some in the Mexican War.) Longstreet, who was the best man at Grant's wedding, according to Smith, "considered Grant 'fragile' and believed his 'delicate frame' kept him out of Sports." He continues:

> Grant's distinguishing trait, said Longstreet, "was a girlish modesty; a hesitancy in presenting his own claims; a taciturnity born of modesty; but a thoroughness in the accomplishment of whatever task was assigned to him. We became fast friends at our first meeting. [He had] a noble, generous heart, a lovable character, and a sense of honor which was so perfect . . . that in the numerous cabals which were often formed his name was never mentioned."

In looking at the patterns of generalship later in the Civil War, Smith writes that Grant modeled himself on Zachary Taylor while the role model for Lee was Winfield Scott, for whom leadership was a ducal legacy. Smith writes: "The business of living and looking the part of a great soldier, with splendor worn as a familiar cloak about starred shoulders; the battle technique of bringing troops to the scene of action and then relying on subordinates to run things; the willingness to rely on sheer audacity in the face of superior numbers—all of these, characteristic of Lee in Virginia, were equally characteristic of Scott in Mexico."

By contrast, Grant chose the Taylor formula of inconspicuous gallantry. Smith quotes a soldier of the Mexican War on the Taylor style:

> He is a very pleasant old man and very sociable not only to officers but to buck privates, also. He is not a proud man at all. When he came to see us he rode a mule and looked like an old man a going to mill. He left us and bid goodbye as though he had always been acquainted with us and told us to be good boys and fight like men if needs be and then left.

Smith continues: "Veterans of the Mexican War who served with Grant in the Civil War recognized that Taylor was his role model. In the spring of 1864, General George G. Meade, who had not seen Grant for almost twenty years, was struck by the parallel. 'He puts me in the mind of old Taylor,' Meade told his wife, 'and sometimes I fancy he models himself on old Zack?'"

Grant himself distinguished between the two styles of generalship when he said, "both were pleasant to serve under—Taylor was pleasant to serve with." Nevertheless, like Lincoln then serving in Congress, Grant came to feel the Mexican War was an imperial excursion, saying: "The war was one of conquest, in the interest of an institution [i.e., slavery], and the probabilities are that private instructions were for the acquisition of territory out of which new States might be carved."

Grant ran afoul of the spit and polish of the postwar regular army and, while serving on the West Coast, was asked to resign his commission, perhaps as a result of his drinking (which, according to Smith, was never the problem that legend has it). Grant struggled on his hardscrabble farms through the 1850s, later agreeing with Sherman that "West Point and the Regular Army were not good schools for farmers, bankers, merchants, and mechanics."

At the outbreak of the Civil War, Grant was living in Galena, Illinois, and the state governor made him a colonel in the militia. Soon he was a general and descending with his troops on Fort Donelson, Shiloh, Vicksburg, and destiny. Smith writes of his affinity for the common solider: "Having survived a number of years on the bottom rung in civil life, he had developed an instinctive feel for how civilians behaved. He recognized that volunteer soldiers were not regulars and never tried to impose the spartan discipline of the old army."

Among Grant's early supporters was John C. Frémont, the failed Republican presidential candidate in 1856, now commanding Federal troops in the West. The irony here is that, as Roy Morris Jr. writes in *The Long Pursuit,* Grant "voted for Buchanan because he didn't know him, and voted against Frémont because he did." Nevertheless, Frémont said of Grant that he "believed him to be a man of great activity and promptness in obeying orders without question or hesitation. For that reason I gave General Grant this important command at this critical period. . . . Grant was a man of unassuming character, not given to self-elation, of dogged persistence, and of iron will."

According to Smith but echoed by many others, Grant's best quality on the battlefield was his unflappable nature (a witness said: "He was the coolest man I ever saw") and his granite-doggedness in bringing the fight to the enemy's army. Smith writes that "the genius of Grant's command style lay in its simplicity. Better than any Civil War general, Grant recognized the battlefield was in flux. By not specifying movements in detail, he left his subordinate commanders free to exploit whatever opportunities developed. . . . Grant was changing the rules. A man who hated war and who could not bear to see the wounded suffer was driving the consequences of rebellion home to the South. . . . Unlike many of his contemporaries, Grant learned from Mexico—not just small-unit tactics and battlefield bravery, but the essence of strategic warfare." Lincoln, as always, was more pithy, saying to the general's doubters: "I can't spare this man; he fights."

On the battlefield, Robert E. Lee looked like a general, with his smooth gray hair, blue jacket with shiny buttons, and imposing horse, Traveller.[5] By contrast, Smith makes much of Grant's democratic mien. He writes: "Some were dismayed to find no trace of breeding or gentility. An observer seeing Grant for the first time noted only an 'ordinary' scrubby looking man, with a slightly seedy look, as if he was 'out of office on half pay.' . . . Another saw someone with 'the look of a man who did, or once did, take a little too much to drink.' . . . Despite his rank, Grant retained what one historian called 'the odd quality of unintentionally vanishing from view in any crowd.'"

One of the ironies of the Civil War is that Robert E. Lee, if he had been teamed with Lincoln, would have ended the war with the South in no time. Lee loved nothing more than taking the fight to the enemy, plus he was a better tactician than Grant (who never won a battle with the brilliance of Chancellorsville). Had Lee been able to fight with the

---

5: Smith writes: "According to his principal biographer, he preferred the company of women, especially pretty women, to that of men, although there was never a suggestion of scandal. Deeply religious, Lee's belief in God was personal, not denominational. He read his Bible and prayer book daily, and spent much time on his knees seeking solace and support. He did not use tobacco, hated whiskey, and rarely drank even wine. Like Grant, he was blessed with great powers of endurance and a strong nervous system. Despite his innate dignity, he met people easily and had a well-developed memory for names. His mind was mathematical, directed toward problem solving rather than abstraction."

resources that Lincoln bestowed on Grant, today we would be writing about President Lee, following Andrew Johnson, not President Grant. Instead, Lee is the elegant outlaw, the noble envoy of the lost cause, while Grant is celebrated for saving the Union but then chastised for turning it over to middlemen.

After Georgetown: President Grant Does a Lot of Deals

IN HIS BIOGRAPHY, Smith works hard to present the Grant administration in a positive light—indicating that Grant's crimes were those of omission or innocence ("Grant rarely met a businessman he did not trust"). He quotes a Grant insider, Adam Badeau, as saying: "His political career was blighted by those he sustained; his Presidency was less brilliant than it might have been because of the mistakes and misdeeds of others."

Smith puffs up Grant's genius in foreign affairs—"Grant kept the United States out of war with Spain, made peace with Great Britain, settled the *Alabama* claims, and established a precedent for arbitration of international disputes. Under his leadership the United States crept onto the world stage, almost unnoticed."—and credits him with slaying the beast of inflation, writing:

> Grant's 1874 veto of the inflation bill is a seminal event in American history. The nation moved away from Civil War soft money and took a massive step toward the resumption of specie payment. The veto message made it clear that Grant was fundamentally opposed to unredeemable paper currency. . . . From 1874 onward, the Republican party became the party of economic conservatism, fiscal restraint, and a sound dollar. Grant imparted to the Grand Old Party a commercial, pro-capitalist stance that replaced emancipation as the party's *raison d'être*.

It might have made a good conclusion to the Grant story, except that during his administration scandal was thick on the ground, with the Black Friday gold panic (James Fisk and Jay Gould cornered the gold market), New York customs house affair (Grant appointees fleeced the nation of tariff receipts), Star Route postal scandal (the auctioning off of profitable postal lines), salary sham (Grant voted himself and Congress a fat raise), whiskey ring (bootlegging and payoffs that reached to Grant's private secretary), trading post offenses (involved the secretary of war), Cattelism (the secretary of the navy was on the take), and safe burglary conspiracy (again involved Grant's private secretary who framed an outsider in the corruption investigations).

In all these scandals, Grant professed to be horrified (along the lines of *Casablanca*'s Captain Renault saying: "I'm shocked, shocked to find that gambling is going on in here!"), but he did his best to defend the accused. According to Smith, this was the same General Grant who after the Civil War had accepted $105,000 from wealthy patrons of the Republican party to pay off the mortgage on his I Street house, which later another group of political insiders bought from Grant and gave to General Sherman. As Smith writes: "Grant leapt at the opportunity to double his money," although in reality he was doubling the money of others.

Grant was an ex-president for almost ten years, leaving office in 1877 and dying in 1885. He would have had an interest in ensuring that Republican Rutherford B. Hayes won the 1876 election, and it was Grant's lieutenants who ensured that popular vote winner Samuel Tilden lost the contest, when Congress adjudicated the votes in the electoral college.

Grant's personal financial dealings, however, were no more successful than his sidewalk firewood franchise. He lent his name (and the time of his son Frederick) to a fly-by-night brokerage house, Grant & Ward, which, when its affairs were wound up, was disclosed to have liabilities of $16 million and assets of $57,000. No wonder he took a trip around the world that lasted almost two years, during which he said to Otto von Bismarck, the German chancellor: "I take no interest in military affairs, and, although I entered the army thirty-five years ago and have been in two wars, in Mexico as a young lieutenant, and later, I never went into the army without regret and never retired without pleasure."

To provide for his wife and children, Grant turned to the writing of his memoirs, and worked at them with the tenacity that had allowed him to take Shiloh. On many days wrapped in a blanket, he turned out his memoirs, nearly all of which dealt with his growing up ("My life in Georgetown was uneventful") and the Civil War. Mark Twain, who knew Grant, stepped in to publish *Personal Memoirs* when he discovered that a publisher was trying to hoodwink the former president.

The memoirs were a commercial and literary success, and earned for Grant's family some $400,000. I have read them and don't buy into the legends that they are among the "best ever" memoirs written by a president or that Twain rewrote the books. They read like a military after-action report, and there's not a line in the books that sparkles with Twain's wit. He could not have written the book without at least inserting a joke or two. As he himself wrote in *Huckleberry Finn* about the author of *The Adventures of Tom Sawyer*: "There was things which he stretched, but mainly he told the truth."

At best the Grant memoirs mesmerized the reading public, much as the life of Grant did Jean Edward Smith. Smith ends his biography with this farewell address that Grant himself wrote:

> It seems that man's destiny in this world is quite as much a mystery as it is likely to be in the next. I never thought of acquiring rank in the profession I was educated for; yet it came with two grades higher prefixed to the rank of General officer for me. I certainly never had either ambition or taste for political life; yet I was twice President of the United States. If anyone had suggested the idea of my becoming an author, as they frequently did, I was not sure whether they were making sport of me or not. I have now written a book which is in the hands of the manufacturers. I ask you to keep these notes very private lest I become an authority on the treatment of diseases. I have already too many trades to be proficient at any.

This farewell address captures Grant's humility, which is no small thing; but keep in mind that Grant lost more men at Shiloh than had died in all previous American wars combined.

Marion: Warren Harding's Home Fires

THE DRIVE ACROSS OHIO from Georgetown to Marion took more than three hours. After having a look at Grant's primary school ("I was not studious in habit"), I took Highway 68 to Interstate 71 and cut through Columbus to Marion, but mostly what I did is sit at red lights, fidget in traffic, and spin the dial on the car radio.

I stopped at a gas station for a quick (prefabricated) sandwich, fuel, and coffee, and to call the Harding Home to say that I would get there at 5:30 p.m., an hour later than I had scheduled. It didn't help my cause that I was sitting in Friday traffic and that I made several wrong turns going through and around Columbus; at least I had kept heading north, but it never felt at much of a speed.

Sheryl Hall, the director of the Harding Home, was in the yard when I pulled up, and she agreed to walk me through the house at 6 p.m., when it would be closed to the public. That way, I could tape our interview as we toured the house that Warren Harding built before his marriage to Florence Kling in 1891, and in which the couple lived (except when they were in Washington) until Warren died in 1923.

Harding was born in nearby Blooming Grove in 1865. He owned and published a newspaper—the *Marion Star*—for his entire adult life, and served in the Ohio state legislature, as lieutenant governor, and as US senator, on and off, from 1897 to 1919, when he became the twenty-ninth president of the United States. He served in office less than three years (a time similar to that of President John Kennedy) and is remembered, if at all, as among the worst American presidents, for the scandals (Teapot Dome) that dogged his administration and for his licentiousness in making love to his mistress on the floor of a White House closet. If there was more to Warren Harding, I had come to Marion to find out what it might be.

Among the museum directors I met on this trip, none was more protective of her subject than was Sheryl Hall about the legacy of the Hardings. As I could tell from our conversation as we walked around the house ("the Hardings had an Airedale by the name of Laddie Boy. . ."), she liked them as people, as the former owners of the house she was entrusted to manage, and as the president and first lady of the United States. More than once she pointed out to me that Warren Harding was a likable man, a successful newspaper editor and publisher, an accomplished speaker on the Chautauqua circuit, a skillful politician, and a president who brought decent values—not just his girlfriends—to the White House. (He had campaigned for a return to what was called "normalcy," a word attributed to him but made up by journalists covering his speeches. He picked it up and ran with it.)

At his Victorian home, Harding liked to read, listen to music on his Victrola, entertain his many friends (he had an affinity for making and keeping them), and, in 1920, campaign for office from the front porch. Hall said he was a man of few vanities, kindly to his staff at the newspaper, and more of a reformer than anyone remembered. (He convened a conference in 1921 to limit the armaments race.) Harding's dalliances with a neighbor's wife (Carrie Philips) and a neighbor's daughter (Nan Britton) were not left off the prepared script, but were explained away by his wife's long-term kidney ailment, which often confined her to bed or made her an unpleasant companion to the gregarious Warren, who had, well, his "needs."

The Harding Home is the only presidential home that I have ever seen that I would not mind living in. The downstairs ("as close to the original as we can make it") is covered with dark wood and, in places, gloomy, but the upstairs is airy, cheerful, and well lighted. What gives the house its presence is the wraparound front porch, which covers two sides of the house on both floors. I am sure the Hardings spent many summer evenings on their porch, greeting the neighbors (at least Warren did, if not Florence). And whenever Warren was in Marion, he would walk from the house to his newspaper office in Marion, less than a mile away. Marion is a prototypical Midwestern town, with angled parking, a main street of now fading storefronts, and a Palace theater. Once Harding had made it in Marion—as the owner, editor, and publisher of the *Star*—he could make it anywhere.

Sheryl Hall and I ended our interview in the director's office, which is in a small cottage in the backyard. The structure went up temporarily in 1920, to house the reporters who came to write about the Harding campaign, and over the years it has been converted into a museum office and gift shop. Standing amidst a collection of Harding biographies, I asked Sheryl for her help in choosing a few. She mentioned one by John Dean (yes, of Nixon and Watergate fame), who had grown up in Marion, and another by James David Robenalt that gave a positive spin on Harding's affair with Carrie Philips, called *The Harding Affair*. At that point I remembered that in 1968 my sister Nanette had given my father a copy of Francis Russell's *The Shadow of Blooming Grove* as a Christmas present (children always struggle with gifts for their fathers), and I remembered him opening the 691-page book and saying, "Wow, that's a lot of Harding."

When I mentioned the book in passing, Hall had something of a fit and said the author was dishonest and had only looked for the dirt on Harding. I didn't say anything more as I had never read the book, even though it had been a fixture on our family's bookshelves the whole time I was growing up. I did, however, get a copy of Hall's Harding biography, *Warren G. Harding and the Marion Star*, and directions to Blooming Grove (the village, not the biography), and said goodbye. I also made a mental note to find the family copy of the 1968 Harding biography. Clearly there was something there that had caused Hall to "spit the dummy" (Australian slang for a pacifier).

Since my visit to Marion, I have now read four biographies of the Hardings (my wife finally asked: "Why do you care so much?") and, with my friend Lee Harris, tracked down the house in Asbury Park where Harding's cronies stashed away Nan Britton and her daughter by Harding.[6] It's not that I care "so much" but that I find Harding an easy subject about whom to read. As Hall said on our tour through the house, he was a likable man, a competent writer, and not overly ambitious, and, to make matters easier for those who would read about his life, he wrote dozens of love letters, many of which

---

6: Robenalt writes: "The first few days at Asbury Park she stayed at the Hotel Monmouth, then moved to a rooming house and finally found two front rooms in a box-like brown-shingled cottage on Bond Street." We found the house on Bond Street, which now is home to a family that did not show much interest in Warren Harding's personal life.

have recently come to light. John Kennedy probably bedded a lot more women in the White House than did Warren Harding, but he didn't leave behind a library of letters to each of the women.

So far in my readings, I have discovered three Hardings (much like the two Grants that plague my thoughts). One Harding is Hall's, the decent editor and publisher whose positive Midwestern outlook made him a success in Marion and, later, in the White House. The next Harding is that of Carl Sferrazza Anthony, who has written a mammoth, page-turning biography of Florence Kling Harding, making the point that most of Warren's achievements were really those of his wife, who made the *Star* a success, got Warren into the senate and White House, and, finally, ran the White House day to day, while he was out carousing with his Teapot Dome pals.

The last Harding is that of Francis Russell, whose biography of Harding I did find, and whose complex portrait of the president draws him as a decent if flawed man, who, like Grant as president, never met a slick businessman he didn't like and whose estrangement from his wife Florence led him down many garden paths, of the sort that Theodore Dreiser (at about the same time) cultivated.

Marion: Warren Harding, Star Newspaper Man

If Hall's Harding is ever turned into a movie, Jimmy Stewart will need to come back to play the decent, optimistic, small-town newspaper editor who rises to the presidency while always carrying a printer's square in his pocket (to remember his honest days when he was, like Twain and Howells, laying out type).

The young Harding attended Iberia College (near Marion), edited the student newspaper, graduated, and, with help from his father and friends, bought the *Star*, which became his ticket to national success. (The masthead reads: "Remember there are two sides to every question. Get them both. Be truthful. Get the facts. Be decent, be fair, be generous.") Hall writes: "Harding always said he 'boomed' Marion—promoted it, stuck by it, loved it. To him, his newspaper's responsibility was to find all of the good in the townsfolk, in the business propositions, in the growing pains and push all of it to center stage. He had little patience for those citizens who picked apart new ideas and predicted doom for the city."

Hall includes insight into Harding from the respected Midwestern journalist William Allen White, who said: "Mr. Harding is not an intellectual giant. He may not be a moral heavyweight. That is as it may be. But he is a courteous, sensible American gentleman, and he does bring home the bacon." And Hall quotes a contemporary of Harding, writing: "There have been better reporters in Marion than Warren

Harding when he covered the town, but we question whether there ever was one more human. Gathering his daily harvest of small stories, he rejoiced in type with the parents of new babies, said pretty things of the newly-weds, jubilated with the jubilant and commiserated with the afflicted." And she picks up on the qualities he shares with Sinclair Lewis's George Babbitt (at least the good ones) when she writes:

> He was an excellent "mixer," he had the inestimable gift of never forgetting a man's face or his name, and there was always a genuine warmth in his handshake, a real geniality in his smile. He was a regular he-man, according to the [standard] of the old days—a great poker player, and not at all averse to putting a foot on a brass rail.

Who wouldn't love such a man? Such was the affection of the staff at the *Star* for their boss that when they formed a union, Hall writes, "the printers asked him to join his own union. He carried his union card in his wallet for the rest of his life." She even adds new research (at least to me) about Harding's role in the release of Eugene V. Debs, recounting:

> Daugherty [the Attorney General] wanted the release to take effect on December 31, but Warren changed the date to the twenty-fourth, saying, "I want him to eat his Christmas dinner with his wife." After he walked out of the prison gates, Debs satisfied Warren's request that he stop by the White House en route to his home in Terre Haute, Indiana.
>
> Writing to friend Malcolm Jennings about the Debs release, Warren said, "I was persuaded in my own mind that it was the right thing to do . . . I thought the spirit of

clemency was quite in harmony with the things we were trying to do here in Washington."

In the archive, Hall also finds words that can be read alongside the farewell addresses of Lincoln, Twain, and Grant. In the 1920 presidential campaign, much of which took place at the Marion home, Harding says of his community:

> There can be no mistaken appraisal of our relationship. It is too extended, too intimate, too thoroughly stamped by community interest. You and I, all of us Marionites, have been boosting this Marion of ours for considerably more than thirty years, and have shared in varying degrees the achievements attending to its development. The thought of development and progress, a desire to find our place on the map of Ohio, inspired us, and there was common interest in spite of the seeming selfishness attending rewards. We were all boosters together, because it is an engaging pursuit.

Leaving Marion, Hall writes, Harding said to his friends and neighbors: "I have been on the square with you and I want to be on the square with all the world." And he continued: "I have a theory of government that if you do for the nation what you do for the community you do exceedingly well; because the nation is only the aggregate of communities."

Marion: Mrs. Florence Harding Runs for President

COMPARED TO HALL'S "HE-MAN" HARDING, with his foot optimistically perched on a brass rail, Carl Anthony's Harding is a puppet, with Florence pulling all his strings. Early on, he quotes a neighbor: "Florence Harding?" piped up one Marionite. "Runs her house; runs the paper . . . runs Warren; runs everything but the car, and could run that if she wanted to."

Florence Kling's father was one of the pillars of the Marion business community, and he loathed his daughter's attachment and marriage to Warren, preferring, as did many locally, to call him "that nigger Harding" or "Nig Harding," in supposition that an ancestor in Blooming Grove had been African American. That rumor lasted until 2015, when DNA testing on Harding relatives disproved the allegation.

Unpleasant as was Amos Kling, he raised a daughter of independent authority, and she ran her life and Warren's as if they were a listed corporation. Anthony writes: "Some men choose women to marry because of sexual passion, others for social prestige, still others for money, but Warren recognized that with Florence he could create a superb partnership. He could count on her." Later in her life, Florence said: "I knew thirty-five years ago that Warren Harding was an exceptional man. He first attracted me by the way he talked. He was interesting."

According to Anthony, Harding's *Marion Star* was a sleepy small-town newspaper, running articles about lost cats and church suppers. After Florence took control of the business side, it developed a sound economic footing, in part because she organized the delivery boys into the Force. (Norman Thomas was one of "her boys," and they remained close to her long after they stopped carrying sacks of newspapers around town.)

Denied the chance to forge her own business career, because of the times in which she lived, Florence channeled her energies into Warren's career. She did have one child, by an earlier, ill-fated marriage, but she had little contact with her son. Anthony writes:[7]

> Instead she would make a profession out of Harding. "Once that they were married, Warren became her hobby," wrote sociologist Chancellor after interviewing former *Star* staff; "she poured out her life for him and for the newspaper on which she worked like a slave."

Without his gift for delivering homilies on American exceptionalism, Warren never would have made it in the political world. But after his career was established—in the legislature and later as lieutenant governor—Florence stage-managed it from afar, making sure he always befriended the right power broker or financial backer. (Chancellor said: "Warren Harding . . . was born to order for her management.")

Left to his own devices, Harding might have sunk in the comfortable life of a country club member, dabbling at golf and other member's wives. Florence wanted none of

---

7: William E. Chancellor collected volumes of dirt on Harding and his family, and while some of what he wrote was true, much of it was scurrilous and false.

that for her senior partner and pressed him to make something of his political career, which reached the national level when he was elected by popular vote to the Senate in 1914. Anthony writes: "She was not the intellectualizing maker of policy but rather the instinctual political manager. The *Star,* the state senate, and the gubernatorial campaigns had proved that."

Of course, among Florence's many worries was that Warren's womanizing would bring shame on the house of Harding. By the time he took up with Carrie Philips, around 1905, the chances are that Florence's health kept her from fulfilling all aspects of her marriage contract. Nevertheless, she devoted much energy to keeping an eye on Warren—by trying not to let him travel alone and prying into his personal papers—although it did her little good. He viewed theirs as an open marriage; she did not. Anthony writes:

> He would honor, cherish, and obey if she asked no questions. Her jealousy never actually abated, but her attempts to keep him from other women became a matter of protecting his career and their work on the career's behalf. There was what one friend gently termed "the perfect understanding which existed between them."

He called her the Duchess, and among his poker-golf-whiskey friends, I am sure he pronounced the term of endearment the way other men might speak of the Warden. He said to Nan Britton about the Duchess: "She makes life hell for me!"

One of the ironies of Warren's newspaper and political life is that he had little to do. After an initial period to get it up and running, and then to establish it as the dominant newspaper in Marion, the *Star* pretty much ran itself. Warren could stop by the office or not, fire off an editorial or not, and still the paper came out every day and earned for the Hardings an excellent income.

So too was his political career on autopilot. In the legislature or even as lieutenant governor, Harding had little to do in terms of executive responsibility. He could attend sessions of the legislature, conventions, meetings, and conferences, and glad-hand as was expected, while others wrote the legislation or delegated authority. Such a schedule left Warren time for winters in Florida, extended trips to Europe, and rail journeys to the West. One of the best parts of the *Marion Star* position was that it came with many complimentary rail passes, and he used them to further his political career—for example, as a delegate to Republican conventions—and to rendezvous with women.

Much as, later in the twentieth century, Hillary Clinton proved adept at managing the fallout from her husband's many affairs, so too did Florence understand how to deal with her husband's spurned lovers. That skill especially came into demand when in 1920 the deadlocked Republican convention passed on the early favorites and chose instead, as its presidential nominee, the clubby senator from Ohio who was a friend to everyone—especially the monied interests—handsome, well spoken, and one of the few politicians who was close to Theodore Roosevelt and William Howard Taft, who otherwise had fallen out of each other's favor.

Anthony has this paragraph on what might have been going through Harding's mind when Republican party officials asked him if there was anything in his background that they needed to know about, before he was given the nomination. He writes:

> Never did Harding discuss his rumination in that room, but certainly Nan and her child, his tempestuous affair with his Senate staffer Grace Cross, the child by Susan Hodder, the pregnancy of Augusta Cole, his more obscure relationships with a Cecilia Hoyle and Ruby Randall all had to weigh on his mind.

By 1920, Harding's affair with Carrie Philips had ended, but she was demanding money to keep quiet during the election. Such news would surely have reached Florence (his unofficial campaign manager), and it says something about her acumen that the Philipses were given $25,000, sent on a round-the-world tour, and never heard from again during Warren's presidency.

Nan Britton was another who was given money and a house (the one Lee and I biked to in Asbury Park), but she also would see Warren from time to time in the White House, sometimes consummating their reunions in a closet near the Oval Office (Bill Clinton style).[8] No wonder a Republican campaign slogan in 1920 was "League Us Not Into Temptation." Later, Washington wit Alice Roosevelt Longworth said of the affair: "My God, we've got a President who doesn't

---

8: Russell has this description, which quotes from Nan Britton's 1928 tell-all memoir, *The President's Daughter*, which the Harding family dismissed as fictional for almost a hundred years: "Whereupon [Nan wrote], he introduced me to the one place where, he said, he thought we might share kisses in safety. This was a small closet in the anteroom, evidently a place for hats and coats, but entirely empty most of the times we used it, for we repaired there many times in the course of my visits to the White House, and in the darkness of a space not more than five feet square the President of the United States and his adoring sweetheart made love."

know beds were invented, and he was elected on a slogan of 'Back to Normalcy'!"

Once Warren was elected—the nation was tired from the war—Florence staged-managed the Harding administration as though the government was the *Marion Star*, and by all accounts, especially Anthony's, she did an excellent job. Warren's business day often ended before lunch, when he would disappear to a crony's hideaway townhouse at 1509 H Street, and there he would drink, smoke, and carouse, until it was time for golf. (Teapot Dome was a foursome gone wrong.) Meanwhile, back at work, Florence was thanking the Boy Scouts for their visit to the White House or laying down the procedures for the US government finally to have a budget. If Warren had any success in his presidency, it was because she followed through on the details. Warren pardoned Debs and greeted him at the White House; Florence saw to the small print of the disarmament treaty and made sure Warren showed up on time to sign it.

So much did Florence choreograph Warren's life—women were his only free time away from her influence—that, ironically, she might also have managed him into an early grave. In summer 1923, Harding was bored, tired, anxious about the scandals, and ready for some new scenery. He was suffering from cardiovascular disease, but his bad moments were always attributed to nervous exhaustion, something Florence knew well. Together they mapped out a trip to the West and Alaska, during which Harding would see the country, recharge his batteries, and give speeches; and the train that took them around would be loaded with cronies, alcohol, and playing cards.

The so-called Voyage of Understanding was to be the ideal working vacation, and to look after Warren's health, Florence decided to bring along the family GP from Marion, "Doc" Sawyer, who treated Florence during her kidney attacks. Sawyer wasn't exactly a quack or a physician with a mail-order degree, but close enough, and after Warren suffered a probable heart attack in Alaska, he said it was simply the result of "bad soft shell crabs," and prescribed bed rest for Harding in a San Francisco hotel, to which the presidential train had raced.

Harding lived on a little while after checking into the suite, but then died suddenly, one reason why rumors have floated ever since that the president had been poisoned. His body returned to the White House on the presidential train, and Harding was buried in Marion, in what is now the Harding Memorial, a monolith at the entrance to the town. For her part, faithful to her "Wurr'en" until the end, Florence spent the month after he died at a friend's house near Rock Creek Park, burning his presidential papers.

Blooming Grove: The Shadows over Warren Harding

THE LAST HARDING that I met during my extended readings developed from two books that need to be read together—Francis Russell's *The Shadow of Blooming Grove,* and James David Robenalt's *The Harding Affair: Love and Espionage During the Great War*—even though, had the two authors ever met, they would have loathed each other.

The "shadow" of Blooming Grove refers to several things, but mostly to the inferiority complex from which Harding suffered for his possible African American ancestry. He was teased at school and later shunned by his father-in-law, and the sense of being an outsider pushed him hard to make a success of his life. The other "shadow" in Harding's life, never reported in depth until Russell's book was published, was Harding's long affair with Carrie Philips.

Russell had obtained copies of Harding's letters to Philips from a local Marion lawyer—she had left them in bags in a closet, and they were found when she died—and the biographer wanted to use long excerpts in *The Shadow of Blooming Grove,* which was published in 1968. Instead, Harding heirs sued Russell before the book was published and prohibited their inclusion in his book. (Under copyright laws, the Harding family claimed ownership of the letters and actually bought them from Carrie's estate. They were locked away in the Library of Congress until 2014.)

The result was that when Russell's book came out in 1968, he left many pages literally blank where there should have been a Harding letter to Carrie Philips (most of her letters to Harding were lost, perhaps in Florence's bonfires at the end of his life). Only much later did the family team up with Robenalt, a lawyer in Cleveland, and he published in 2009 the content of many letters in *The Harding Affair: Love and Espionage During the Great War.* However, the book attempts the near impossible—that of both publishing the love letters to Carrie Philips and putting Harding in a favorable light. (Robenalt writes: "Ironically, letters showing his adultery, and the story surrounding their discovery, may be Warren Harding's salvation.")

The espionage aspect of the book, alluded to in the subtitle, is that the Wilson government suspected Mrs. Philips of working for the enemy in World War I, as before the war she had gone to live in Germany and remained sympathetic to all things German during the fighting. Only by reading Robenalt together with Russell was I able to get a full sense of Warren's relationship with Carrie Philips. Although it was not at all his intention, Robenalt literally fills in the blanks in Russell's *Blooming Grove.*

As a postscript, the subsequent DNA tests in 2015 negated several important features in both books. When Harding's relatives submitted DNA samples to Ancestry.com, they proved that, despite a lifetime of denials, Harding was the father of Nan Britton's daughter, Elizabeth Ann Blaesing (Robenalt was skeptical, although he left open the door of possibility),[9] and

9: He writes: "Nevertheless, since so many of her dates and 'facts' are corroborated by the Philips letters, her story could be true, though not as she has embellished it."

it proved that the Hardings never had any African American blood mixed into their line in Blooming Grove (an important theme in Russell's work).

For his part, Harding always assumed he was the father of Britton's child, who was born two weeks before Harding was elected president; and while he was alive he paid her child support and saw Britton in the White House. As for the charge of African American ancestry, it wounded him as a child growing up with insults and taunts, but later he grew more philosophical and even joked about it with a newspaper friend, knowing it would be printed: "How do I know, Jim?" he remarked. "One of my ancestors may have jumped the fence."

Despite his insecurities, the Harding in Russell's book—while besotted with Mrs. Philips, the wife of his close friend in Marion—is more a professional politician than the newspaper man of Hall's biography or the henpecked husband in Anthony's. To Russell, journalism was only a stepping-stone to Harding's calling as an office seeker, and he devotes much of the biography to his political dealings, in which there are few references to Florence managing the stage. Russell writes:

> Politics was a game he understood thoroughly—as a game. He had read little beyond the exchanges that came to the *Star* from other Ohio newspapers. His background in history and economics and literature had not progressed beyond the days when he sat on the hard benches of Iberia College. His mind accepted the world of Marion as he found it, and applied it to the world at large. Nevertheless, in his challenge to the Republican county elders, he appeared progressive, almost *a* progressive.

Harding's evolution into politics came through his public speaking, and he rode the Chautauqua circuit with a set speech about Alexander Hamilton that worked for most occasions. Russell writes about Warren's fascination with Hamilton: "He stood for a nation, whereas Jefferson and his Democrats wanted merely a confederacy for self-protection—the issue that was decided finally by the Civil War. Hamilton was 'the commanding figure that riveted the Union, laid the broad foundations which underlie our Federal government today, and laid the plans for the future development which his prophetic vision enabled him to see.'" Once Harding had memorized the talk, he could use it endlessly on his trips across Ohio and, later, the country. He even said to a friend: 'If I say so myself, I do think I turn out a good speech.'"

In politics, according to Russell, Harding was the ideal front man—good-looking, charming, and with only some vague notions about America the beautiful. Harry M. Daugherty—an Ohio Republican politician who many credited with making Harding president—spotted Harding early on and said: "What a great-looking President he'd make!"

At his best in politics, Harding was what he called himself, a "harmonizer," a noncontroversial figure who could appeal to all wings of the party, in part because he had no firm convictions himself besides the obvious faith in community, town, and country. Russell writes: "For all his amiability he possessed neither the knowledge, training, nor energy to be a good debater. Never in the seven sessions that he served did he champion any measure from the Senate floor." Russell quotes Senator Watson saying: "The simple fact is my dear old friend just did not like to work." Russell says of his days in the Senate: "Between sessions, golf, poker, travel, convivial associates, and the occasional dalliance consumed his days."

According to Russell, Carrie Philips, with whom he had an affair for more than ten years, beginning in 1905, was Harding's alter ego, not the domineering Florence. Russell describes Philips: "She was a head taller than her husband, high-breasted and her hair had the reddish tinge that the Greeks called golden. Her face itself, though full, was classical—or at least pre-Raphaelite—in profile." Her husband, Jim, ran a dry-goods store in Marion, and the Hardings and Philipses often took trips together, even for several months to Europe. (Russell describes the differences between the travelers: "For Jim and the Duchess Europe was a more elaborate outing. For Harding it was a series of colored postcards. But for Carrie, even within her tourist insulation, it seemed a more rooted and more varied way of life than anyone could have conceived of in Bucyrus or Marion." It suggests why later Carrie packed up her daughter and moved to Germany.) In explaining the affair, Robenalt is more direct, writing that "Harding was childless, stuck in a complicated and sexually arid marriage to a woman five years his senior."

I am still not sure about the John Dean and James David Robenalt thesis that publishing Warren Harding's love letters to Carrie Philips proved that he was a better president than history had remembered. In the foreword, Dean makes the case this way: "This suppression [of the letters] often gave the false impression that there was something to be hidden, when, in fact, there was much to be revealed that showed what a fine man, and able president, Harding had been."

At best, I think, it says that Harding could have had a future as a writer of soft porn or, perhaps, if cleaned up,

Hallmark greeting cards. Here's one passage from a letter to Carrie Philips: "Impassioned love for you is an expression of the soul of reverent love, and the joy of it has been the miracle that *only real love* knows." There are many more passages with the same soupy sentiments throughout the correspondence, and some letters, such as this one, go further. He writes to Carrie on September 15, 1913: "Honestly, I hurt with the insatiate longing, until I feel that there will never be any relief until I take a long, deep, wild draught on your lips and then bury my face on your pillowing breasts. Oh, Carrie! I want the solace you only can give. It is awful to hunger so and be so wholly denied." Some of the letters to his mistresses were written on US Senate stationery while Congress was in session, although clearly Harding wasn't following the debate. And, as with the Language of the Fan, Harding invented a code for his letters, so that they could be read aloud to Carrie's husband.[10]

In their letters, Harding made hints that he was prepared to leave Florence for Philips, but he never did, and things cooled when she moved to Germany for a year and later when Harding was a senator in Washington. Russell writes: "There were times enough when Harding wished that his wife were dead. Although he played with the idea, he could never assert himself to the point of leaving her. She was in her grim way part of him, a part he could not discard.

10: Robenalt has this passage: "Other words were more personalized love messages, and he continued to use them in private letters even after she returned from Europe. 'Matrix' was such a word, meaning 'I am utterly and gladly all yours—today and always.' 'Cloudy' was intended to be read as 'Message not clear.' 'Mellow' meant, 'I want to come to you in your dreams tonight, oh, so close.' He was even comical and ribald with some of the terms: 'Sismine' meant 'You, my adored,' and 'Govhard meant 'Hungering me.'"

Their dark and cluttered house represented home, with all the emotional overtones the word had for him."[11]

Russell does track down an illuminating vignette from Harding's 1920 front porch campaign in Marion. This was after Harding's physical affair with Philips had ended, although they were still neighbors and friends. Professor Arthur Hirsh of Ohio Wesleyan University went to Marion to hear Harding speak, and he describes the following exchange:

> I stood some distance back one forenoon when Mrs. Phillips was standing only a few feet away, on the Harding front lawn, talking to Mr. Harding who sat on the porch corner that he used as a campaign headquarters. With one eye on him and the other on the front door of the residence, she would take one cautious step, then another, toward the porch. Suddenly, Mrs. Harding appeared. A feather duster came sailing out at Mrs. Phillips, then a wastebasket. Mrs. Phillips did not retreat. Next came a

---

11: When I walked around the Marion house, as a book person, I had especially admired Harding's collection in his library. Sheryl Hall had implied that he loved nothing more than to spend his evenings with the classics, many of which are behind glass. Such a detail made me think better of Harding (as a reader of books like Thomas Hardy's *Jude the Obscure* or Henry Merman's *The Isle of Unrest*). Then I came upon this passage in Russell, which implied Harding had a Potemkin library. "Now, in his rising dignity," Russell writes, "he was an easy touch for every book salesman. He scarcely needed reminding that it was befitting a statesman to have a library. Soon the brown alcove at the rear of his parlor at Mount Vernon Avenue filled up with sets of Hawthorne's works; Bulwer-Lytton's works. . . .The unread volumes stared at each other from a tall mahogany bookcase with swinging doors on one side of the room and an expanding range of Globe-Wernicke portable shelves with leaded glass fronts on the other." Finally, Robenalt extracts from Harding's letters to Philips, and figures out exactly what the president read in his evenings or on trips. He writes: "The books all had common themes of love, scandal, mystery, poetry, and passion, and included: *Love Affairs of Lord Byron*, by Francis Gribble; *Eugene Field's Poems*; *Rest Harrow*, a novel by Maurice Hewlett about a "difficult" girl and her love affair; *At the Villa Rose*, a mystery by British author A. E. W. Mason; *Married Life of F: Carrols*; and *Cupid's Cyclopedia*, by Oliver Herford with John Cecil Clay."

> piano stool, one of those old, four-legged things with a swivel seat by which it could be lowered or raised. Not until then was there a retreat. She tossed him a kiss and left quietly.

According to Russell, the political skill that enabled the amiable, if lazy, Senator Warren Harding to become president was his ability to maintain friendships with both Theodore Roosevelt and William Howard Taft and, by extension, their factions in the party. Those two men broke in 1912, when Teddy ran for president as a third-party candidate, ending Taft's chance at reelection. A party stalwart, Harding had sided with President Taft, one of the few mainstream Republicans to do so, and that ended Harding's cordial relationship with Roosevelt.

Nevertheless, as a senator and Republican elder, Harding worked hard through the 1910s to reconcile with Roosevelt. He succeeded to this extent. Roosevelt told Daugherty that he wanted the presidency in 1920 and that, according to Russell, "he had Harding in mind as his vice president." Roosevelt, alas, died suddenly in 1919, and Harding won the nomination on the eighth ballot of the Republican convention, as one delegate said, "because there was nothing against him, and because the delegates wanted to go home."

Although Russell goes into great detail about the financial scandals that would ruin Harding's presidential legacy (many details only came out after he was dead, along with the revelation that he might have had a child outside his marriage), he does paint a more positive picture of Harding's presidency—that he negotiated an end to World War I; spoke out for equal rights, especially for African Americans ("Congress ought to wipe out the stain of barbaric lynching"); asked for new legislation abolishing child labor; and suggested that the United States become a member of the Permanent Court of International Justice established at the Hague by the League of Nations (something even President Barack Obama refused to consider). Russell reports that he spoke with eloquence before Congress, saying "that the democracy of the United States was a lie until the Negro was granted political and economic equality."

They might be insurmountable "ifs," but if Harding's friends had not stolen the government blind and if he had not used the presidential mansion as a shag house, there is a chance that Harding would be remembered at least as favorably as John Kennedy or certainly no worse than McKinley or Hayes.

In the end, however, Harding could not say no to his wife, girlfriends, cronies, political masters, golf buddies, drinking pals, insiders, and confidence men, and together they brought him down, with demands for money, power, fame, and influence—all of which they were sure Harding could provide them. Little did they know that all he wanted was a good time.

Late in his presidency Harding confessed to a friend: "Frankly being President is rather an unattractive business unless one relishes the exercise of power. That is a thing which has never greatly appealed to me." Had Harding lived, when told by the world he was "a very bad man!", he might have responded, as did the celebrated Midwestern writer Frank Baum for his character from Oz: "Oh, no, my dear; I'm really a very good man; but I'm a very bad Wizard."

Fremont: Ohio After Dark

Over and over on this trip, I kept coming across the name Frémont. It was the name of the Stevensons' street, the name of the general who had run as a Republican in 1856, and the same man who had promoted Ulysses Grant in the western theater of the Civil War. He had also inspired the ugly Democratic ditty in the Richmond newspaper, "free niggers, free women, free land, and Frémont," and the quip from Grant that he voted Buchanan because he didn't know him, and against Frémont because he did.

A Southerner who made his way to the Republican Party, Frémont had helped to open up the American West, was a friend of "Kit" Carson, fought in the Mexican and Civil wars, ran for president, and was later governor of Arizona, as before the war he had been briefly the military governor of California. Alas, he had eluded me in my readings, and every timeout my glasses, which were packed into the trunk of the car. I called a friend, Allen Rhodes, on my cell phone and found him in front of a computer, from which he guided me through the dark to Blooming Grove, not entirely sure why I was heading for an obscure village in Ohio. (He has a master's in American history from Columbia University, where we met, but clearly had missed the lectures on Warren Harding.)

If in Blooming Grove there is a plaque with Harding's name on it, I could not find it. The hamlet is little more than a collection of houses, and none of the streets have streetlights.

I took a picture of the sign outside the town—to verify to Erroll that I made it there—and departed on more back roads to Bucyrus (where Carrie Philips had lived for a while) and Tiffin, arriving in Fremont around 11 p.m.

My problem in Fremont was that I could not immediately find a place to stay, and that meant losing another twenty minutes (remember, the day had started on the 6 a.m. bus from Indianapolis) when I was tired and hungry. The Travelodge (motto: "We'll leave the dust on") I found finally was on the edge of the town, backed up against vacant lots and what looked like a swamp. Next door was a Denny's restaurant, where I ate a depressing meal at midnight in the company of obese teenagers having enormous plates of fries and burgers, washed down with container jugs of soda. (I was reminded of the *Onion* headline: "Obama Drastically Scales Back Goals for America After Visiting Denny's.") At least I had positioned myself to be at the Rutherford B. Hayes house on schedule the next day at 9 a.m.

Fremont: The Fraud of the Century Embraces Rutherford B. Hayes

EVEN BEFORE I PULLED UP in the rental car to the magnificent Spiegel Grove—the name of the Hayes home in Ohio—I was prepared to like the nineteenth American president. From my reading, I knew he had fought bravely in the Civil War (aside from Grant, Washington, and Jackson, he might have seen the most frontline combat of any US president) and been wounded five times. He was a successful lawyer—in the mold of Benjamin Harrison—congressman, and governor, and had agreed to serve his Republican party in the 1876 election, which was tilted in his favor.

As president, Hayes ended federal occupation of the South. Some said he ended the occupation in exchange for winning the election. He championed the cause of Native American rights, as had Ulysses Grant, that would allow Indians to prosper while the nation moved west into their lands. (The museum has many pictures of Hayes in conferences with Native Americans.) Tired of political infighting, Hayes left the White House in 1881, happy to return to Spiegel Grove, which is largely unchanged from when he came home. Members of the Hayes family lived in the house until 1965, when it was given to the foundation that now runs it.

Nancy Kleinhenz, on the museum staff, walked me around the Hayes house and gardens. The Hayes of her walking tour was a happy warrior, who doted on his wife, Lucy, his lifelong companion. (She only earned the nickname "Lemonade" Lucy in the twentieth century, long after she had died in 1889.)

Hayes kept a diary from age thirteen and wrote many letters, most of which have survived. He got his undergraduate degree from Kenyon College, in Gambier, Ohio, and a law degree from Harvard. (President Obama is the only other Harvard Law graduate to become president.) He was married with children when the Civil War broke out, but enlisted anyway, and the governor of Ohio encouraged him to form the Twenty-Third Ohio Volunteer Infantry, which would be his home from 1861 to 1865, and in which he would rise from lieutenant to major general. Also, while Hayes was serving in the Twenty-Third Ohio, he was elected as a representative to the US Congress, although famously, according to Nancy, he refused to leave the front lines to campaign.

Hayes's regiment was mostly engaged in what is now West Virginia and Virginia, and saw heavy action at Carnifex Ferry, Kanawha, and South Mountain. He missed the fighting at Antietam, because of a serious wound, but came back later to serve with distinction in the Shenandoah Valley. Grant said of his service: "His conduct on the field was marked by conspicuous gallantry as well as the display of qualities of a higher order than that of mere personal daring."

In addition to serving in Congress, Hayes was elected three times as governor of Ohio, from which he moved to the White House. Nancy said Hayes was a happy man, who never took himself too seriously, and who, in retirement, was content in his home office, surrounded by his books and papers, or in the library parlor, where he would meet his guests to Spiegel Grove (many of whom were distinguished).

Hayes liked gardening with his wife, and whenever he was besieged with callers, he would hide in his modern bathroom, in which he even had a desk. (No one would ever interrupt someone in the bathroom, was his logic.) Nancy said Hayes had a puckish humor and few airs, although he did mount his White House portrait in the front room. He died in 1893, some four years after he had lost his wife, saying, "I know that I'm going where Lucy is." He looks like a Boy Scout in comparison to Warren Harding, although there are skeletons in his ample closets at Spiegel Grove from the 1876 election, among the most corrupt in American history.

The best two books I have read about the 1876 election are by Roy Morris (*Fraud of the Century: Rutherford B. Hayes, Samuel Tilden, and the Stolen Election of 1876*) and Gore Vidal (who set *1876*, one of his Narratives of Empire novels, in and around the election). The election featured the popular war hero and Republican governor from Ohio (although the writer Henry Adams called Hayes "a third-rate nonentity, whose only recommendation is that he is obnoxious to no one") against the sitting Democratic governor of New York, the pious corporate lawyer Samuel Tilden, whose tombstone in New Lebanon, New York, reads: "I Still Trust the People." At issue was whether the United States would embrace a third term of Grantism (the shorthand term for the general's many corruptions) or vote Democratic for the first time since James Buchanan beat John C. Frémont in 1856.

The Republican nomination was a contest of wills between Congressman James G. Blaine (New York congressman Samuel "Sunset" Cox called him "the honorable hyena from Maine") and New York political boss and Grant man

Roscoe Conkling (Blaine had once noted his "haughty disdain, his grandiloquent swell, his majestic, supereminent, turkey-gobbler strut").

When delegates could not choose between Blaine and Conkling, they nominated the pleasant-to-all war hero Hayes, about whom a newspaper editor said: "The nominee's chief recommendation seemed to be that 'Hayes has never stolen.' Good God, has it come to this?" Such was Hayes's estrangement from the political process that when told who would run with him for vice president, Hayes asked Lucy: "I am ashamed to say, who is Wheeler?" (He was a New York congressman.) In the closely contested election, cartoonist Thomas V. Nast liked to caricature Tilden wearing a dress. His high moral tone, not unlike that of Al Gore before he ditched his wife, Tipper, rubbed a lot of people the wrong way.

So close was the general election that Tilden won the popular vote by 250,000, although in early returns Hayes carried the electoral college, especially when you added in the contested state delegations of Louisiana, Florida, and South Carolina, which both Hayes and Tilden claimed as victories.

Louisiana, Florida, and South Carolina sent two slates of electors (one pledged to Tilden and the other to Hayes) to the electoral college in December 1876. The election would be decided depending on which electors would be allowed to cast their votes.

In response (almost as happened in 2000 during *Bush v. Gore*), the Republicans hired influence peddlers while the Democrat Tilden cranked out a short book, *The Presidential Counts,* which Morris calls "a massive, book-length study of previous presidential elections." (It was said of Tilden's style that "he writes like a schoolmaster of finance. His letter is like a chapter from some German work in metaphysics.")

According to Morris, Tilden argued "that the Senate and the House had the ultimate right to examine the ballots and decide which, if any, of the disputed ballots (in Louisiana, Florida, and South Carolina) to accept. In the event the two legislative bodies could not approve a majority of the electoral votes for either candidate, the election should be thrown into the House of Representatives, as prescribed by the Constitution."

The Republicans, however, didn't want the House deciding the election, as Democrats controlled more state delegations than did Republicans, so they favored an "electoral commission" that (with a majority of Republican members) chose to recognize the Republican delegations from the contested states. In short, the Republicans stacked the deck.

The suggested deal that allowed Hayes to win the presidency, many thought, was that the Republicans agreed to withdraw federal troops from the South and turn over local control there to the Democratic party—something to which not even Tilden might have agreed. It was the end of Reconstruction. According to Morris, "Even before the vote was concluded, the nation's new president-elect was already en route to Washington, riding in comfort aboard a luxury train provided free of charge by Tom Scott and the Pennsylvania Railroad."

The jingo press stepped into high gear, calling Hayes: "His Fraudulency," "His Fraudulence," "Old Eight to Seven" (that was the vote of the electoral commission for Hayes), and "Returning Board Hayes." It was said he was "commissioned" as president, and that "the monster fraud of the century is consummated." Not even philandering Harding ever stole an election, and here the beneficiary was an entirely decent man. Later, as one Democrat said, "He did such a good job I almost wish he had been elected."

Fremont: Gore Vidal Spins 1876

GORE VIDAL'S NOVEL *1876*, among the finest ever written about an election, gives the reader an insider look at the personalities in the contest. The narrator is Charles Schermerhorn Schuyler, who has recently returned to New York and Washington from a life abroad (he sounds a lot like Vidal, who lived much of his life in Rome), and he explains the election to his daughter, Emma, as they move among the drawing rooms of power in New York and Washington. Here are a few of the portraits that he passes along:

- Of Tilden, Schuyler says: "I record only Apgar Senior's view of Governor Tilden. 'The man is so often drunk that he cannot get up in the morning.'" He goes on: "If Governor Tilden has a fatal flaw, it is his curious notion that men can be compelled by good argument to be honest, to show disinterest where there is only interest and greed."
- About Grant, he says: "Grant is—well, not deep but puzzling. For one thing, the hurt face is perfectly contradicted by the confident voice, by the swift intelligent gaze that simultaneously takes in and dismisses—reflective of a military genius that for some reason has not translated into politics as it ought to have done, for, contrary to legend, generals are almost by definition adept politicians."

• On Blaine, Schuyler recalls: "'He could sell the White House to a speculator,' I heard myself observe to Emma, 'pocket the cash, and the people would still love him.' I do admire the man's audacity."

• On the Republican Party: "More to the point, the noble new party that freed the slaves and preserved the Union is the very same party that is now in cahoots with the crooked railroad tycoons and with the Wall Street cornerers of this-and-that, thus making it hard for a noble creature like Bigelow—like Stedman?—to confess to the bankruptcy of what only ten years ago was the last or latest, best or better, hope or dream of an honourable system of government."

• On the Democrats, Schuyler says: "It's the Tildens I can't abide, and the Bigelows and the Bryants and the whole moaning tribe of old women who think we would have had all this wealth, these railroads and manufactories, just by going to church!"

• On Mark Twain: "My dislike for Twain is inevitable. The professional vulgarian wandering amongst the ruins and splendours of Europe, making his jokes to reassure the people back home that in their ignorance, bigotry and meanness they are like gods and if they ever should (Heaven forbid) look about them and notice the hideousness of their cities and towns and the meagreness of their lives, why, there's good old Mark to tell them that they are the best people that ever lived in the best country in the world, so let's go out and buy his book!"

• On those supporting Hayes: "Known as the Stalwarts, they are the enemies of every sort of reform and hence fierce supporters of General Grant and of the spoils system."

• On the outcome of the election: "Nordhoff assures me that one of the chief reasons behind the last-minute coalition to support Hayes is that he is willing, unlike Grant, to withdraw Federal troops from the South, and allow that febrile region home rule."
• On Americans: "Some new race has obviously replaced the Yankees: a plump, voluptuous people, expanding gorgeously beneath their golden sun."

Saying goodbye to Nancy, I toured through the ample gardens around the house. There is a marker for the president's son Webb Hayes, a military officer who helped relieve Beijing during the Boxer Rebellion, fought with Theodore Roosevelt on San Juan Hill, and received the Congressional Medal of Honor in the Philippines, for which the citation reads: "Pushed through the enemy's lines alone, during the night, from the beach to the beleaguered force at Vigan, and returned the following morning to report the condition of affairs to the Navy and secure assistance."

In the spirit of Harding in Europe, I bought some postcards in the gift shop and looked again at the museum, before pointing the car in the direction of my next stop, Canton, Ohio, and the presidential museum of William McKinley, who followed in the footsteps of his Ohio compatriot, both in the Civil War and later in the White House. Between 1868 and 1900, the White House, with few exceptions, was the campground of Civil War veterans and bewhiskered Republican generals.

Across Ohio: Oberlin Plays by the Rules

FROM FREMONT, I drove east on Highway 20 for an hour to Oberlin, where I had decided to stop for lunch. I had never seen the college that is famous for its music education, and I got there around 12:30 p.m., just as the town of Oberlin was setting up a fall fair in the town's central park. (There were books and bikes for sale, along with food and face painting.)

I unloaded my bike from the trunk of the car, and biked the contours of the campus, learning from various inscriptions that the college and town date to 1833 and that Willard Van Orman Quine ("one of the greatest philosophers and logicians of the 20th century" but until then unknown to me) had gotten his undergraduate degree from Oberlin in 1930.

The police on duty around the square didn't like the idea of bikes getting near the crowds, so I walked to a Subway restaurant to buy a sandwich and ate sitting outside on the grass. Afterward, I went over to the campus bookshop (another run by Barnes & Noble) to look at course readings—it's a good way to tell what a particular college is like—but the unfriendly clerk said that part of the store was closed. I drove away from Oberlin—it's a New England quadrangle spliced into the Ohio farmland—happy that I would never need to come again. For a little town, it certainly did have a lot of rules.

According to the map, it was only an hour and a half to Canton and the McKinley Museum, and I figured I would arrive in the midafternoon. In that part of Ohio, largely a rectangle of county roads, I could pick my way south and east, almost like a sailboat tacking into the wind. Once I found Canton, however, I made a few wrong turns finding the museum (it's not well signposted), and when I rolled up to the front door, it was just after 4 p.m. and closing.

I couldn't believe that yet another museum on my route was closing before 5 p.m., so I threw myself on the mercy of two men still in the museum office. Using phrases like "came all the way from Switzerland," "wanting to tape a radio interview," and "wrote ahead to the management but never heard anything back," I struck a sympathetic nerve with Buzz Ream and Larry Bullough, the last two volunteers in the office. They were roughly my age, clearly good friends with each other, and it seemed to me that they loved their part-time work with the McKinley Museum. Buzz agreed to answer a few of my questions for radio, and then suggested, "Why don't we tape this upstairs in the museum?" which was music to my ears. Despite my late arrival, I would make it inside the McKinley Museum after all, although while standing around the office, I learned that McKinley's Canton house and its famous front porch were torn down in the Depression. So much for historical preservation, at least in Canton, a city of vacant lots, if not broken dreams.

Canton: William McKinley Works from Home

JUST AS I WAS PREPARED to like Rutherford B. Hayes before showing up in Fremont, I had my doubts about William McKinley long before I set foot in Canton. I hold him responsible for the Spanish-American War of 1898, in which the US army and navy drove the Spanish out of Cuba, the Philippines, Guam, and Puerto Rico. In high school I had tried reading William Appelman Williams's *The Tragedy of American Diplomacy*—a teacher said it would provide some keys to my thinking about the world—and while I didn't get very far into the history (although his subjects are excellent, his prose can be leaden), I did get far enough into the book to take on his thesis that America had opened its imperial doors in 1898, when McKinley was president. The neocolonialism of American foreign policy, as seen in Vietnam and the Middle East, began with the Spanish-American War. McKinley, Williams believes, as the front man for expansionist capitalism, went abroad in search of new markets and cheap labor, but instead had only brought back monsters.

I didn't think it right to start in with McKinley's warmongering with Buzz and Larry. They had invited me, at closing time, into their museum, and clearly both held McKinley in high regard. The least I could do was hear their story, which was told as we balanced my tape recorder on a cabinet upstairs in the museum. Around us were the artifacts of McKinley's life and lost house, including the desk he used in Congress and at the White House, many photos of him as a young officer in the Civil War, and a replica of the pistol that assassinated him in 1901.

Buzz outlined for me the William McKinley story—his childhood in Niles, Ohio, near Youngstown, his college studies at Allegheny College in Pennsylvania, and his time at Albany Law School. In between his college studies and the law came the Civil War, in which McKinley served with distinction as a canteen officer in the Twenty-Third Ohio Volunteer Regiment of Rutherford B. Hayes.

Supplying the troops with coffee and sandwiches while they are in mortal combat is more dangerous than it sounds, and McKinley, in particular, was mentioned in dispatches for his heroism at Antietam (the battle that Hayes missed). On several occasions around Burnside's Bridge, he managed to bring his wagons close to the troops while they were heavily engaged. Hayes later wrote that "he passed under fire and delivered, with his own hands, these things, so essential for the men for whom he was laboring." At Antietam, McKinley was a sergeant; he was a major when the war ended, and by then had an important patron in General Hayes.

After the war, McKinley finished his legal studies and passed the bar in Canton, where in 1871 he married Ida Saxton, to whom he remained devoted for the rest of her life. (In the White House and even before, her health was marginal, because of epilepsy, and much of McKinley's free time was spent caring for and worrying about his wife's health.) His political career took off in 1876 when he was elected to Congress, the same year that his friend and mentor Hayes was elected president.

His friendship with the president (who wasn't well regarded in Congress) didn't help McKinley win choice committee assignments, and he crossed his friend Hayes on the question of allowing silver to back the American dollar (McKinley approved; Hayes did not). Nevertheless, they remained on good terms, and McKinley further enhanced his standing through his close dealings with another Ohio Civil War general, James Garfield, who would succeed Hayes in 1881.

During the 1880s, McKinley achieved prominence for passing the McKinley Tariff, a piece of national legislation that protected the American manufacturing base—much of which was in Ohio—from cheap foreign competition. He became known for his leadership of the Republican party in Ohio, the breeding ground for postwar presidents.

McKinley failed to win reelection in 1890, after the Democrats gerrymandered his congressional district into a Democratic stronghold. Undaunted—McKinley was always of positive mind—he ran the next year for governor and won, while at the same time his political ally John B. Sherman (brother to the Civil War general William T. Sherman) was elected to fill one of the Ohio seats in the US Senate. Helping Sherman was the Ohio magnate Mark Hanna (he had shipping and oil investments, among many others), who subsequently would play a key role in the future political career of William McKinley.

In particular, Hanna and some other businessmen stepped in when it became clear that McKinley had foolishly guaranteed the borrowings of a friend and associate, who promptly went bankrupt, threatening to bring down the governor with him. Instead, Hanna managed the collateral pool, raised money from businessmen working with the state, and retired the notes without having recourse to McKinley's money. The governor was saved from financial ruin, and Hanna, among others, held an IOU from McKinley. The stage was set for him to run for president while beholden, in effect, to the Fortune 500 of its day.

I asked Buzz about McKinley the man, and he answered by describing him as kind, warmhearted, a caring family man (the McKinleys lost their two daughters at young ages, and never had more children). A neighbor said of him: "He was of kindly disposition, of no hatreds, and mistreated no one." One historian concludes that McKinley's overriding trait was an unstinting affability. In later years, he was preoccupied with his wife's health. She didn't like being apart from her husband, and he did his best to stay close. (Unlike Harding, McKinley found a calling in nursing his ailing wife.) Thankfully, as a presidential candidate in 1896 and again in 1900, McKinley never needed to leave her. The voters came to Canton in droves, and he spoke from his front porch, with his wife close by. It was the ideal solution for a work-from-home presidential candidate.

Canton: Bimetallism Underwrites the 1896 Election

Before coming to Canton, I had read an account of the 1896 presidential election between McKinley and William Jennings Bryan from Nebraska. The summer before, I had found Paul W. Glad's *McKinley, Bryan and the People* and had to endure jibes about my choice of vacation reading. (They were along the lines of, "Is that one in Oprah's book club?")

In Glad's opinion, the 1896 election offered the American people a clear choice between silver and gold, monied interests and those of farmers, East and West, and, overall, a battle between labor and capital. As much as the 1860 election pointed the way out of slavery, so did 1896 offer workers (in the cities and on farms) a chance to break free of their industrial servitude. Except that McKinley won, and he brought into the White House a clear rejection of the issues raised in the Haymarket or later during the Pullman strike. Eugene Debs can be seen as another big loser in 1896, one reason he might have chosen, four years later, to run for president.

In setting up the opposites of the 1896 election, Glad describes how each candidate subscribed to beliefs that had probably long since vanished from the landscape. He writes:

> The two myths which dominated American thought in the nineteenth century were real enough in themselves precisely because they did dominate American thought. Bryan's acceptance of the agrarian myth and

> McKinley's belief in the myth of the self-made man help to explain why neither candidate offered a completely new departure, a radical alternative, in 1896. Each spoke in an idiom to which Americans had grown accustomed. Each held a position ultimately justified by a traditional myth.

Of the two candidates, Bryan was the better orator while McKinley had the better organization, led by Mark Hanna, who was a new kind of political boss—more interested in making one man president than in running a city or a county. Glad writes of the symbiotic connection between McKinley and Hanna:

> A direct telephone line connected the McKinley home in Canton with Hanna's office in Cleveland. Always ready for consultation with the formal, platitudinous, moralistic exemplar of Republicanism and Americanism was the realist who had few thoughts about dignity and decorum except to admire those qualities as they appeared in McKinley. "Together," writes Margaret Leech, "these two made one perfect politician."

Such a new political relationship explains how, with a straight face, McKinley could run for the Republican nomination with the watchwords "McKinley against the bosses."

The economic issues that divided America in the 1890s were tariffs and currency, whether the United States should block cheap imports from flooding the nation and whether the dollar should only be pegged to gold or whether it could just as well be convertible into silver (thus allowing more money to circulate, which would help farmers, who for so long had remained at the mercy of Eastern capitalists and their gold fixation).

For Wall Street, McKinley was the ideal big business candidate, having gotten a protective tariff passed through Congress in 1890. Bryan stood opposite such a position. He wanted "a more flexible currency, for free coinage of silver, for an increase in the circulating medium, for a graduated income tax, for a subtreasury, for postal savings banks, for an increase in the circulating medium, for a government ownership and operation of railroads, and for the reclamation of lands held by aliens and railroads."

Unlike McKinley and Hanna, Bryan had to consolidate the left wing of the political spectrum, which in the 1890s was fragmented not only between conservative and liberal Democrats but among many other parties on the fringes as well. At the Democratic convention in 1896, Glad writes, "There were Coxeyites and Debsites, Prohibitionists and Suffragists, Socialists and Bellamy nationalists, all of them hoping to get a hearing for their special causes. Leaders of the Bimetallic Democratic National Committee also appeared on the scene early."[12]

Bryan staked his position early on the silver question—asking an ally to read to the convention the following: "We demand the free and unlimited coinage of both silver and gold at the present legal ratio of 16 to 1 without waiting for the aid or consent of any other nation." In his acceptance

---

12: Some critics of the two-party system forecast the end of their days, when Republicans and Democrats would be joined together in a forced, arranged marriage. One wit said: "The ceremony will be performed at the altar of plutocracy. Grover Cleveland and Ben Harrison will act as brides-maids, the devil will give away the bride, and Jay Gould will pronounce the benediction."

speech, Bryan uttered what were to become his most famous words: "You shall not press down upon the brow of labor this crown of thorns, you shall not crucify mankind upon a cross of gold."

The Republican convention was less exciting. Glad writes that the Republican chairman said, "The great questions for debate . . . were 'Free Trade and Free Silver against a Protective Tariff and Sound Money.'" And he quotes from journalist William Allen White about how scripted were the proceedings: "The applause is hollow; the enthusiasm dreary and the delegates sit like hogs in a car and know nothing about anything." Glad concludes: "Probably McKinley and Hanna would never rival Gilbert and Sullivan in showmanship, but they did achieve most of their objectives. There is something to be said for that."

It would be impossible today to hold a national election on the convertibility of the currency, as now the American dollar is pegged only to political expedience. But in 1896 silver became the adjective that modified many political positions. Believe in silver (they were called Silverites), and you believed that farmers were due a break, that Wall Street's hold on the American economy was too onerous, and that inflation would put prosperity into the laboring classes.

During the campaign, Glad writes, McKinley continued to work away at the theme that silver meant a fifty-cent dollar, despite Bryan's attempt to destroy the effectiveness of the argument. McKinley said: "We do not want any cheap money, any more than we want cheap labor in the United States." Truth be told, he wanted cheap labor more than cheap money, and by fixing the dollar to gold, the Republicans got both. In response, Bryan would say: "The poor man is called a socialist if he believes that the wealth of the rich should be divided among the poor, but the rich man is called a financier if he devises a plan by which the pittance of the poor can be converted to his use."

The election was closer on the stump than in the final tally. McKinley won New England, the Midwest, California, and a majority in nearly every big city, and took in 271 electoral votes. Concentrating only on silver, Bryan won the South and the agricultural West. The popular vote was closer, 7.1 million for McKinley versus 6.5 million for Bryan. The interesting thing about the electoral map in 1896 is that one hundred years later, in the election of 2000, Democrats would win most of the states that McKinley won, and Republicans would win those that had been Democratic in 1896.

Along the lines of Adlai Stevenson II, Bryan ran a bold and exciting campaign—he said: "One of the most important duties of government is to put rings in the noses of hogs"—but Hanna had pulled out all the stops with McKinley's campaign ("Prosperity at Home, Prestige Abroad") and for most voters, protectionism seemed like a better deal than detaching the dollar from Grant's gold.

Canton: McKinley Remembers the *Maine*

DURING THE INTERVIEW IN THE MUSEUM, Buzz and I talked about the Spanish-American War of 1898, and he took the position, which later became mine, that McKinley was swept along on a current that wanted war with Spain at all costs. The president was less a warmonger, in this telling, than the victim of a national mania that saw war with Spain as a way to strike a blow against European colonialism, open up new markets in the Caribbean and Asia, bring democracy to the downtrodden around the world, and remain competitive against the European imperial powers.

On a personal level, McKinley was not in favor of jingoism or the war ("I shall never get into a war, until I am sure that God and man approve. I have been through one war; I have seen the dead piled up; and I do not want to see another"), but on a political level, he never commanded his own ship, and the forces behind him, especially after the 1898 sinking of the USS *Maine* in Havana harbor, saw war with Spain as the only way forward for national and international redemption.

Among those most vociferous for war was Teddy Roosevelt, who only in the 1900 election became McKinley's vice president and eventual successor, after McKinley's assassination. Confronting Hanna during a speech in Washington, TR said: "We will have this war of freedom." Roosevelt was serving as McKinley's assistant secretary of the navy (a job his cousin Franklin would hold for Woodrow Wilson), but he dreamed of leading men in combat, and a war with Spain seemed like his best option.

Scott Miller in his history *The President and the Assassin: McKinley, Terror, and Empire at the Dawn of the American Century* describes the bind in which McKinley found himself in 1898. Economically, the United States suffered from surpluses, which were thought to be the reason for recessions, then called panics. Only with new, captive markets—say those in the Caribbean, Hawaii, or Asia—could the US hope to remain competitive with other world powers.

Miller describes the problem this way: "Too many bikes, too much steel, too much cotton. The self-inflicted predicament unfolded upon American businessmen as a nightmare of catastrophic proportion. In the economic logic of the day, this was no business cycle; it was a crisis that spoke to the very core of the economy and, more than a few felt, threatened even the democratic principles on which the country was founded." He quotes a friend of McKinley's saying all the president ever wanted "was to create new markets for American producers and manufacturers."

Miller writes that, for a while, McKinley thought he could avoid war: "More out of intuition than calculation, [he] began pursuing a third alternative. The United States would extend its influence abroad, but it would be neither political nor territorial. Rather, the country would aim to establish a commercial hegemony." But then the *Maine* exploded (its source was a gas tank, not an enemy bomb) and William Randolph Hearst was cabling to a correspondent: "YOU FURNISH THE PICTURES I'LL FURNISH THE WAR." Miller writes: "In the spring of 1898, Americans treated the prospect of war in Cuba like a cross between a debutante's ball and

'Buffalo Bill' Cody's Wild West Show." In the costume drama that followed, the United States swept Spain from the world stage.

Peace proved a lot harder than war against Spain. Never sure what the war had been about, McKinley had few ideas what to demand in victory. He took the Philippines, Cuba, Puerto Rico, and Guam; gave Spain $20 million; and called off the fighting.

Before the war, Congress had passed the Teller Amendment, in which the United States proclaimed "that the people of the island of Cuba are, of right ought to be, free and independent." The wisdom of that decision was confirmed during the fighting, when soldiers would write home their impressions of the enemy, as did one member of the Massachusetts Volunteers, who wrote about the Spanish: "They are a filthy, indolent, thievish, immoral set, and it is a burning shame." By contrast, the historian and commentator Henry Adams said: "I find America so cheerful, and so full of swagger and self-satisfaction, that I hardly know it." Mark Twain wrote the stinging essay, "To the Person Sitting in Darkness," which reads, in part: "There must be two Americas: one that sets the captive free, and one that takes a once-captive's new freedom away from him, and picks a quarrel with him with nothing to found it on; then kills him to get his land."

After the war, it became clear that Cuba wasn't ready for home rule, as one witness there wrote (as quoted by Miller): "Self-government! Why those people are no more fit for self-government than gunpowder is for hell." Cuba would remain a confused American possession for much of the next century, some might even say, even until today. The Philippines were only granted independence in 1944.

Guam remains an American protectorate, and Puerto Rico is a so-called commonwealth, neither a state nor independent, but most recently on the edge of bankruptcy.

In short, the Spanish-American War signed up the United States for taking on what Rudyard Kipling called the "white man's burden" in a poem that he wrote in February 1899 during the war with Spain. One verse reads:

Take up the White Man's burden—
The savage wars of peace—
Fill full the mouth of famine
And bid the sickness cease;
And when your goal is nearest
The end for others sought,
Watch Sloth and heathen Folly
Bring all your hopes to nought.

The belle of the ball in Cuba was Theodore Roosevelt and his Rough Riders, and the victory on San Juan Hill earned Teddy the vice presidential nomination on the Republican ticket in 1900. Hanna, among others, hated the idea of putting the erratic Roosevelt so close to McKinley. He exclaimed: "Don't any of you realize that there's only one life between this madman and the Presidency?"

Canton: Eugene V. Debs Misses the Football Hall of Fame

THE MEMORIAL HOLDING William McKinley's tomb is up the hill from the museum, but it was closed. I looked at it from the parking lot and followed Buzz's directions, driving past the location on North Market Street where the McKinley house and its front porch had been located (now the space is used for library parking). A plaque on the site reads: "During the campaign McKinley addressed about 750,000 people who came to his home in Canton."

During the 1896 campaign, Hanna wanted him to hit the trail and debate directly with Bryan, but McKinley, who wanted to stay home with Ida, said Bryan was too good of a speaker. He told Hanna: "I might just as well set up a trapeze on my front lawn and compete with some professional athlete as go out speaking against Bryan. I have to think when I speak."

The former home of Ida Saxton McKinley, where the couple lived when they first came to Canton, is farther down Market Street and serves as the National First Ladies Library. The stately, well-maintained Italianate building, with a wrap-around porch, was trimmed with bunting but had long since closed when I drove past. (The last tour is at 2:30 p.m.) Later I did get some amusement when I read about the library online and found this reported in 1998: "First Lady Hillary Clinton makes first 'hit' on web site; accesses her own bibliographic records." No mention was made whether or not she deleted them, or where the server was located.

I drove from Market Street over to Nimisilla Park, where Eugene Debs gave the speech in 1917 that landed him in jail for sedition. If there is a marker in the park that says, "On this spot the administration of Woodrow Wilson arrested labor leader Eugene Debs under the Espionage Act and later sentenced him to prison for ten years, for speaking out against war and wage inequality," I didn't find it. The park has basketball courts, a band shell, playground equipment, and assorted outbuildings, but otherwise is silent on its role in American history. Besides, in the accepted narrative, Wilson is a good guy ("he kept us out of war"), Harding is a bad guy (Teapot Dome), and Debs is a troublemaker, if well meaning. Nimisilla Park only complicates the story.

Although I knew it would be closed, I also wanted to drive by the Pro Football Hall of Fame, which was three miles west on 12th Street. It, too, had long been closed, since 5 p.m. From the street, the buildings look more like a mall that has outgrown its footprint than a museum. The round building that shows up in news reports is just the tip of an iceberg that has many additions, and a stadium next door. In a way, I was relieved that it was closed. I would not have been keen to fork over $24 to see the exhibits ("Visit Tom Brady's draft card . . ."), and more on my mind was getting to the campus of Kent State University. To paraphrase what Georges Clemenceau said about Woodrow Wilson and the League of Nations: I like the National Football League; I just don't believe in it.

Canton was among the saddest cities I saw on my travels. Some houses were abandoned, and even the downtown part of the city looked forlorn. No doubt McKinley had moved to Canton because it represented the center of the nation, as Buzz had told me, "halfway between New York and Chicago, and the center of much industry."

Now Canton is an industrial black hole, with a Rust Belt infrastructure, although later I was pleased to read that the unemployment rate was only 5.1 percent when I was there. *Forbes* magazine featured Canton in its report on America's fastest-dying cities, and from that I inferred unemployment was low because so many people have chosen to leave northern Ohio. I am sure most visitors come to Canton for the "Hall of Fame village" (conveniently by the interstate), or maybe the McKinley Museum, and then beat a quick retreat out of town. You can see why McKinley liked to say, just down the road: "I am a tariff man, standing on a tariff platform."

Kent State: Democracy Under Fire

I WAS FREE THAT EVENING and decided to spend the time in Kent—thirty-seven miles north of Canton—trying to understand the shootings on May 4, 1970, that cost the lives of four students and wounded nine others.

The massacre at Kent State defined the protest era of the Vietnam War. I was in the tenth grade when it happened and read the *Life* magazine accounts of the shootings. But I never had understood exactly what happened and why. I thought if I could spend time on the campus, find some books on the subject, and maybe interview some surviving witnesses, I might have a better idea of its events. At the very least, Kent was halfway to Cleveland, and my friend there who was putting me up that night would not be home until 10 p.m.

For once in my travels without GPS, I had no trouble finding where I wanted to go. I made a short detour through Akron (some of the tire companies still have their headquarters downtown, but there was no sign of LeBron James) and took an interstate in the direction of the university, although it faded into a highway before reaching the town of Kent.

The state university is a short distance from Main Street. I found an empty parking lot on the southwest side of the campus and there reassembled the folding bike, so that I could ride around. From the size of the parking lots and the paucity of cars in them, I sensed Kent is a commuter school. And as I biked around on that Saturday evening, I saw few students.

In what looked like the campus center (the buildings around the entrance are new and imposing, with lots of glass and red brick), I asked an older man walking his dog if he knew where I could find the site of the shootings. He pointed me up a hill through some parking lots, and a short time later, I was on the hill, looking down at the Commons where the demonstrations had taken place in spring 1970, after the Nixon administration invaded Cambodia.

Before coming to Kent, I had tried to arrange an interview with Alan Canfora. He was wounded in the wrist during the shootings, appears in many books, and now works with the May 4 Center, a small memorial museum on campus that has continued to research the question—still elusive today—why members of the Ohio National Guard opened fire on unarmed students demonstrating against the war. Canfora had said he would be away that weekend but that I could easily access on my phone a tape-recorded walking tour of the site. (The narrator is Julian Bond, the civil rights activist and former US representative in Congress.) He also said I could interview him afterward by phone, although when I followed up he lost interest in talking to me.

For the longest time that evening, despite pressing the pound sign on my phone to access the next recording, I had trouble orienting myself to what happened where during the 1970 confrontation. The hallowed ground at Kent State covers two sides of a hill. In the Commons, a practice field and frisbee area on campus close to Main Street, the National Guard first confronted the demonstrators, who slowly retreated up the hill behind them (to a more central part of the campus) where they scattered.

For some reason, the guard went up the hill and then way down the other side, to a practice football field, where no one was protesting. On leaving the field to return to the Commons, they marched back up the hill. Only at the top of the hill did the guard turn toward the campus and fire randomly at students below, many of whom were milling around a parking lot.

When the guard shots were fired, there were few students close to them and none at that moment throwing rocks or firing guns. The students killed and wounded in the shooting were, in some cases, more than fifty yards from the guardsmen.

Why the retreating guard turned and fired their military weapons (which were carrying live ammunition on the campus) remains a mystery. Some guardsmen said they heard gunfire and started shooting. Others said they heard a pistol go off. Others said they heard no orders to shoot but followed the lead of other guardsmen who began firing their guns. In all, about sixty-seven shots were fired. Thirteen students were hit, four fatally.

In several trials—both civil and criminal—some of the guardsmen were charged with manslaughter, and lawyers on both sides tried to get at the reason why their guns had been fired. In all the trials, the guardsmen were acquitted of manslaughter or of using unnecessary force. (Later the state paid the victims some small compensation for their wounds or the families of the dead for their loss.) Never did the trials, however, uncover the sequence of events that explained why the guardsmen decided to shoot at the students in the first place. At best, the trials and inquiries made the shootings sound like a forest fire or natural disaster for which no expert had a reasonable answer.

Like the shootings in the Haymarket, the events at Kent State on May 4 and the subsequent trial verdicts continue to divide the nation—at least those who still remember them. Defenders of the National Guard and Ohio's then governor, James Rhodes, believe that civil protest on campus during those days had crossed the line to domestic violence. The night before, demonstrators had set fire to the ROTC (Reserve Officers' Training Corps) center on campus.

Supporters of the student demonstrators argue that the assemblies were peaceful (certainly on May 4, the day of the shootings), that the students had a First Amendment right to assembly and free speech, and that, besides, none were carrying weapons. And they point out that some of the killed and wounded were simply walking to class and had played no role in the demonstrations.

Without Canfora to guide me and tiring of the phone messages, I rode my bike around campus sidewalks until I had a good idea of the routes taken by the students and the guard, where the shots were fired from, and where the students were killed. (Some of the student memorials are in a parking lot, with lights on stanchions to show where they fell.) But it wasn't until I got to New York, went to the Strand bookstore, and found some histories about Kent State that I began to grasp the issues that surrounded the shootings and those of the subsequent trials and investigations. I bought Peter Davies's *The Truth About Kent State: A Challenge to the American Conscience*, because it got good reviews for presenting the facts in the case, and a second book, *The Kent State Coverup: The*

Definitive Account of the Kent State Shootings and the Trial That Followed by Joseph Kelner, chief counsel for the victims, and James Munves, because I thought that the defense lawyers for the students would best plead their case.

As with the Haymarket or the death of Martin Luther King Jr., I am sure it is possible to read forever on the subject, but I stopped at these two volumes, plus a bunch of documentary films on the Internet. What did I learn? That Ohio governor James Rhodes, running for reelection that year, wanted to stand up to student radicals; that the Ohio National Guard had no experience in crowd control, and guardsmen were sent to the campus with live ammunition in their rifles, incompetent officers, and confusing orders, if any; that when the killings took place, the Kent State president was having lunch with his staff in a nearby restaurant; that a probable FBI informer in the crowd or near the guardsmen fired a pistol just before the guard turned and shot the students; and finally that neither the state nor federal government had any interest in finding out the truth about the shootings, fearing that any condemnation of the National Guard would reflect poorly on public officials, Governor Rhodes, or President Richard Nixon. Best, it was decided, to leave the story as an unsolved mystery, in which much of the blame came to rest on the dead students.

From reading Peter Davies, I learned many details that were not available to me on the bike that night in Kent. For example, he writes about the pistol shot: "There were scores of witnesses, and the only conflict in their testimony revolves around such questions as whether there were one or two shots, whether there was a signal, whether it was an officer or a sergeant who gave the signal, and whether he was wearing a gas mask or not. On the key question of whether there was a reason for the soldiers suddenly to start shooting, the witnesses are almost all agreed: there was none." He quotes a Department of Justice conclusion: "At the time of the shooting, no student posed a threat to the lives of the guardsmen." So what happened and why?

One thing that became clear in my reading is the extent to which the Kent State campus, on the day of the shootings and those preceding it, was in turmoil. By invading Cambodia on May 1, the United States had escalated the war in Vietnam, after years of telling citizens that it was winding down. And in 1970, draftees were still going to the war and dying. In response, the Kent students, like those at many other campuses, had protested, although the marches down Main Street and the burning of the ROTC building had brought out the Ohio National Guard.

On May 4, to add to the atmosphere of chaos, the National Guard had fired off rounds of tear gas at the students and buzzed the demonstrations with an army helicopter, like those in *Apocalypse Now*. (Kilgore: "How're you feeling, Jimmy?" Door gunner: "Like a mean motherfucker, sir!")

In response to the tear gas, some students threw rocks at the troops, but not that many, and one guard senior officer, Major General Sylvester Del Corso, threw rocks back at the students (so much for professional crowd control). He said: "If those goddamn kids can throw rocks, I can, too."

Finally, at the time of the shooting, many guardsmen were wearing heavy rubber gas masks, giving them the appearance of ghouls and, more dangerously, cutting them off from understanding the general situation and hearing the orders from their officers.

Another variable that led to the violence was that the guardsmen were deployed not simply to protect campus buildings (which were not under any threat) or to end the protests (which would have been unconstitutional) but also to make a general political statement that the governor of Ohio would not tolerate such dissent. They were pawns in a reelection campaign game. Davies writes: "In essence, what Governor Rhodes had said to the guardsmen was: You men are up against the scum of America but be careful. They are vicious, organized, and dangerous. Your job is to protect the citizens of Kent and Portage County, where no one will be safe if we fail, and remember, your commanding officer has said, we can stop them with gunfire if necessary."[13]

In other words, the guardsmen (or at least some key leaders) were sent in spoiling for a fight. The head of the National Guard, General Canterbury, said before the shootings: "These students are going to have to find out what law and order is all about."

The most difficult event to comprehend in the lead-up to the shooting is what the National Guard discussed after they had been led up and down Pagoda Hill to a practice field on the far side of the campus. Put simply, the guard had marched themselves out of the demonstration. If what happened next wasn't so serious, it would have seemed burlesque to watch the guard march down the hill and

---

13: Kelner quotes a tape recording of Governor Rhodes's statement at the May 3 press conference advocating the use of all necessary force: "We are going to eradicate the problem. We are not going to treat the symptoms. . . .These people just move from one campus to another and terrorize the community. They are worse than the brownshirts and Communist element and also the night riders and the vigilantes. They are the worst type of people that we harbor in America. . . .There's no sanctuary for these people."

occupy a football field where there were no student protestors nearby.

On the practice field, well away from the demonstrations, some members of the two companies met in a huddle, as if calling a football play. What they discussed has never been revealed. In his history of the Kent shootings, James Michener writes: "We know almost exactly what happened, save the crucial matter of whether there was, at the practice field, any kind of order or agreement which triggered the firing a few moments later." Davies writes: "Had some of the guardsmen gotten together just minutes before the shooting and decided among themselves that upon a signal they would fire at the students who had been harassing them ever since they started out to disperse the noon rally of May 4?"

From their football huddle, the guardsmen marched back up Pagoda Hill above the Commons. At the top, however, they turned and fired some sixty-seven shots. At the subsequent trials, some guardsmen said that they felt threatened by the students. But Davies writes: "If the guardsmen's claim that a crowd was charging them to within ten, fifteen, twenty, and thirty feet was true, then obviously most of the casualties would have been less than two hundred feet away. Why were they shooting at students two hundred, three hundred, and four hundred feet away from them, distances that removed any danger whatever to the soldiers? . . . The closest person killed, Jeffrey Glenn Miller, was at least 85 yards away."

Davies quotes several conclusions from a US Justice Department report that "there was no sniper; that the guardsmen had not been surrounded; that they could have resorted to tear gas rather than shooting; that the rock throwing had not been as widespread or as dangerous as claimed by General Canterbury; that no guardsman had been seriously injured; and, finally, that the shooting was 'not proper and not in order.'"

Today, anyone wandering around the campus parking lot, as I was, and lining up where the individuals were killed against the location of the troops can only conclude that the guard fired blindly across a wide area—not unlike the police shooting in the Haymarket.

After the shootings, local, state, and national bodies conducted investigations and, in some cases, handed down indictments. As Kelner writes, however, "This special grand jury . . . indicted not the guardsmen, but twenty-four students and nonstudents and one professor and issued a report condemning students and the university administration." (File this under blame the victims.) One student charged said: "This isn't an accident case where someone has been run over by a car. We've been run over by the governor and the whole state of Ohio. Any jury we get is going to think of themselves as protecting Ohio against a bunch of Communist hippies."

This group came to be known as the Kent 25, although only five of those accused went to trial, all relating to the burning of the ROTC building on May 3, 1970. One nonstudent defendant was convicted on one charge. Two other nonstudents pleaded guilty to lesser charges. The rest of the charges against the others were dropped for lack of evidence. Later on, in other trials, evidence was presented that the National Guard and the local fire department had let the ROTC building (a temporary shelter dating to World War II) burn, so that the governor would have an excuse to crack down on the students and make his points in the press.[14]

The subsequent Kent State trial was a civil suit that the families of the killed and wounded brought against the National Guard and other officials. Kelner writes: "In some ways the trial was worse for them [the parents] than the nightmare of the five preceding years: the obscene letters, the telephoned threats, the alienation from neighbors and relatives, and the pain of empty rooms and old letters found unexpectedly at the bottom of a drawer."

Although the plaintiffs' lawyer was told, "You'll never get an Ohio jury to vote against the guardsmen," he presented a case with the latest forensic evidence that showed few students around the guard when it fired. He also argued, on behalf of his clients, that whoever had ordered the banning of the May 4 rally on campus had violated the students' First Amendment rights. In his opening argument he argued that "the photographic proof . . . showed that many of the statements . . . to validate the shooting were false and not worthy to believe." He also showed other pictures "showing that the guardsmen were neither surrounded nor menaced before they fired their weapons."

One witness for the plaintiffs showed photographic evidence "that the total number of students in front of the guardsmen as they fired, to a distance of 325 feet, was between 80 and 143 . . . The evidence of the film is that at no time before Troop G opened fire were they being approached by more than 17 students, that none of the approaching stu-

---

14: Early on the night it burned, the fire department had come and put out the fire. While the guard was surrounding the building, the fire reignited. Kelner later asked, "How was a building. . .guarded by police set on fire?"

dents was closer than 85 feet, and that 10 of them were more than 175 feet away."

More damning was the audio evidence introduced that showed sixty-seven shots were fired, "thirty-two of which came from M-1s. A minimum of three shots were fired from a 45 automatic, and there were at least two from a 12-gauge shotgun." Who was carrying a .45 automatic and a shotgun were never identified. The shooting lasted 12.53 seconds. Another witness said: "You do not act individually in military formation. You react to orders."

An expert witness for the plaintiffs was James F. Ahern, and he was a police chief in New Jersey. After analyzing the evidence in the case, he summarized well how to apportion blame in the shootings. According to Kelner, he blamed the following people:

- Governor Rhodes for authorizing that demonstrators be dispersed instead of protected, for leaving provocative armed guardsmen on the campus, and for inadequate assessment of intelligence
- General Del Corso for the loaded rifles, improper training, and inadequate assessment of intelligence
- General Canterbury for improperly ordering the dispersal of a nonviolent assembly, for leading the men to the practice field, for chasing a crowd after it had been dispersed, and for inadequate assessment of intelligence
- The officers on the field for inadequate control of their men
- The enlisted men for unauthorized and unjustified shooting

The case against the guard was dismissed, although the government later paid out a total of $675,000 to the wounded and the families of those killed. The value placed on the life of Alison Krause, one of two young women killed on the day and often shown in pictures of the shootings, was $15,000.

Unavailable to the plaintiffs in their case against the guardsmen was an audiotape, which surfaced only in 2007, that a Kent State student had recorded during the shootings. Alan Canfora discovered the so-called Strubbe tape, on which can be heard the commands "Guard!" and then after a short pause, "All right, prepare to fire!" I listened to the enhanced tape on YouTube, and I could clearly hear the words "prepare to fire!" Other words are harder to decipher. Nevertheless, the Department of Justice refused to reopen the case against the National Guard. Nor to my knowledge have any guardsmen confessed to receiving orders from their officers.

Missing from the exhibits on campus is the extent to which the Nixon administration in 1970 tried to blame all its problems in Vietnam on "campus bums." I thought about Nixon raging against students when I biked one more time across the Kent State battlefield and stood next to the hilltop pagoda, around which the National Guard was clustered when they fired.

In 1970 much of America wanted to believe that the fighting in Vietnam was just and that if only the students would put down their protest signs, the war could be won. As much as anything, that attitude doomed the slain students at Kent State, and the shootings could have happened at any campus in America. In the aftermath of the Kent State shootings, I remember many Americans saying that the students had "got what was coming to them," and that this was the fate of traitors.

May 1970 was an ugly moment in American history, with students dead on other campuses (Jackson State in Mississippi had a similar incident about the same time) and many other young Americans dead in Southeast Asia. That month in Vietnam, 428 US soldiers were killed in the fighting, and another 2,100 were seriously enough wounded to require hospitalization. Who remembers their names or that the protestors on campus were trying to bring them home? Or that it was the McKinley administration, from nearby Canton, that first took American arms and soldiers to Asia?

As Kipling wrote:

Take up the White Man's burden—
Send forth the best ye breed—
Go bind your sons to exile
To serve your captives' need;
To wait in heavy harness
On fluttered folk and wild—
Your new-caught, sullen peoples,
Half devil and half child.

Cleveland: Dollar Mark Hanna Goes for the Gold

I SPENT THAT NIGHT IN SHAKER HEIGHTS, with my boyhood friend Nick Lubar. We also turned back the calendar to 1970, although this time it was to recall getting our certificates that summer to work as lifeguards.

The drive from Kent should have been straightforward, but instead I made a wrong turn and embarked on a grand tour of Cleveland's inner-city neighborhoods, which have lost some of their luster since the McKinley administration, when John D. Rockefeller lived on Euclid Avenue. I am sure it didn't help my cause that I was using the map that came with the rental car, not one with any detail. A world globe might have been nearly as effective.

Nick was off the next morning to a sailing regatta, and I had to return the rental car. Before dropping it off, I had thought of driving to Mentor, Ohio, to see the home of James Garfield, who was assassinated in the first year of his presidency, 1881. The Internet, however, reported that the Garfield home was closed for renovations, and Nick told me that I would not see much, if anything, from the street. Besides, Mentor was a forty-minute drive from Cleveland, along Lake Erie. Instead, I contented myself with a drive-by visit to Garfield's tomb in Lake View Cemetery and a Mark Hanna statue in the University Circle neighborhood (through which I had been wandering the night before).

I found Mark Hanna seated on stone not far from the Cleveland Art Museum, Case Western Reserve University, and Lake View Cemetery. Almost more than downtown Cleveland, which is largely limited to office buildings, the Rock and Roll Hall of Fame, and some stadiums, University Circle is the cultural heart of Cleveland, so it makes sense that Hanna is here, presiding over the optimistic quarter of the city. Hanna "boomed" Cleveland the way Harding did Marion, but here he had more with which to work.

All I had to decode Hanna in bronze and stone was Thomas Beer's biography *Hanna*, published in 1929 and a favorite book of my friend Lewis Lapham's, of *Lapham's Quarterly*. For years Lewis "boomed" the biography of Hanna for its portrait of the Gilded Age and that of McKinley, but on several attempts, I had never gotten past page one hundred. I did like Beer's writing—his father had worked with and liked Hanna—but, living in Europe, I was distant from the robber-baron culture in Cleveland, until I made the turns through University Circle, and I could reread the biography as one might a friend's high school yearbook.

Beer starts his biography when Hanna (born in 1837) comes of age in the Civil War—he enlisted and toward the end guarded some forts near Washington, DC. Although Hanna was far from the drawing rooms of the Lincoln administration, Beer captures the side of the Civil War that was an elaborate craps game played by placemen who besieged the White House and overwhelmed the otherwise thrifty Lincoln. Beer describes the game:

> But the war's interior effect on American manners had no immediate students and certain modern writers seem to

> fancy that a period of corrupt legislation, fantastic morals in public affairs, and ethical sloth commenced only with the end of the war, as if Booth's bullet had released seven devils on the nation. Yet the Gilded Age set in with 1861; no phenomenon appeared after Mr. Lincoln's death that was not plain by the close of 1862, and of many concurrent phenomena during his presidency he, himself, was the innocent producer.

Of the war's end, Beer writes: "Looked at from this angle, the victory of the North in the American Civil War meant the economic victory of the concentrated energy of coal over the simple energy of the muscles." And he quotes John Hay, later secretary of state, on "the mob in Willard's Hotel, where 'you are mixed up with office seekers, wire pullers, inventors, artists, poets, prosers, clerks, diplomatists, mail contractors, railway directors, until your own identity is lost among them. . . . You adopt the universal habit of the place and call for a mint julep, a whisky skin, a gin cocktail, a brandy smash or a glass of Pure Old Rye.'"

After the war, as a young businessman in Ohio, Hanna was a work in progress, investing in oil refineries, rail spurs, and lake steamers, but never finding his voice among the affluent.

Ohio was the place to make both a fortune and a political career, and in another ten years of dealmaking, Hanna would be on a first name basis not just with Grant but with Hayes, Garfield, and later, of course, McKinley as well. Hanna got his political start gathering up contributions from the party faithful. As Beer writes: "Still, someone had to collect from the local committees. Mr. Hanna, genially persuasive, had been useful in 1876. He roamed northern

Ohio, smoking cigars, and collected. It was a weary job and it had no dignity. It was like the function of some trusted priest in the Middle Ages, arranging the loans of Holy Church to the Jews and Italian bankers. It was business to be done quietly, by a solid man."

According to Beer, Hanna understood that in the great American divide between silver and gold, it made sense to bet with the golden, hard-money men. Congressman Garfield, also from Cleveland, bemoaned the inflation that was a legacy of the Civil War. Beer quotes him saying: "We are cut off from the money currents of the world. Our currency resembles rather the waters of an artificial lake which lie in stagnation or rise to full banks at the caprice of the gatekeeper. Gold and silver abhor a depreciated paper money and will not keep company with it." Grant was elected in 1868 (Beer writes: "Next March, as per prophetic schedule, the first of Mr. Hawthorne's bulletheaded generals entered the White House"), but "amusement hunters, power-seekers, and orators swarmed on the guileless, tired soldier [Grant]." In the Gilded Age, according to Beer, "everyone was tired and wanted to be entertained."

Beer is sympathetic to Rutherford B. Hayes, but thinks he was unable to skate with the likes of Roscoe Conkling and James G. Blaine. Beer writes about Hayes: "He had not been President two weeks when a breach showed between the Executive Mansion and Capitol Hill, nor was it ever filled in with any help from General Hayes. He had a vanity, but it was not wide enough to hold much oil in the shape of flatteries dispensed by Roscoe Conkling: he did like to be called General." About Conkling Beer writes: "He had the kind of sarcasm which covers a shortage of real wit, and the effrontery of a practiced harlot. All this equipment was mottled and disfigured by the most humorless egoism. He liked power."

In the 1890s, Hanna found his calling as a kingmaker behind the scenes. (Beer writes, "Behind this apparatus was a point of reality: one might quietly rule in politics without being a politician. One might be an engineer.") Hanna liked McKinley as a man, and as an Ohio industrialist, he was happy to ride the hobbyhorse of the tariff. (Beer writes: "Tariff is a method of deliberated stealing from foreigners—that is, from a class of human beings in which the native has no sentimental interest.") And 1896 became his year, as Beer's father later told Theodore Roosevelt: "He has advertised McKinley as if he were a patent medicine!" Beer adds as an aside a conversation between his mother and Hanna's wife: "My mother asked her if Mr. Hanna had not great power over Mr. McKinley. Mrs. Hanna said that he had power, of a kind. I remember the qualifying phrase so distinctly."

Whatever the qualifier, Hanna understood the men dealing political cards in 1896 better than anyone else. He later said of Bryan: "Bryan's mistake . . . was a constant appeal to self-pity," although he probably agreed with him on the need to keep America away from imperial follies. Beer writes:

> He [Hanna] might have understood just the last sentence in William Sumner's arraignment of the colonial idea. "The notion is that colonies are glory. The truth is that colonies are burdens—unless they are plundered, and then they are enemies." This last he would have realized; he had been plundered. He was the enemy of the East, where all his good money, taken by the railroads, went to join the interest on his mortgage.

Much the way Otto von Bismarck hated the idea of colonies for Germany, so did Hanna recoil from the war with Spain, which was to be his undoing. Beer writes: "In June, John Pierpont Morgan sent an agent to Washington to represent to Mr. Hanna that a victory in Cuba might make Germany recoil. Mr. Hanna rudely answered that he was not in the victory business. Still, a victory was supplied."

The war showed that others besides Hanna had McKinley's ear. ("You have no idea," Abner McKinley, the president's brother, wrote on January 26, 1898, "of the pressure on William from religious people.") And the war brought to the fore the phenomenon of Theodore Roosevelt, who was everything Hanna abhorred in politics. Before he was, according to Beer, "an amusing oddity who could be jocosely presented to strangers as 'our police commissioner.' Now he was atop San Juan Hill and soon on the ticket with McKinley, despite Hanna's foreboding."

In the 1900 election, Hanna managed again to help McKinley defeat Bryan (Thomas Beer writes: "Mr. Bryan duly swarmed into sight, talking against imperialism, advocating more free silver, and, of course, anxious to preserve the nation from the Trusts"), but a year later Roosevelt was president and Hanna was eclipsed. Beer writes his political obituary:

> For all Americans are credulous about other Americans. As they had arranged a seraglio for Roscoe Conkling, delirium tremens for Grover Cleveland, originality and sincerity for William Bryan, and inhuman valor for Theodore Roosevelt, so they now built up an unqualified loathing of Marcus Hanna among the plain people.

> Dramatically, this should be. . . . Dollar Mark, the Red Boss of Cleveland, the fat brother of the Trusts in cartoons, was now to appear.

Hanna could have dealt with the insult of investigations, but not ridicule, and his several years in the Senate watching Roosevelt run the country were too much for him. He died in 1904 and is still scandalizing the nation with his 1899 observation that "all questions of government in a democracy were questions of money." Americans, I am sure, prefer something grander from a man sitting on marble.

Cleveland: James Garfield Takes One for the Team

ALTHOUGH LATER I WENT TO LONG BRANCH, New Jersey, where James Garfield died, and the battlefield at Chickamauga, where in the Civil War he was an aide-de-camp to General William Rosecrans, I feel now that I did not do justice to the life of the twentieth president. I missed his house in Mentor, Ohio, completely—although, for a change, that wasn't my fault—and all I did in Cleveland was drive by his tomb. But I could not face parking the car and climbing up a long set of stairs to look at his coffin. Houses I like; tombs less so.

Perhaps for those reasons I never could reconcile Garfield in my mind. Was he yet another malleable general there to do Grant's bidding in war and peace? Or was he his own man who, had he lived, would have bridged the divide that later stretched between Bryan and McKinley? For sure Garfield had many good qualities. He had steered Hayes into the White House, and he had a calming effect on the boisterous personalities around Grant. His record in the Civil War was exemplary. He was well read, humane, and had a close (non-Harding) relationship with his wife. On the downside, Chickamauga was a military disaster, and, as president, Garfield lacked the spine to drive a knife into the political back of Roscoe Conkling, whose forces, three months into Garfield's presidency, put a bullet into his.

For the record, the Garfield tomb is in Lake View Cemetery, near University Circle in Cleveland. It sits on a hill, and the dark, brooding stone gives it the feel of a marker over some Napoleonic battle. Garfield was brought here in the fall of 1881, after he died that September from the wounds he suffered at the hand of an assassin, the office-seeking, delusional Charles Guiteau. (He thought Garfield should make him the consul in Paris.) When he shot Garfield in the Baltimore and Potomac Railroad Station in Washington, DC, Guiteau shouted: "I did it. I will go to jail for it. I am a Stalwart and Arthur will be president," a reference to Chester Arthur, who spent most of his career as Conkling's bag man in the New York customs house.

With modern medicine, Garfield would have easily recovered. He died from an infection that his doctors caused, by probing for the bullet with unsanitized hands. The shot had missed all vital organs, and he would have been fine, except for the germs his doctors brought to the table. The reason he died in Elberon, next to Long Branch, New Jersey, is because his desperate wife, Lucretia, thought maybe the Atlantic sea air would help him recover.

Among the first to console the widow was Ulysses Grant, also then on vacation in Long Branch. She received him but silently recalled how wounded her husband had been when Grant tried to deny Garfield the nomination in 1880.

Garfield died at age forty-nine, which is relatively young for a politician, although by that time he had served four years in the Civil War, been a member of Congress for more than twenty years, was a confidant of presidents Grant and Hayes, and would have joined the Senate in 1881, had he not been elected president. In death, Garfield was also held up as an idealist in politics, someone who had taken on the bosses, notably Roscoe Conkling, and won. That said, many of the scandals after the Civil War came close to Garfield, and his idealism could also have been mistaken for naivete about his many benefactors.

Like Harrison and Hayes, Garfield raised a regiment of Ohio volunteers in the Civil War, and that allowed him to march toward the guns as a colonel, and not go over the top of the stockades as a private. Before the war, he had attended Hiram College and graduated from Williams, before reading law and being admitted to the bar. He was also active politically at an early age, and when home on medical leave during the war in 1862, he was elected to the House of Representatives (as was Harrison), which didn't hurt his chances of getting better assignments at the front.

Early in the war, Garfield led his brigade into action in Eastern Kentucky. On another trip I saw the plaque in Pound Gap (north of the Cumberland Gap over the Appalachians) that credits Garfield with driving the Confederates from Kentucky, an important goal for Lincoln in the Civil War. From there he served as a commander at Shiloh.

In 1863, when he was recovered from a long illness, Garfield fought in the bloody battle of Chickamauga, as aide-to-camp under General William Rosecrans. The battle would haunt Garfield and Rosecrans for the rest of their lives, political and otherwise.

Chattanooga, Tennessee: Garfield Checks Out of Chickamauga

Chickamauga is south of Chattanooga, to the east of Lookout Mountain and south from Missionary Ridge, and the entire area was a crucible of the Civil War until 1864. Under orders from Grant, who had been victorious at Vicksburg and promoted to the command of the western theater, Rosecrans had pursued the Confederate General Braxton Bragg south of Chattanooga, where the two armies met (facing east and west) along the banks of the Chickamauga Creek.

Garfield's job in the battle was to draft the orders that Rosecrans was issuing to his corps commanders, and, a careful writer and thorough soldier, Garfield did his job well. In the midafternoon, however, Rosecrans dispatched an order to General Thomas J. Wood through another subordinate, which read "The commanding general requests that you close up on Reynolds as fast as possible, and support him."

The problem with the orders was that, if Wood complied, he would leave a gap in the front line and move his troops illogically to another sector. Rather than disobey an order, he followed the instructions, withdrew from the front lines, and opened a divide through which Confederate General James Longstreet (Grant's best man!) poured eight divisions.

Instead of a closely contested battle, Chickamauga became a Southern rout that was only stanched when General George Thomas held the Union lines on what became known as Horseshoe Ridge. Meanwhile, seeing his line breached, Rosecrans left the field of battle, with Garfield trailing behind him.

When it became known that Thomas was still fighting for his life on Horseshoe Ridge while Rosecrans was back in Chattanooga, the Union command was shaken. What saved Garfield from ignominy in this retreat was that he rode back to Chickamauga, with Rosecrans's blessing, and ordered General Thomas to take command of the battle, which he did, successfully.

From that day forward, Rosecrans, who had his own political aspirations, and Garfield would be estranged—each blaming the other for the bungled orders to Wood, the collapse in the line, and the retreat from the enemy.

Rosecrans would never recover his reputation. Grant relieved him, but in 1880, in the same election that saw Garfield elected president, Rosecrans was elected to the House of Representatives from California, and he would have been among those mourning the dead president in September 1881.

After the war, Garfield remained in Congress and added to his portfolio a lucrative legal career. During the administration of Andrew Johnson, however, Garfield was entrapped in the Crédit Mobilier scandal, which involved the front company of the Union Pacific Railroad, padded invoices that ran into the millions, and shares in the company sold below cost to members of Congress, including—maybe—to James Garfield. James G. Blaine, Garfield's mentor in Congress, deflected the same charges, but Garfield had to duck and weave before a congressional investigation. He was exonerated, although only in the lax climate of the times, by arguing that certain payments had been "loans," although the take of Charles Francis Adams on the scandal was more decided. He wrote of Crédit Mobilier:

> The members are in Congress; they are trustees for the bondholders; they are directors; they are stockholders; they are contractors; in Washington they vote the subsidies, in New York they receive them, upon the plains they expend them, and in the "Crédit Mobilier" they divide them.

Garfield's relations with President Ulysses S. Grant were close, even though he resented, after the relief of General Rosecrans at Chickamauga, that Grant chose to replace the commanding general with General Thomas (the so-called "Rock of Chickamauga") and not the fleet-footed Garfield. Nevertheless, as a player in the Ohio congressional delegation, Garfield served Grant well, in particular, in steering through legislation that would link the American dollar to gold. Garfield also took some heat in the "salary grab" scandal, in which raises for members of Congress and the president were backdated to 1871. Garfield's congressional committee had approved the structure of the deal.

Garfield was also a key operative in the Hayes presidential campaign of 1876, helping first to secure the nomination for Hayes (after Garfield's man Blaine ran out of steam) and then wheeling and dealing in Congress to see that the hastily formed Electoral Commission would elect Hayes as president. (Uncomfortably for Garfield, Roscoe Conkling had also played an important hand in electing Hayes.) Hayes wanted Garfield for his cabinet, but Garfield demurred. Hayes tried to persuade Garfield to run for Ohio governor in 1878, as a stepping-stone to the White House, but Garfield preferred to run for the Senate, and would have been seated there in 1881, had he not been elected to the presidency.

Cleveland: The Republicans Serve Garfield from a Poisoned Chalice

More than any of the post–Civil War elections, the race in 1880—at least that for the Republican nomination—brought out the many factions in the party. Garfield went to the convention pledged to support Senator John Sherman, also from Ohio, but came away, after thirty-six ballots, with the nomination for himself. Among those who contested the election were Grant, Blaine, and Sherman.

Only after thirty-four ballots did Garfield get more than two votes. By the last, he had 399 and the nomination. Although he won the electoral vote comfortably (214 to 155), his margin in the popular vote against Democrat Winfield Scott Hancock (a corps commander at Gettysburg) was 1,898 votes (out of about nine million cast). Unfortunately for Garfield, he had to deal with the devil (Conkling) to win the election, and that bedfellow cost him his life.

The best history of the 1880 election that I have come across is Kenneth Ackerman's *Dark Horse: The Surprise Election and Political Murder of President James A. Garfield.* A long-time staffer on Capitol Hill, Ackerman prefaces a long account of Garfield's assassination with a description of how rivalries within the Republican party—involving Grant, Conkling, and Blaine—spilled over into the election and the Garfield presidency.

With Grant and Blaine stalemated at the convention, Garfield emerged as the dark horse, but for him to win in

November, he was forced to accept Chester Arthur as his vice presidential candidate and grovel at the so-called Fifth Avenue Summit, at which he agreed, according to Ackerman, to "consult with [Conkling's] friends and do only what was approved by them." That bargain allowed Garfield to carry New York and the election, but when he appointed an enemy of Conkling's to the customs house (where all the money was), the Stalwarts (as Conkling's loyalists were known) vowed revenge.

The 1880 Republican convention was especially vitriolic. Ackerman writes about Blaine's early successes:

> Reluctant candidate or not, Blaine had succeeded remarkably in 1880. Even running against a living legend like Ulysses Grant and weighed down by old scandals, Blaine had attracted enormous national support. He championed hard money (backed by gold), support for business enterprise, a strong tariff to protect American jobholders, Irish independence, and a stiff backbone against the old Confederacy—what some called "bloody shirt" politics, exploiting old Civil War passions long after Appomattox, but what Blaine touted as loyalty to Republican values of Union and civil rights for freed blacks.

In his way for the nomination was Grant, the first president in the republic to seek more than the two terms that George Washington had set as a precedent. Conkling was Grant's man at the convention, and, according to Ackerman, he played to the crowds. He writes of the first ballot:

> Conkling waited, then began to build the crowd's energy with a parade of cascading metaphors. "The election

before us is to be the Austerlitz of American politics," he said, "it will decide for many years whether the country will be Republican or Cossack." Quickly he turned to his candidate. "New York is for Ulysses S. Grant. Never defeated—never defeated in peace or in war, his name is the most illustrious borne by living man."

In praising Grant, Conkling made sure to run down Blaine—the friends of Ulysses Grant, he said, "have never threatened to bolt unless the convention did as they say," unlike "the charlatans, jayhawkers, tramps, and guerrillas—the men who deploy between the lines, forage now on one side and then on the other."

Later it would be Blaine who would push the nomination away from Grant and Conkling, and to his protégé Garfield. Ackerman adds: "The thirty-six ballots of 1880 stand as a record, the most ever cast to choose a Republican nominee for president, far more than the second- and third-longest Republican face-offs: ten ballots to choose Warren Harding in 1920 and eight to nominate Benjamin Harrison in 1888."

More ominously, Ackerman writes that "Grant never sent Garfield any congratulations at all: no telegram, no letter, no private message." That omission should have put Garfield on guard, but he was out of his depth.[15] Senator Henry Dawes of Massachusetts said: "Garfield is a grand, noble fellow, but fickle, unstable, [with] more brains, but no such will as Sherman, brilliant like Blaine, but timid and hesitating. It

15: One biographer wrote: "Grant, it was widely remarked, stood for nothing but himself."

has saved us from the third term and its jackals." But he could not save himself.

As president, Garfield lost an early showdown with Conkling and Arthur. Ackerman describes the humiliation: "The party boss finally had wrested control of New York patronage away from the president. Within hours, Half-Breeds [followers of Blaine] and moderate journals in New York, Boston, and Philadelphia began a drumbeat of dismay. It was 'weakness,' 'surrender,' and 'ingratitude.' There had been pressure, and weak-willed Garfield, the accidental president with no mind of his own, had crumbled." In such a test, Garfield had no choice but to fight back. As he liked to say: "I will not compromise with traitors."

Ackerman makes the fight between the president and the New York party sound fair, almost noble, but Conkling held all the high cards, and Garfield was stuck playing a losing hand. Ackerman writes:

> As president of a great country, once he'd made a decision, even a close, dubious one, he [Garfield] had to stick with it. People respected backbone, and without their respect his authority meant nothing. Garfield could no longer live with Roscoe Conkling's petulant demands hanging over his presidency. Conkling could not be dealt with nor tolerated. If that meant political war, then he had no choice but to fight it.

At the beginning of his administration, the clueless Garfield, hoping to keep everyone under the same tent, had even proposed bringing both Conkling and Blaine into the cabinet, by giving Blaine Treasury and Conkling State. Blaine exploded: "His appointment would act like strychnine upon your Administration—first bring contortions, and then be followed by death." Even without Conkling in Garfield's cabinet, the results were the same. Several months later Garfield was shot down in a Washington, DC, train station.

While I have never read anything that proved Conkling had any direct involvement in Guiteau's assassination of Garfield, he was the beneficiary of the shooting, and such was his influence among the Stalwarts that it was hardly necessary for him to order the hit, so clear would his intensions have been understood among the faithful.

The spot in Elberon, near Long Branch, New Jersey, where Garfield died, is now marked with a small headstone on a beach road that states: "Died on this site September 19, 1881." Ackerman wrote a fuller epitaph when he pointed out: "Garfield had made a bargain [at the political convention] in Chicago; the presidency for himself and the vice presidency for the Stalwarts. The Stalwarts had won the second spot on the ticket. To redeem the bargain's value, one simply had to remove the holder of the first spot." That's what happened.

Cleveland: Amtrak Runs Away from the Rails

By Sunday afternoon, I was back on the bike, riding around Cleveland and out to Chagrin Falls, for lunch with a teacher from my high school. Anyone who thinks Ohio is flat should climb the last hill on the way into Chagrin Falls from the west.

I had last been in a class with Robbie Thomas in 1972, but we picked up the conversation as though I was just back from spring break. Next time, he said, he would take me around Akron, where he had grown up and just finished writing a book, *Our Mister Ensworth*, about an influential teacher he had in high school. Sitting at lunch with him and his wife, Becky, I hoped someday I could do the same for him.

My Amtrak train for Buffalo was scheduled to leave from downtown Cleveland at 5:55 a.m., but before I began setting up alarms around my guest room, I had a text message from the railroad, saying the *Lake Shore Limited* would be forty-five minutes late. That delay meant I could sleep in until 5 a.m. and take a commuter train to Tower City Center, from where it would be a short ride to the Amtrak station near Lake Erie.

By the time I showed up at the station, the train was scheduled to be two hours late, which meant that I had time to bike around downtown Cleveland (the sunrise along the lake was stunning) and buy breakfast from a diner. Even after all that touring, when I got back to the station, the train was announced as three hours late. Finally it showed up around 9 a.m., although it never moved until three that afternoon, putting us into Buffalo nine hours behind schedule, around 6 p.m.

Only once in my life—on a night train in Bulgaria—had I ever been so late on the rails. On that occasion, I had a berth in a sleeping car and didn't mind the delay. Here, like the rest of the passengers on the train, I spent the day pacing up and down the platform, reading, and working on my computer.

The given reasons for the delay varied. Amtrak said it was "holding signals." A rumor on the platform said the problem was with CSX, which owns the tracks. I liked the theory of someone in the train diner, who said that thieves in Cleveland liked to steal copper wires from the signals and sell the valuable metal on black markets. The shame was that I missed all my appointments in Buffalo, where a friend had waited for me at the station, at least for a few hours.

Just before arriving in Buffalo, we passed the wreck of the Penn-Central, in the form of the Buffalo Central Terminal, the grandiose station of the New York Central that now lies in ruins.

Amtrak stopped using the terminal in 1979, and in the 1980s, Conrail—the successor company to Penn-Central—sold the station to speculators, who stripped it of its architectural details, leaving the station an empty monolith. The only reason is wasn't torn down is because no one had the money to do so, and later because it was given landmark status. Now owned by the Central Terminal Restoration Corporation, a nonprofit company that is seeking the money to redo it as an arts complex, the station is occasionally open for tours and events and always open for fundraising, which the new owners do well.

Amtrak now uses two stations in Buffalo, but the *Lake Shore Limited,* even when nine hours late, only stops at Dick Street in Depew, a Buffalo suburb about eight miles from downtown. The new Amtrak station, like so many in the system, looks like a dry cleaning establishment, while, in its heyday, Central Terminal had the soaring elegance of Istanbul's Blue Mosque.

Happy finally to be off the train, I unfolded my bike in Depew and decided that I would ride into Buffalo and defiantly make my planned tour at night. At 9 a.m. the previous morning, my friend Earl McElfresh had waited for my train, hoping to show me the historic sites around Buffalo. He's an expert on American history—also one of the country's finest Civil War mapmakers—and I had briefed him on the places I wanted to see. But he had now long since departed. I knew the places in Buffalo I wanted to see and that the bike would take me to them, even though nearly all would be closed. At least, I figured, the stone showing where McKinley was assassinated would be "open."

While putting together the bike, I stood with a British man who was riding his bike across the United States and now on his way to Niagara Falls. Unfortunately Amtrak had lost or (as the conductor said) "misplaced" his bike. I thought of helping him deal with Amtrak's bureaucracy, but there wasn't much I could do, so I wished him well and biked into the setting sun.

Buffalo, New York:
Fleeing Demons Along Broadway

ACCORDING TO A MAP that I had carried in my saddlebag (better than anything I found in Ohio), I could ride west along Ellicott Road to Broadway and that would take me directly into downtown Buffalo.

Because it was still rush hour when I started and Ellicott is a major road, I stuck to a sidewalk and rode in front of suburban malls. Later, around North Ogden Street, the neighborhood changed to an inner-city slum, although one made up of small frame houses, not high-rise projects.

After a few miles, it was close to dark. I was hungry and felt increasingly lost, although on the horizon I could see the glittering towers of downtown Buffalo. From my map, I sensed that Broadway did run into the city, but in places it would shift directions.

During one map consultation, a teenager, also on a bike, came up to me and said, "Gimme that fucking bike." Saying nothing, I looked at him and his old bike, and in a flash I was sprinting down the road away from him. I didn't think his bike was up to the chase. Nor did I think he had a gun.

For a circus bike, the Brompton can push a big gear. He gave a half-hearted chase, for a block or two. I weaved along Broadway (Tour de France sprint style) until he faded in the distance.

A few minutes later, panting heavily, I was in the empty canyons of downtown Buffalo after dark. I found a hotel (and not a cheap one at that), left my bags in the room, and went out in search of William McKinley, Theodore Roosevelt, Mark Twain, and Grover Cleveland, all of whose ghosts haunt the once-great city.

Buffalo is relatively small and the bike worked well for getting me around, although when I stopped a taxi to ask directions to the McKinley marker on Fordham Road, the driver tried to talk me out of it, saying: "I wouldn't go there in this cab."

Fortunately, I ignored him, and I rode up elegant Delaware Avenue until I cut west toward Buffalo State University (which was swaddled in spotlights and gleaming in the darkness) and crossed a river on Elmwood Avenue. From there, despite all the forebodings of the cab driver, it was two short blocks to the place where in September 1901 anarchist Leon Czolgosz assassinated McKinley at the Pan-American Exposition while the president was greeting the public.

Buffalo: William McKinley Dies of Revolutionary Fever

THE MARKER IS ATTACHED to a rock that sits in the median of a street in an affluent suburb. It reads: "In the Pan-American Temple of Music which covered this spot President William McKinley was fatally shot Sept. 6, 1901."

Ida McKinley hated to be apart from her husband but chose not to make the quick trip with him to Buffalo. In turn, McKinley had said he would only be gone a short while.

The motives of McKinley's assassin were never very clear. At his trial, the interest was in convicting him and packing him off to his execution (all in about sixty days), not in delving into his mystical, revolutionary beliefs.

Of Polish origin but living in Cleveland, Czolgosz had converted to anarchism through the words of Emma Goldman, whom he heard speak shortly before he killed McKinley. He said: "Miss Goldman's words went right through me, and when I left the lecture I had made up my mind that I would have to do something heroic for the cause I loved."

Like terrorists today, anarchists at the turn of the twentieth century believed in what they called "the propaganda of the deed," which more often than not was a prime-time killing—as was the case with the anarchist bomber who killed Czar Alexander II on the waterfront in St. Petersburg. Czolgosz would also have been sympathetic to the working men shot down in the Haymarket or during the Homestead Strike (between steelworkers and Andrew Carnegie). A few days before the shooting, Czolgosz had bought a pistol that, he said, he thought "would look good in a museum."[16]

He fired two bullets at McKinley. One lodged in his abdomen; the other missed. After shooting McKinley, Czolgosz said to one of the men who subdued him: "I done my duty." When word of the shooting reached Mark Hanna, he said: "Now that damn cowboy will be president of the United States."

When McKinley was shot, "that damn cowboy" was on vacation in the Adirondacks. He rushed to the side of the president, who showed some signs of recovering, so Roosevelt returned to his vacation. Eight days later, the president died, and TR returned to Buffalo to take the oath of office. Again, modern medicine would have allowed him to recover.

On my bike, I found the elaborate house, with a front portico and columns, where Roosevelt took the oath of office in September 1901. It's now called the Theodore Roosevelt Inaugural National Historic Site. As a Peeping Tom of tourism, I yet again looked through the windows of a closed museum and, this time, saw a book-lined library and an elegant parlor.

The house had belonged to a Buffalo lawyer, Ashley Wilcox, when it was used to swear in TR. At midcentury, the house fell into ruin (despite its location in downtown Buffalo), and only in 1966 were funds appropriated for it to be

---

16: A replica of the Czolgosz pistol is on display in the McKinley Museum while the original is in the Buffalo Historical Museum around the corner from where McKinley was shot. Buzz and Larry asked if I would put in a word with the folks in Buffalo for them to send the original pistol to the McKinley Museum, but Amtrak kept me from that appointed round.

done up as a national historic site. I doubt Hanna would have given to the cause.

In the small world of presidential politics, when he was in Buffalo, Roosevelt made his headquarters at the Buffalo Club, which was nearby and easy to find on the bike. It was illuminated with spotlights and had the appearance of an elegant bed-and-breakfast. Millard Fillmore, from East Aurora, a Buffalo suburb, was its first president in 1867, and Grover Cleveland was later a member.

Just down the street from the Inaugural Site is the address of Mark Twain's house in Buffalo. He lived at 472 Delaware, in another splendid mansion of the period. The family of Clemens's wife, Olivia Langdon, gave the couple this house in 1871, just after their marriage, when Clemens was hired to work for the *Buffalo Express* newspaper. The house was torn down in the 1960s, when so much of old Buffalo was in ruins. In 1960, a local Mark Twain society had tried to raise $100,000 to save the property, but it failed. No wonder Twain wrote in *Autobiography,* "It is less trouble and more satisfaction to bury two families than to select and equip a home for one."

Buffalo: Grover Cleveland's Dating Game

Another house on my tour that night belonged to Grover Cleveland, who was sheriff (1871–73) and mayor (1882) of Buffalo before serving as governor of New York from 1883 to 1885. He was president from 1885 to 1889 and again from 1893 to 1897. Harrison was president during the interregnum, and McKinley took his place in 1897.

The Cleveland house stands at 51 Johnson Park, although it took me a few tries to find the cul-de-sac. No plaque marks the house, and it remains a private residence, as best as I could figure. The only giveaway that Cleveland had lived there was the presidential bunting that hung from the second floor. Some owner subsequent to Cleveland also added White House columns to the front porch. The house is small and squeezed into a narrow lot, and it speaks to Cleveland's modesty.

The only other Buffalo memorial to Grover Cleveland is a statue near Niagara Square, which is at the heart of Buffalo's government and city hall. I biked there from Johnson Park, pedaling through the canyons of the empty downtown district at night. I was the only one about, except for a slow-motion police car. On the back of the statue there is a quote from Cleveland, who says: "I have tried so hard to do right."

On an empty square in downtown Buffalo, I wasn't prepared for Grover Cleveland's earnest confessions or even to discover that so much of his political life was set in Buffalo. I had pegged him as a New Jersey man. His birthplace home, now a modest museum, is in Caldwell, New Jersey, and once with my father I found the house in Princeton (behind Nassau Street) where Cleveland had lived in retirement. It, too, remains a private residence. Instead, I now realized that he was Buffalo's president, even though the city has him locked away in remote corners.

While in Buffalo and even after he was elected president, Cleveland was a bachelor and rarely gave much thought to how and where he lived, which may explain why he's one of the few former presidents who is without a library museum or a presidential site. All Teddy Roosevelt did in Buffalo was take the oath of office, and he has been rewarded with a National Park Service–maintained house. By contrast, Cleveland was Buffalo's mayor and from the city became governor and president, yet his only remembrance is an obscure statue near City Hall. For a big man, he left a small footprint.

Again, I blamed Amtrak for my Cleveland ignorance. Had I arrived at 9 a.m., not 6 p.m., I would have toured with Earl and maybe found a Cleveland expert somewhere in the historical society. Or perhaps I would have tracked down a Cleveland biography in a local bookstore. Instead, I felt that I had come late to class without having done the reading. My only consolation was that Buffalo didn't seem to care much for the local connection to its president.

Cleveland was the only Democratic president between James Buchanan and Woodrow Wilson, unless Andrew Johnson, who ran with the Republican Lincoln, counts as a Democrat. All the other presidents between 1860 and 1913 were Republicans, and many of the "bullet-headed" Ohio general variety.

The problem with judging Cleveland is that he was often a sheep in wolf's clothing. One biography calls him "a Bourbon who stood neither for reform nor against it." And just when you are sure that Cleveland was a Democratic reformer, he does something like call out the troops to put down the Pullman strike. Eugene Debs campaigned three times for Cleveland, but he became embittered over the president's armed suppression of labor and eventually went his separate way.

Nor do Cleveland's White House policies align with his reputation as someone who took on civil service reform, tackled the Republican bosses, and pulled back on American expansionism.

For example, even more than his interloper Benjamin Harrison, Cleveland was a hard-money man who hated the Silverites (William Jennings Bryan included, later on). He thought the McKinley tariff excessive, but still he supported protection for American industry. In terms of government spending, his positions were close to Ronald Reagan's, famously vetoing additional pensions for Civil War veterans. Many of his supporters, so-called Gold Democrats, left the party in the 1896 election and voted for McKinley. Cleveland said nothing during the election, which helped to doom Bryan.

For all his talk about financial responsibility in government, Cleveland presided over the Panic of 1893 and left a deficit in 1897. He warned of going abroad, as John Quincy Adams had said, "in search of monsters," and refused to go along with a commercial cabal that was for annexing Hawaii.

But the warships that were built during his heady naval expansion came in handy when McKinley lowered the boom on Spain. And during the McKinley administration, when teetotalers confronted Hanna about the glories of Prohibition, he would answer by quoting Cleveland: "If you suppress the use of alcohol in America, you must seize Canada or build a string of forts all along the Canadian border."

In foreign affairs, it counts somewhat against Cleveland's record that at the Berlin Conference in 1884–85, his administration embraced King Leopold of Belgium as the rightful ruler of the Congo. In his time, Leopold would preside over the deaths of some ten million Congolese.

Biographies about Cleveland tend to portray him as either a saint or a sinner, and there is not much in between. Well after the fact, H. L. Mencken liked Cleveland and gave his reputation a boost when he wrote:

> We have had more brilliant Presidents than Cleveland, and one or two who were considerably more profound, but we have never had one, at least since Washington, whose fundamental character was solider and more admirable. Put beside him, even Lincoln begins to look a bit pliant and irresolute: as for Roosevelt and Wilson, they become limber mountebanks, worked by strings. There was never any string tied to old Grover.

Another of Cleveland's hagiographers, Professor Allen Nevins, writes: "He possessed honesty, courage, firmness, independence, and common sense. But he possessed them to a degree other men do not."

The reason I think history has not been kinder to Cleveland is because the public never could grasp some of his inner motivations. He would often say one thing and do another.

For example, he championed open, transparent government—and in the White House often answered his own telephone—but then he hid a possible cancer operation on his jaw by having it done in secret on a yacht in Long Island Sound and later telling the public that he had two teeth removed.

And Cleveland's love of country rings slightly hollow when you read that he paid $150 to George Benninsky, a Polish immigrant, to serve in his place in the Civil War.

Finally, there are Cleveland's relations with women and his child born out of wedlock who in the 1884 election spawned James G. Blaine's ditty, "Ma, Ma, where's my Pa?" (After the election, Cleveland supporters liked to chuckle, "Gone to the White House, ha ha ha!") In fact, the story behind the son that Cleveland conceived in 1873 with a Buffalo salesclerk, Maria Halpin, is darker than a campaign smear.

A new book on the subject by Charles Lachman, *A Secret Life: The Lies and Scandals of President Grover*, argues that after a chance meeting on the street and an oyster dinner with the thirty-seven-year-old Buffalo lawyer and promising politician, Cleveland forced himself on the woman, who subsequently became pregnant. Lachman reports:

> Cleveland sexually assaulted her . . . "[b]y use of force and violence and without my consent," . . . adding that when she threatened to notify the authorities, Cleveland . . . "told me he was determined to ruin me if it cost him $10,000, if he was hanged by the neck for it. I then and there told him that I never wanted to see him again [and] commanded him to leave my room, which he did."

Cleveland loyalists later said that he acknowledged paternity of the child in an honorable way, not because he was sure he was the father, but because the three other men also seeing Miss Halpin at the time were married. One of them was his close friend Oscar Folsom, whose daughter Cleveland would one day marry.

The child was given the name Oscar Folsom Cleveland, but he was forcibly taken from his mother and made a ward of the Buffalo Orphan Asylum. For her part and against her will, Maria was bundled off to the Providence Lunatic Asylum, where medical evaluations proved her only illness was that she had fallen afoul of Buffalo's male elite.

On her release, Halpin had to live only with the stigma, painted by Cleveland and his pals, that she was an alcoholic tramp who used sex to chase powerful men. It was a smear tactic worthy of the Clintons in the 1992 election, and later, when Cleveland was running for president, it explained away how the clean-living, good government, reformist politician bachelor, Grover the Good, had become ensnared in a honey trap—he fell for the bait.

Cleveland's romance with and marriage to Frances Folsom, Oscar's daughter, was presumably less violent than his encounter with Halpin but still not without a degree of creepiness. Oscar died in a carriage accident in 1875, when Frances was eleven, and Cleveland, as her father's lawyer and best friend, looked after the girl's trust and financial affairs. He had known her since she was born.

Frances was in college in upstate New York when Cleveland was elected president, and shortly thereafter—according to the official history—he received permission from her mother to write letters to her. A year later, in 1886, Cleveland married Frances. He was forty-nine, and she was twenty-one. By all accounts, it was a happy marriage that produced five children, including their daughter "Baby" Ruth, who gave her name to a candy bar and a baseball slugger.

While living in retirement in the house behind Nassau Street, Cleveland died in 1908. He was buried in Princeton, not Buffalo. He remained active in his retirement and consulted some with President Teddy Roosevelt, but one of the few public stances he took was to come out against women's suffrage, saying: "sensible and responsible women do not want to vote. The relative positions to be assumed by men and women in the working out of our civilization were assigned long ago by a higher intelligence."

Maybe there are local reasons why he's the forgotten man in Buffalo?

Olean: Only Men with Maps Won the Civil War

UNDER MY ORIGINAL, PRE-AMTRAK SCHEDULE, I was to spend the next morning riding my bike south from Buffalo to East Aurora, where I had an interview with the head of the Millard Fillmore Museum. (In the 1858 senatorial election, Lincoln's people said: "our whole problem there [in the decisive central Illinois counties] has been & is Fillmoreism.")[17]

Instead, because the day before I had left my friend Earl McElfresh sitting for hours at the Amtrak Depew station, I decided to bypass East Aurora and Fillmoreism, and head on the bus straight to Olean, where he lives and works.

The Coach USA bus left the Buffalo terminal at 7:30 a.m. By now I was a pro at loading my bicycle onto a bus, and the driver never said a word. The route south went through East Aurora (I looked for the Fillmore house but didn't see it), Arcade, and Machias, but mostly what I remember is that the leaves were beginning to turn color in the autumn sunshine.

Olean, where we arrived at 9:45 a.m., is a pretty town that lies on the back roads of upstate New York, between Binghamton and Buffalo. I pushed my bike from where the bus dropped me, and found Earl in the office of McElfresh

---

17: Whigs in 1856 had supported Fillmore, who ran for president on the ticket of the independent American Party, also called the "Know-Nothing Party." It was a nativist party and a successor to the Native American Party. Apologists for Fillmore said he was unaware of the party's xenophobic views when he agreed to run on the ticket. I had hoped a visit to East Aurora would clear up this hanging chad of the 1856 election, but it was not to be.

Map Company, on the main street. There I apologized for his Amtrak stranding in Buffalo the day before, and then turned on my tape recorder to pick his fine mind about the Civil War, a subject he has been studying since college in the 1970s.

Earl's fascination with the Civil War began when a friend in the 1970s took him to Gettysburg. Since then, he has filled his waking hours, not to mention his houses, with histories of the Civil War, and that led him to form the McElfresh Map Company, which produces maps of the battlefields that show them in their original state (not as they are today remembered by the Park Service).

In explaining what led to this calling, he described the experience of finding William Frassanito's *Antietam: The Photographic Legacy of America's Bloodiest Day*, looking at the pictures "then and now," comparing them to maps of the battlefield, and realizing that the maps in his hand were wrong.

To make his maps as accurate as possible, Earl visits the town of the battle, goes to the local survey office, talks to agronomists about local crops, researches pictures in the Library of Congress or elsewhere, and consults the memoirs of soldiers who fought there. (He once got aerial pictures of a battlefield to search for a road he sensed had been there in the 1860s that had vanished from the maps.) He said it was amazing how much variance there is between the battlefields we know today at Gettysburg, Antietam, Vicksburg, and so on, and what they would have looked like in the 1860s. He laughed when I asked him whether Gettysburg got its multimillion-dollar visitors center before or after the fighting.

Because Earl has spent his lifetime reading about the Civil War, I asked him what he thought were the best books about specific generals on each side. He said Lloyd Lewis, with help from Bruce Catton, had written the best biography of General Grant. Volume one is called *Captain Sam Grant*, and it ends in 1861. He likes Douglas Southall Freeman's multivolume biography of Robert E. Lee, and James I. Robertson Jr.'s account of Thomas "Stonewall" Jackson.

Earl had less good things to say about Joshua Lawrence Chamberlain (commander of the Twentieth Maine at Gettysburg and the hero of Little Round Top), feeling he invented the story about the salute Union soldiers gave to Confederates at Appomattox.[18]

When I asked, Earl said that the best books about the Civil War are those written before the photocopy machine was invented. "Now," he said, "I just get the feeling books are endless quotes, connected by an 'and' or a 'but.'" He does like James McPherson's one-volume history, *Battle Cry of Freedom*, saying, "He covered everything, not just the battles."

The best part of our conversation was when Earl used what I would call his "mapmaker's perspective" on the Civil War to argue that when generals used their intelligence corps and cavalry groups to draft accurate maps, good things usually followed in battle. When troops had no maps or bad ones, they tended to lose. He went further in saying he had less respect for Southern generals, describing how

---

18: My wife's great-uncle commanded I Company, Twentieth Maine, at Little Round Top, and served under Chamberlain. But I had always wondered about the Appomattox story, which appears in Chamberlain's memoirs about the end of the war. He writes: "At such a time and under such conditions I thought it eminently fitting to show some token of our feeling, and I therefore instructed my subordinate officers to come to the position of 'salute' in the manual of arms as each body of the Confederates passed before us." Great imagery and story, but, alas, according to Earl, not true.

they often won "in their own backyards" (Bull Run or First Manassas) but lost decisively when they were out of their comfort zones (Antietam or Gettysburg). He quoted an aide to Robert E. Lee as saying that Confederate soldiers were half as effective north of the Potomac as they were to the south, and says of Stonewall Jackson's flanking operation at Chancellorsville that "he knew that little road" while the Union forces did not. He also said that one of Lee's key mapmakers, possibly Jedediah Hotchkiss, was unavailable after Chancellorsville and that Lee never properly replaced him. Earl criticized Lee for not bringing with him proper maps of southern Pennsylvania and says that when his army of the Potomac crossed its namesake river in June 1863, "it was lost. He didn't know where he was, and he could not ask the locals for help." Call this the mapmaker view of history, but it makes perfect sense.

I asked Earl, based on his mapmaking and study of the Civil War, which generals he had come to admire. He began by saying, "Grant and Sherman were the two great generals of the war." He didn't think Sherman was as violent as history has described him ("he never went after civilians"), and that coming into the war, he was the Union general with the most sympathy for the South, having lived there. About the others in the Civil War, he had this to say:

- Of Robert E. Lee, Earl said he was "a great tactician, but a terrible strategist. He lost too many men to stay in the war. He should have followed George Washington's lead. Washington lost every battle but won the war. Lee won every battle, or almost, and lost the war." If the fighting had dragged on and if Lee had adopted a purely defensive strategy ("a porcupine in a ball"), he believes that the North would have given up the war.

• On Lincoln, he said: "I think if Jefferson Davis had been president of the Union, and Lincoln had been the commander in chief of the Confederacy, that the South would have won the war. I have no question about that. Lincoln was a true genius."

• On the South, he said, "I think the leadership in the South was a terrible case of arrested development." His point was that Southern culture, dependent on tradition and slavery, was such that no one had ever questioned the leading politicians or generals. He said: "Many in the South didn't have to grow up. These people were immature."

• On Grant, he said: "People forget, but when he was just a lowly brigadier general, people would find him studying maps of the entire war. He was thinking big, right from the beginning."

After our conversation, I went with Earl in his car to drop his daughter off at college. St. Bonaventure University is right in Olean, and I liked seeing the campus. Then I said goodbye to him, and I waited on North Union Street for my friend Tom Leonard to collect me for the drive to Elmira, New York, to see where Mark Twain wrote many of his celebrated novels and stories.

Ithaca: The Burned-Over District

In my original plan, I would have taken the Coach USA bus from Olean to Elmira and met Tom at the center there for Mark Twain studies. Instead, because of my lost Amtrak day, I had missed the daily bus that connects those towns. Tom had no choice but to drive west and collect me. Once again, I regretted that the ripple effect of the Amtrak fallout was spreading so far across New York State.

In the 1970s, Tom and I both went to Bucknell University, and since then we have met all over the Northeast, in the cause of American history. It was with Tom that I first saw the Garfield tomb in Cleveland (he was a law student at Case Western). In recent years, we have met in Pennsylvania at the Brandywine battlefield (outside Philadelphia) and in Chambersburg (near his house in Harrisburg), and have even gone together to Shanksville, to make sense of the crash of United Airlines 93 on September 11, 2001. When I knew I would be coming through Elmira and the Twain center, I invited Tom to join me for the day, and he had agreed instantly and with enthusiasm. He even handed me a book as I got into his car, entitled *Huck Finn Among the Critics*.

We decided to have lunch in Olean at a diner and to drive across upstate New York on Interstate 86. Left to our devices and with more time, we would have preferred the local road, Highway 417, to see more of what is called the "burned-over district." The term comes from the evangelist Charles G. Finney and the Second Great Awakening

(1790–1840), a Protestant revival movement that worked magic with Methodists and Baptists. So successful was Finney in western New York that he spoke of the area as having run out of fuel (unconverted population) and that there was nothing left to burn (convert).

We were invited to taste wine at the Dr. Konstantin Frank Vinifera Wine Cellars on Keuka Lake that afternoon, and the fastest way to Hammondsport and the Finger Lakes was on the interstate to Bath. (My favorites were a 2012 Reserve Gewürztraminer, I am sure, because it tasted the most like home, and a 2010 Merlot Reserve that cost $49.) So involved did we get with the wines that we postponed until the next day our visit to the Twain center. We were sure Sam would have approved. After all, he did like to say in his lectures: "My books are like water; those of the great geniuses are wine. Fortunately, everybody drinks water."

We spent that night in Ithaca as neither of us had ever been to the town that has Cornell University, Ithaca College, and, nearby, a community college. Maybe if the sun had been shining that afternoon or if the rain had stopped that evening, we might have liked Ithaca more. Instead, it gets my vote for the most disorganized small town in America—a dismal exchange of one-way streets, broken sidewalks, confusing streetlights, and blind alleys—that has a few (overpriced) bars, few bookstores, and the feeling of Despond, if that slough in *Pilgrim's Progress* had come with aboveground parking garages. We toured around Cornell in the fog, and I thought better of Kurt Vonnegut for getting tossed out of it.

Elmira: Huckleberry Finn Comes to Life

At 10 a.m. we met Barbara Snedecor at Mark Twain's Study on the campus of Elmira College. She is a professor at the college and the director of the Center for Mark Twain Studies, which, in addition to housing some of his papers on campus, runs Quarry Farm, Twain's summer house where he wrote *Huckleberry Finn* and many other novels.

Barbara found us outside the Study, which is an octagonal structure, about the size of a garden house, where Twain did all his writing during his summers in Elmira. The reason Twain came to Elmira was because his wife's family was from the town and Twain enjoyed their company. (He also enjoyed their generosity, as they had given the young couple the house at 742 Delaware Avenue in Buffalo.)

The Study is mostly an octagon of windows, and when Twain was in residence, it sat on a hill above Quarry Farm, from where he had an expansive view of the Chemung Valley around Elmira. He would go there after breakfast, carrying a handful of cigars, and work undisturbed until late afternoon.

In that way, over many Elmira summers, he wrote not just *Huckleberry Finn*, but *The Gilded Age*, *Tom Sawyer Detective*, *Pudd'nhead Wilson*, *Life on the Mississippi*, and *The Prince and the Pauper*.

During the rest of the year, Sam and Olivia lived in Hartford, but their life there was that of the showman Mark Twain, and his many speaking and business engagements. In

Elmira, Sam Clemens the writer was at work, and only in the late afternoon, by some prearranged signal, would he allow his children to bother him in the Study. Sometimes, to his delight, they brought the kittens.

After our look around the Study, where I interviewed Barbara on tape and we looked through the facsimile editions of Twain on display, we drove with her the short distance out of town (past a statue of Syracuse University football star, Ernie Davis, who grew up in Elmira) to Quarry Farm, which is up a steep hill from the town. Barbara said that during his summers, Sam would often walk down the hill late in the afternoon to visit a local bar, but that sometimes he needed a ride back up the hill, at the end of his pub crawling.

Quarry Farm is closed to the public (we could only get in with Barbara) but operates as a retreat for authors and puts on lectures and other events. That night, we had planned to return to Quarry Farm to hear a lecture by Professor Daniel Royot of the Sorbonne, entitled "Comparative Aspects of Benjamin Franklin's and Mark Twain's Cosmopolitan Legacy." But the professor had fallen ill in Paris and never made his trip to America. So the house was quiet. We wandered freely around the parlor (faithful to the Twain era but without much Twainiana). What I enjoyed the most was seeing his rocking chairs (well, descendants of them) on the back porch. Many familiar pictures of Mark Twain show him in a rocking chair, and all of those photographs would have been taken at Quarry Farm.

American literature owes a debt to Susie Crane, Olivia's sister, who conceived the Study, had it designed and built, and gave it to her brother-in-law Sam as a gift. Twain wrote to William Dean Howells on June 11, 1874: "Susie Crane has built the loveliest study you ever saw, it is octagonal, with a peaked roof, each face filled with a spacious window, and sits perched in complete isolation on top of an elevation that commands leagues of valley and city and retreating ranges of distant blue hills."

Of his time at Quarry Farm, Twain wrote: "The three months which I spend here are usually my working months. I am free here and can work uninterruptedly. . . . Yes . . . this may be called the home of *Huckleberry Finn* and other books of mine, for they were written here."

Here he was at his most productive, as he wrote to Howells in 1883: "I haven't piled up MS [manuscript] so in years as I have done since we came here to the farm these three weeks and half ago. Why, it is like old times, to step right into the study, damp from the breakfast table and sail right in and sail right on, the whole day long, without thought of running short of stuff or words." He also said of Quarry Farm that it was "a place in which to take a foretaste of Heaven."

From Quarry Farm we drove back to the campus and said goodbye to Barbara. There was an exhibition of Mark Twain things in the main building of the old campus, and Tom and I wanted to see his typewriter and some of the early pictures of the Study. (It was moved to the campus in 1952, and now has pride of place at the center of the college.) Barbara gave us each a copy of a book, *Mark Twain in Elmira*, about his New York State summers, and she pointed us in the direction of the local cemetery, where Twain is buried, as are his children and many Langdons. When later we went to see the grave, we found that someone before us had left a cigar on the headstone.

Walking around the campus, seeing some of the Twain statues they have put up, made me promise to myself that, when I was back home, I would finish Twain's *Autobiography*, which I had started and put down on several occasions. Alas, the copy I own is an abridged edition that Charles Neider edited. Since the *Autobiography* came out in 1917, there have been many editions. Most recently the University of California, which is publishing his complete works, brought out two volumes of the *Autobiography* that contain 1,512 pages of densely packed type.

I might like to own those books, but I know I will never read them, in part, because as much as I admire Twain, a lot of his prose is lost on me. It is likely just a question of age—his and mine—but I will never be able to read *A Connecticut Yankee in King Arthur's Court*. And *The Gilded Age*, which covers so much of his era, is also written in a style that I find hard to access. I am sure if I had been a contemporary of his, I would hang on every word, as I do, for example, with the books and journalism of Tom Wolfe. But even they might be hard to read in a hundred years, such are the contemporary allusions.

As a middle-aged reader, I do like reading the older-age Twain. The wit is still there, but without any of the clowning. For example, of the mistakes made in his life, he writes about a friend who was encouraging him to invest in something new:

> He was with Graham Bell and was agent for a new invention called the telephone. He believed there was great fortune in store for it and wanted me to take some stock. I declined. I said I didn't want anything more to do with wildcat speculation.

And Twain has a lovely passage in his memoirs about going back to Hannibal, which reminded me, on this trip, of the many nights I had spent in the company of childhood friends. It reads:

> The other Mary, now a widow, was upstairs and, presently, sent for me. She was old and gray-haired but she looked young and was very handsome. We sat down and talked. We steeped our thirsty souls in the reviving wine of the past, the pathetic past, the beautiful past, the dear and lamented past; we uttered the names that had been silent upon our lips for fifty years and it was as if they were made of music; with reverent hands we unburied our dead, the mates of our youth, and caressed them with our speech; we searched the dusty chambers of our memories and dragged forth incident after incident, episode after episode, folly after folly, and laughed such good laughs over them, with the tears running down.

Of his summer writing, Twain says simply: "I was roving far and wide on the lecture beat but I managed to arrive in Elmira every now and then and renew the siege."

Until I picked it up again, I had not known that *Autobiography of Mark Twain* is a book about death. I had assumed he wrote it, little by little, over the years, but instead it was written after his wife and all but one of his children had died. In the book, he is alone with his thoughts—of Hannibal in his childhood, and about Quarry Farm when his girls were young.

Although he is still Mark Twain and amused with the world ("Reader, suppose you were an idiot. And suppose you were a Member of Congress, but I repeat myself"),[19] there is

19: I was pleased, as well, to find this quote in the Adlai Stevenson *Black Book.*

also a darkness in the writing, a longing to be, if only for a minute or an hour, with his beloved wife and children.

The book ends with Twain's own farewell address, as haunting and sad as Lincoln's. It reads:

> When Clara went away two weeks ago to live in Europe, it was hard, but I could bear it, for I had Jean left. I said would be a family. We said *we* would be close comrades and happy—just we two. That fair dream was in my mind when Jean met me at the steamer last Monday; it was in my mind when she received me at the door last Tuesday evening. We were together; *we were a family*! the dream had come true—oh, precisely true, contentedly, true, satisfyingly true! and remained true two whole days.
>
> And now? Now Jean is in her grave!
>
> In the grave—if I can believe it. God rest her sweet spirit!

Syracuse: "Certain Half-Deserted Streets"

As he needed to head home to Harrisburg, Tom dropped me at the Elmira Transportation Center, which for the most part is a bus station with some taxis parked out front.

When I discovered that it was a two-hour wait until the next bus to Binghamton, I biked around Elmira and went back to the campus. I was seeing Elmira on a sunny autumn afternoon. I am sure, in midwinter slush, it can take on the air of Ithaca. Still, I liked the wide streets, the elevated train tracks running down the center, that senators Patrick Moynihan and Alfonse D'Amato had pushed to convert the Erie-Lackawanna railroad station into the transportation center, and that the campus mixes so easily with the town. (In Kent, Ohio, you sense a wall between the two worlds.)

As I did at Oberlin, I went to the campus bookstore and began looking at the books assigned in various college courses. This time, instead of being shooed away, a bookstore associate, David Rundle, came over to ask me if I had any questions and ended up spending about thirty minutes with me, taking me through many of the courses, their professors, and the assigned readings. Elmira, as all colleges should, owns its own bookstore, and Rundle, along with his colleagues, works closely with the professors. He knew what books were in print, how long it would take to order a title, and even what editions worked better than others. (We talked about differences, in the classics, between Norton, Oxford, and Penguin.)

From his spontaneous bookstore tour, I learned that Elmira is a small college—about 1,400 students—and that to get the most out of it, undergraduates do best by embracing the liberal arts and spending the four years dividing their time among all the disciplines in the college. Elmira has some departments, such as English and its Twain center, that lend themselves to in-depth study. In general, each academic department only has about four or five professors, which isn't enough for a student to do a proper concentration. (You would run out of classes pretty fast.)

What makes Elmira great, I thought, is the totality of its liberal arts courses, not just one department. Besides, any school that assigns its students *Minerva's Owl: The Tradition of Western Political Thought* by Jeffrey Abramson (Plato to Marx, but in readable English) ought to be better known. And, for nervous parents of young freshmen, how many distractions or vices can there be in a snow-belt town that is an hour from Binghamton and four hours from New York City?

From Elmira I was headed around the Finger Lakes to Auburn, New York, where the next morning at 9 a.m. I had arranged an interview with a director of the William Seward House. Seward was a senator and secretary of state for Lincoln and, afterward, Andrew Johnson.

To complete the administrations between Lincoln and Roosevelt, I needed a proxy for Johnson, who was born in Raleigh, North Carolina, but spent his adult life in Tennessee, not near any of my bus stops. (Seward, who always thought he should have been president, would not have minded filling in.) Seward is famous for "Seward's Folly," the acquisition of Alaska in 1868.

Although I did not relish taking three buses from Elmira to Auburn (changing in Binghamton and Syracuse) over six hours, I did want to learn more about Seward, sometimes called "Lincoln's indispensable man," and other times called things, by the Democrats, that are unprintable here.

It amused me that the bus drivers, in speaking to each other on the radio, referred always to Binghamton as "Bingo," a name the staid upstate New York city hardly deserves. All I saw of it, however, was the bus terminal, as thirty minutes after arriving, I had purchased dinner and was on a bus heading to Syracuse, where I had to change from the airport to downtown, and catch a bus to Auburn.

The downtown Syracuse bus station (okay, the Syracuse Regional Transit Center) felt like a wasteland, or at least Prufrock's "certain half-deserted streets." I huddled with my bike and bags on a bay in the loading area, waiting for the bus to Auburn, which was posted to arrive around 9:30 p.m. but was late ("streets that follow like a tedious argument").

When it arrived, there were only six passengers who boarded. I loaded the bike underneath and took a seat in the darkness. The only break in the midnight spell came when we went through Skaneateles, and the lights from the antique stores and main street boutiques flickered into the bus.

I was headed for the Super 8 motel in Auburn, which I had booked during a stop that had Wi-Fi. (It was all I could find.) The directions were attached to the confirmation, but inaccessible when I was on the bike. I got out of the bus at what looked like a central stop in Auburn and asked directions to the motel, which turned out to be off James Street, near downtown.

I would not have wanted to walk, but on the bike I could afford to make wrong turns and backtrack, which I did several times. It was much closer to Genesee Street than I had guessed, and the parking lot, which was half full, glowed in the klieg lighting of the state prison across the meandering Owasco River, which had the feel of a reassuring moat.

Auburn:
William Seward Doffs His Whigs

ALTHOUGH THE MOTEL BREAKFAST was limited to juice, coffee, Cremora, and a plastic-encased muffin, I made the most of it, and arrived at the Seward House just after 9 a.m., where Andy Roblee was expecting me. We had been corresponding online, and he had said he was free to tape an interview in the morning.

As there was no one visiting the house at such an early hour, we spoke first in Seward's library—imagine a small room lined with leather-bound first editions, floor to ceiling—and then made the rounds of the mansion, in which Seward lived for his entire adult life, when not on official duties in Albany or Washington.

The house had belonged to his wife's father, Elijah Miller, and Seward moved there when he married Frances in 1824 and only departed when he died in 1872. From the 1830s until his death, Seward was a central political figure in American politics and, like Lincoln's hero Henry Clay, among the most prominent men of the nineteenth century who never became president.

I liked Andy Roblee, a man in his early thirties, I guessed, who was in charge of the facilities around the Seward House. Since our meeting, he left that job to attend graduate school at Cornell in historical preservation management, something I know he will do well. His Seward was similar to that of Walter Stahr, the author of *Seward: Lincoln's Indispensable Man*, but when I went through the house, I had yet to read the 2012 best-selling biography.

All I knew about Seward was what I had read about him in Lincoln histories. In those he comes across as supercilious and vain, someone who had little time for Lincoln until he was dead. By contrast, I found the Seward of the Auburn house to be sympathetic and intellectually engaging.

And, more than Lincoln in the 1850s, this Seward took a stand against slavery, when only crusading abolitionists were calling for its elimination. It might have cost him the presidency, but he was never one to bite his tongue on a political issue.

Seward was born in 1801 in Florida, New York, upstate from New York City but today within commuting distance. He graduated at the top of his class from Union College in Schenectady in 1820, after taking a short break in his junior year to travel south with a friend. In the Seward files, Stahr turns up a letter written in 1866 by a Rosetta Alexander, claiming that she had heard from her mother and her former owner that Seward was her father (dating to his junior year excursion to Georgia). In a life that is otherwise untouched by scandal, the suggestion that Seward might have fathered a child with a slave girl in 1819 is intriguing, but Stahr takes the story no further. Nor does Seward, who ignores the letter (although he does keep it in his files).

Seward was elected to the New York state legislature in 1830 and was active in the Anti-Masonic Party in the early 1830s before he joined the nascent Whig Party, which dates to 1834. The Whigs (Lincoln would become one also) were opposed to Andrew Jackson, who they believed to be tyrannical and prone to mob rule. At this time Seward also became a "river and harbor" man, believing that the government should get behind big infrastructure projects (not unlike the Erie Canal, which comes close to Auburn), while Jackson, for his part, was shutting down the Second National Bank and taking the government out of the improvement business.

Stahr writes this about the Whig Party:

> The Whigs, in the words of the leading historian of their party, "believed government must promote prosperity. Especially in hard times, the government must take positive action to stimulate economic recovery." Whigs favored a national bank and state support for internal improvement projects, such as roads and canals, that would not only provide jobs but also lay the groundwork for future growth.

Around this time, Seward met (accidentally, in a carriage accident) Thurlow Weed, who was from the Rochester area. Seward and Weed would become one of the great tandems in American politics—not unlike Hanna and McKinley. Roblee quoted Seward's expression that "Seward is Weed and Weed is Seward. What I do, Weed approves. What he says, I endorse. We are one."

Seward said of his new, lifelong friend: "Weed is very much with me, and I enjoy his warmth of feeling. A politician skillful in design and persevering in execution, whose exciting principle is personal friendship or opposition, and not self-interest—that is just Thurlow Weed."

During the 1830s, on something of a political pilgrimage, the Sewards visited Monticello in Virginia, the home of Thomas Jefferson. Stahr writes:

> They were unable to enter the house at Monticello—"we found every door closed"—but they strolled around the immense gardens and visited Jefferson's grave—"in a very rough, dilapidated condition."

A sample of New York State politics can be glimpsed in the presidential election of 1836, when Seward, according to Stahr, "reportedly called Martin Van Buren, the Democratic presidential candidate, a 'crawling reptile, whose only claim was that he had inveigled the confidence of a credulous, blind dotard' (Jackson)."

Auburn: Seward Plays for the Presidency

Seward entered the national stage, so to speak, in 1838, when he was elected governor of New York State, but a decision in office there, according to Roblee, might have cost him the Republican nomination twenty-two years later in 1860. Seward embraced the idea of free education for the children of Catholics, an important New York constituency, but always suspect to the nativist element in the early Republican Party. In 1860 Senator Thaddeus Stevens spoke out against Seward for the nomination, just because of this decision that "ruined free education in New York."

Seward was New York's governor for two terms, leaving office in 1842, after which he returned to his law practice and settled a huge land dispute in western New York (around the "burned-over district") that made his fortune.

In the 1840s he also tried a celebrated murder case, in which he acted for the accused black man William Freeman, arguing an early form of the insanity defense. Freeman lost, but Seward won an enhanced reputation for sympathy with the downtrodden. At the end of the case, according to Roblee, Seward said that on his grave he wanted the words, "He was faithful."

Like Lincoln and Grant, Seward opposed the Mexican War, saying, according to Stahr, that "the Democratic desire to acquire Texas would lead to 'a war with Mexico—an unjust war—a war to extend the slave-trade and the slave-piracy.'" In 1949 the New York state legislature sent him to the US Senate, where he arrived in time to take part in the debate over the Compromise of 1850. In that debate, he challenged Senator John C. Calhoun, saying there was a "higher law" (than the Constitution) when it came to the slavery question. Seward became well established as an opponent of slavery.

In the US Senate throughout the 1850s, Seward took part in the national debate on the extension of slavery that came up not just over the Compromise of 1850 but in the Kansas-Nebraska Act (1854) and the Dred Scott decision (1857) as well, both of which pushed Lincoln back into politics. Roblee described a well-known confrontation between senators Seward and Stephen Douglas:

> During the Kansas-Nebraska debate, Douglas rounded on Seward (who was trying to interrupt him) and said: "Ah, you can't crawl behind that free-nigger dodge." Seward responded (prophetically): "Douglas, no man will ever be president of the United States who spells 'negro' with two *gs*.

After the 1852 election, the Whig Party dissolved, and many, like Seward and Weed, ended up in the Republican Party, which ran its first candidate, the omnipresent John C. Frémont, in 1856. So sure was Seward that he would win the 1860 Republican nomination, in 1859 he took a trip to Europe and met Queen Victoria, among other dignitaries, all of whom thought they were meeting the next president of the United States.

Although Weed managed the Seward campaign for the nomination at the 1860 Republican convention in Chicago, he could not muster the support needed for the senator.

(Stahr writes: "On the first ballot, Seward had received 172 votes, about 60 short of the number he needed. Lincoln had received 102 votes, and the remaining votes were scattered among various candidates, including Cameron.") In *The Long Pursuit,* Morris has an excellent summary of why Seward did not get the nomination:

> Seward was also weakest in precisely those states the Republicans needed to carry to win what was universally expected to be a close election—Pennsylvania, Indiana, and Illinois. Stephen Douglas, if he managed to nail down the Democratic nomination, was historically formidable there, and even old John Bell might siphon off precious votes with his appeal to tradition-minded Whigs. . . . With the crescent of states in the Old Northwest shaping up to be the major battleground of the election, Kentucky-born, Indiana-reared, Illinois-based Lincoln was well positioned to contend for those rustic votes, one hand-split fence rail at a time.

Nor did it help Seward that the nativist elements in the Republican Party (here is Fillmoreism rearing its ugly head again) were bitterly opposed to him.

Prior to the 1860 election, Seward had only met Lincoln once, in 1848, when they both were campaigning in Massachusetts for Zachary Taylor. As we were walking around the house, Roblee said: "Seward, like everyone else, underestimated Lincoln." Seward remembered their conversation about slavery, and Lincoln followed up the meeting, after Taylor won the election and Seward was his confidant, asking for an appointment as a federal land commissioner. Seward, however, never answered the letter.

Auburn:
Lincoln and Seward Go to War

NOT ONE TO HOLD A GRUDGE, Lincoln appointed Seward to be his secretary of state, and Seward assumed, given that he thought Lincoln a nonentity, he would, as Roblee said, "lead from behind." Early in the administration, on April 1, 1861, Seward wrote Lincoln a letter, outlining how he (Seward) wanted to proceed, given that Lincoln was paralyzed by non-action. (In effect, Prime Minister Seward was writing to King Lincoln about how he proposed to run the government.) Lincoln did not answer Seward in person, but met with him. Neither man shared the contents of this visit to the woodshed, but clearly Lincoln—gently, kindly, and no doubt with many jokes—did with Seward what James Garfield was unable to do with Roscoe Conkling: he let him know who was the boss, and how the relationship could work, if Seward wanted to remain on board.

After this encounter, Lincoln had no more loyal cabinet member than Seward, and the unlikely pair (Mary Todd Lincoln hated Seward, thinking him a "sneaky" abolitionist, with his hand in her family's pocket) was successful in running American foreign policy during the Civil War. As secretary of state, Seward had less to do with the prosecution of the war, although he sat in on all the major political decisions, such as that surrounding the Emancipation Proclamation.

Among Seward's and Lincoln's finest moments was their handling of the Trent Affair, in which Southern diplomats on the high seas were forcibly removed from a British ship, the *Trent*. Stahr writes: "The *Trent* crisis was the Cuban missile crisis of the nineteenth century: a moment when the United States faced possible war with the world's other major power, a period of intense emotion and apprehension."

The incident could easily have escalated into forcing Britain to side with the South in the Civil War, which could have tipped the balance against the Union. Working in tandem as two lawyers, drafting and redrafting each other's letters and briefs on the crisis, Lincoln and Seward managed to keep Britain out of the war, just as later in the war, they defused the tensions in Mexico (Napoleon III had put Maximilian on the throne there) so that France would not aid the Confederacy.

Seward skillfully managed American foreign relations during the Civil War. At one point, he organized a tour of New York State for the diplomatic corps and took them from New York City to Buffalo (with an appropriate stop in Auburn) to show the world the extent of American wealth, and that just in one state. The subtle message: "Don't interfere with us." He also worked hard to ensure that no European power tried to mediate the conflict, as Stahr writes: "If one or more of the major European powers offered to mediate between the North and the South, the offer itself would imply that both the United States and the Confederate States were separate, sovereign nations."

In Stahr's book, there are several descriptions of Seward's conduct and personality in the Lincoln administration. Gideon Wells wrote that Seward "is obtrusive, never reserved, or diffident of his own powers, is assuming and presuming, meddlesome, unreliable, and uncertain, ready to exercise authority always, never doubting his right until challenged, then he becomes timid, doubtful, distrustful, inventive of schemes to extricate himself." Journalist Noah Brooks said: "He is affable and pleasant, accessible—from a newspaperman's point of view—smoking cigars always, ruffled or excited never, astute, keen to perceive a joke, appreciative of a good thing, and fond of 'good victuals,' if not of luxurious furniture." Alas, Seward never won over Mary Todd Lincoln, who during the war told her husband that Seward was "a hypocrite who simply could not be trusted." (She also called Ulysses Grant a "butcher" and asked that he be kept away from the White House.)

Seward was famous for working hard and speaking his mind, although not all the advice and comments he shared with Lincoln have stood the test of time. Lincoln consulted Seward on the address at Gettysburg, and afterward Seward said to Edward Everett (who was the main speaker that day) that Lincoln's speech was "a failure, and I am sorry for it."

Auburn:
Bailing Out Andrew Johnson

FORGOTTEN IN HIS HISTORY is that Seward was the target of an assassination attempt the same night in April 1865 that John Wilkes Booth shot and killed Lincoln. Recuperating from a fall off his horse, Seward was at his house when Lewis Powell knocked on the door, claiming to have medicine for the secretary of state.

The assassin brushed past the servant and mounted the stairs. Fortunately, Seward's son Frederick heard the intruder and confronted him on the second-floor landing, although Powell beat him with a pistol and then—pushing past Seward's daughter Fanny—attacked Seward in his bed with a dagger. Hearing the struggles and screams, an aide and a servant came to Seward's assistance, and they drove off Powell (who was arrested the next day at the boarding house of Mary Surratt and hanged).

Although both Sewards, father and son, were badly wounded in the attack, perhaps the most grievous wound to William was the subsequent loss of his wife and daughter. His wife, Frances, worried that her son Frederick would die from his wounds (he did not), collapsed and died of a heart attack in June 1865. Seward's beloved daughter Fanny never recovered from the emotional shock of the incident, and she died a year later of tuberculosis. She was twenty-one. Her library in the Auburn house remains intact and under glass; Roblee said it is among the best surviving collections to show what a young girl was reading in the 1850s, and her girlhood diary is one reason so much is known about Seward's home life.

Seward recovered from his stab wounds and served another four years as secretary of state for President Andrew Johnson, although, as Roblee said, they never enjoyed the intimacy that Seward had developed with Lincoln. Johnson was often drunk and always erratic, and he and the precise Seward were a bad match. Nevertheless, Seward contributed what few successes can be attributed to the Johnson administration, although his association with the Democrat Johnson again cost Seward respect among certain Republicans, who already suspected him for his earlier Catholic sympathies. Some called Johnson Seward's puppet or lackey boy, but they exaggerated Seward's influence. He was a Lincoln man, although he proved indispensable for Johnson as well.

Andrew Johnson never had a mandate to act as president, and the impeachment charges brought against him were the culmination of the struggle over how and by whom Reconstruction would be administered. (Hardliners wanted to sow salt in the Southern soil, while Lincoln liberals favored a more accommodating peace.)

When Johnson fired a hardline cabinet officer, Republican Edwin Stanton, the Congress passed the Tenure of Office Act, which required Senate approval before any other cabinet officer could be fired. After its passage, Stanton tried to reclaim his office as secretary of war (Grant and Sherman had turned it down in the meantime) and actually barricaded himself in his office.

When Johnson fired him, in effect, a second time, the president was impeached. It turns out that what saved Johnson's presidency was that Seward, among others in the cabinet, followed the advice of an intermediary who said the solution was simple: "Buy your way out." The estimated cost of purchasing Johnson's acquittal was about $200,000, of which the intermediary kept $50,000.

Later, according to Stahr, Seward said wistfully: "$10,000 more were to be given to poor Thad Stevens but no one would undertake to give that to him so I undertook it [my] self. The poor fellow died [on August 11] and I have it now." Clearly Seward had made up with one of the men who had doomed his 1860 nomination.

Touring the Auburn house that has artifacts of the Alaska acquisition, Roblee spoke at length about "Seward's folly" that in 1867 cost the government $7,200,000 ($121 million in today's dollars). Seward got interested in Alaska because of whaling, and the need for oil for naval warships. Alaska was also called "Johnson's polar bear garden" and proved a delight to political cartoonists.

As secretary of state, Seward also worked on the outstanding claims with Britain, through arbitration in Geneva, over the USS *Alabama,* which the British had built for the Confederacy and which had wreaked havoc on Union shipping during the war. Earlier Seward thought of trading the *Alabama* claims for British Columbia, to link up the continental United States with Alaska, but that deal fell through. Nevertheless, Seward's moves and his desires—he secured guano islands in the Pacific in perpetuity through the Guano Islands Act[20]—points to him

---

20: The act is still binding. It explains why, for example, Midway Island was considered an American possession in World War II. What the act allowed is for any American to claim possession of any island where there was guano (important for gunpowder) and where that territory was not claimed by another government. Some fifteen islands, including Johnson Atoll, are still considered guano islands.

(more than William McKinley) as laying (Stahr writes) "the foundations of the American empire." Roblee talked about other moves Seward wanted to make as well—the purchase of the Virgin Islands from Holland, and the takeover of the Sandwich Islands (Hawaii), both of which Congress turned down.

Toward the end of my visit, Roblee and I stood in the upstairs hall, called the Diplomatic Gallery, where Seward displayed his collected portraits of political leaders he admired (it has some 132 pictures on the walls), and Andy talked about the end of Seward's life, which was as eventful as his active political career. A widower whose life had been government, he left office in 1869 and immediately set out on two long world tours—the first around the Americas, including to Alaska, and the second to all the continents, except Antarctica. He was gone more than two years, and collected for the Auburn house many souvenirs, including pictures of the world leaders that he had to know and like—Pope Pius IX and Bismarck among them. Needless to say, much of the interior of the house is done in Alaskan cedar.

Coming home, he began work on a book of his travels, but died in 1872 in a small back room off the kitchen. Although he had his library and parlor in the main part of the house, Seward would come back here to write, and he died next to a specially designed desk chair that allowed him to recline comfortably and write. His last words to his assembled family, according to Roblee, were: "Love one another," although on his tomb are the requested words from the Freeman trial: "He was faithful."

By good fortune, the Auburn house remained in the hands of the Seward family until 1951, when it was given to a local historical society, and in 1955 it opened for tours. Their uninterrupted ownership explains why everything in the house belonged to Seward and why the thousands of books in his library are original.

Cortland:
Harriet Tubman's Famous Landlord

When my Seward visit ended, I was stuck in Auburn. I wanted to get to my sister's house in New Paltz, New York (near the Hudson River, Newburgh, and Poughkeepsie), that night, and the only direct way to get there was on the train from Syracuse or the bus from Binghamton.

Originally, I had planned to go from Auburn to Utica, where Roscoe Conkling, who figures in so many stories here, had his upstate New York house. The house is not a museum, but it remains standing, and I had directions in my bag on how to get there. Alas, if I detoured to Utica, my only chance of getting to Poughkeepsie that night would have been on Amtrak's *Lake Shore Limited* (for which I had a ticket). Were it running on time (arrival time 4:49 p.m.), that would have worked perfectly.

The problem with that plan, however, was that since my disaster in Cleveland I had been tracking its on-time performance, and on most days it was between five and seven hours late. (Clearly those copper-wire thieves in Cleveland were doing a land-office business.) Such a train would only get me into Poughkeepsie between 10 p.m. and midnight, which was too late an hour for my sister to collect me. That left me at the mercy of the bus system, for which the closest connection to Binghamton and Newburgh (near Poughkeepsie) was from Cortland, New York.

I knew about Cortland because it was where the New York Jets had trained in summer and because I had seen it listed in my Russell's bus guide. Fortunately, Andy Roblee said he didn't mind driving me there, which he said was about an hour away. Otherwise, I might still be on my bike, riding southeast from Auburn on Highway 41A, which is between lakes Owasco and Skaneateles.

On the drive south, Andy stopped so I could see Seward's modest grave site—his generous father-in-law and former law partner is also there—and we slowed down so that I could see the small house and plot of land that Seward had sold to fugitive-slave activist Harriet Tubman, who had herself escaped from slavery.

In the 1850s (when Seward sold her the house), she was a chief engineer on the Underground Railroad. (She made thirteen trips south to help slaves escape, many on Maryland's Eastern Shore.) She was also friendly with John Brown and supported his causes, although she was not present in Harper's Ferry during his 1859 raid (which troops commanded by Colonel Robert E. Lee put down).

No doubt Seward's sympathy for Tubman (the house is just down the road from Auburn) was known in political circles and did him no good with his national aspirations. Nevertheless, he stayed behind her. Stahr writes that "he offered Tubman very easy terms—only $25 down and $10 per quarter thereafter—and he did not object when she failed to make even these payments." Who would have thought that William Seward could have been an easy touch as a landlord? Maybe that was his bond with Lincoln, who lived in his own house as if Mary Todd's tenant.

Andy dropped me on the main street of Cortland, and I had forty-five minutes to catch the Greyhound bus to Binghamton. Unfortunately, no one in Cortland knew where the bus stopped or where I could buy a ticket. I was sent in every direction, depending on whom I asked. At least I passed the "Official Headquarters of the NY Jets Summer Camp," which was a bar serving Genesee beer.

I rode twice to the SUNY Cortland campus on this fool's errand, and finally gambled on a bus shelter in town as the logical place for a Greyhound bus to stop. No one else was waiting there, but the bus showed up at 1:15 p.m. I bought a ticket for $10 from the driver. By 2:10 p.m. I had made the connection in Binghamton for Newburgh, which got me, so to speak, home to New Paltz for dinner.

Route 17: A Hoosier Holiday

IF I JUST WANTED TO DESCRIBE the bus trip that afternoon, I would be tempted to write that, in the rain, the Short Line bus followed Route 17 down to Middletown, where there was a rest stop in a parking lot (only the smokers needed rest), and that we arrived in Newburgh, in another parking lot, just before 6 p.m.

All I now remember of the ride is a boarded-up rail terminal near Middletown, which I later discovered was an Ontario & Western station (although it only went, ironically, from Weehawken, New Jersey, to Oswego, New York) dating to 1892, which, in the familiar modern story, a local group is trying to save while the owners are letting it go to ruin. For now, it is a homeless shelter.

I didn't think more about the bus ride south toward New York City until I later read Theodore Dreiser's *A Hoosier Holiday*, and I was struck how his route in 1915 and mine on this trip had followed the same path. He left from New York, crossed New Jersey and part of Pennsylvania, entered New York State around Elmira, and then drove across Ohio to Indiana, where he ended his touring around Terre Haute and the houses of his unhappy childhood. I had traveled in the opposite direction and had not intentionally followed in Dreiser's footsteps. But when I discovered a reprint of the 1916 edition, I read it with amusement that I could easily track his drive a hundred years before. He liked the automobile for the reason that I like the folding bike: because it gave him freedom to go where he pleased. Dreiser traveled in the company of an artist friend, Franklin Booth, who did the illustrations for the book, and with a chauffeur, which is one way to deal with the frustrations on the road.

After reading W. A. Swanberg's biography of Dreiser, I approached *A Hoosier Holiday* with some trepidation. Which Dreiser would be in the car: the werewolf who stalked women across the United States or the bright-eyed observer and novelist, who in *Sister Carrie* and so many other books had managed to preserve the look, sounds, and behavior of America in the late nineteenth and early twentieth century?

By good fortune, the Dreiser motoring to Indiana is excellent company: he is alert, observant, humorous, and game for anything. (If he used the trip to chase women, he wrote away those particular rest stops.) For three weeks, he's in the back seat of a convertible, as though part of a homecoming parade that is traveling across America. Of his first glimpse at upstate New York, he writes: "I wasn't on the high road between Binghamton and Elmira at all but in some happy land that hadn't anything to do with motoring—a land of youth and affection."

For his day job, as the poet laureate of crooked corporations and compromised executives, Dreiser only has his eye out for swindles, stock waterings, inside trading, monopolistic pricing, and the usual financial sleights of hand. (In *An American Tragedy*, the story is the dark heart of man's soul, which finds even murder acceptable in the service of ambition, fame, pleasure, and fortune.)

In *A Hoosier Holiday*, however, that America is left behind on the Manhattan side of the Hudson River, and mostly what Dreiser sees in front of him are amber waves of grain. For example, he writes:

> Oh, the lovely roads by which they came, the sylvan nooks where their homes are, the small schoolhouses, the wide spacious fields with crows and blackbirds and bluejays for company, the grey snowy fields in winter, these black filigree trees for a border—and the great cities which haunt the dreams of these boys and girls and finally lure so many of them away.

Even his rages are short-lived, as when he writes: "Dear, crude, asinine, illusioned Americans! How I love them!"

Nevertheless, not even Dreiser can write a five-hundred-page book with only Whitmanesque homilies about the life of the road (the introduction calls this kind of writing "Thoreau at 29 cents a gallon"). Between the purple mountain majesties, he does, occasionally, remember the world he left behind in New York, as when he writes: "American cities are not given to imagination outside the walks of trade" or "the American world of that day wanted you to eat, sleep and dream money and power."

The irony of the upbeat travel book is that, amidst the growth and expansion of American industry and power—essentially he is visiting McKinley's Canton or Harding's Marion—Dreiser senses the country is in decline, despite all the factory smoke on the horizon. In one of the longest discourses about the vanishing age of industrial steam, he writes:

> When America is old, and its present vigor and life hunger has gone and an alien or degenerate race tramp where once we lived and builded so vigorously, perhaps some

> visitors from a foreign country will walk here among these ruins and sigh: "Ah, yes. The Americans were a great people. Their cities were so wonderful. These mouldy crumbling skyscrapers, and fallen libraries and post offices and city halls and state capitals!"

These passages are few and far between—like the few bad meals he eats in charming roadside diners serving homemade pies. Most of the time, the motoring Dreiser is singing the praises of the open road:

> If anyone doubts that this is fast becoming one of the most interesting lands in the world, let him motor from Buffalo to Detroit along the shore of Lake Erie, mile after mile, over a solid, vitrified brick road fifteen feet wide at the least, and approximately three hundred miles long.

Now the roads outside Buffalo look headed to the back of beyond.

Dreiser finishes his Hoosier holiday with a quick drive east. He was gone for three weeks, and then spent a year writing about it. He never did return to his native Indiana (as Twain did to Hannibal as an old man), but on the road Dreiser must have felt he had buried some of his past in Terre Haute. He ends the book with his own farewell address, suggesting that the country has lost something of the optimism of his youth. He writes:

> "Once," will say those historians of far distant nations of times yet unborn, perchance, "once there was a great republic. And its domain lay between a sea and sea—a great continent. In its youth and strength it dared assert

that all men were free and equal, endowed with certain inalienable rights. Then came the black storms of life—individual passions and envies, treasons, stratagems, spoils. The very gods, seeing it young, dreamful, of great cheer, were filled with envy. They smote and it fell. But, oh, the wondrous memory of it. For in those days men were free, because they *imagined they were free*—"

Of dreams and the memory of them is life compounded.

The difference between Dreiser's mostly idyllic, sometimes scheming America and mine is that my only moments of idealism came when I was meeting someone—the many people that I describe in these pages—or later when I could hear the voice of a writer describe the places I had been. Except on the bike, when I was on the road, such as on the bus ride from Binghamton to Newburgh, the travel was numbing, and I doubt even the homeward-bound Dreiser could talk up a traffic jam in Ohio or a delay on Amtrak.

New York City: Chester A. Arthur Collects on His Debts

I TOOK TIME AWAY FROM MY TRAVELS in New Paltz, where my younger sister Julie lives. We were still sorting through my parents' estate, and spent some days in her barn, sorting boxes of papers, pictures, and books. (I never did find my father's copy of *The Shadow of Blooming Grove*, the Warren Harding biography, so I ordered another online. Nor did I find Porter McKeever's biography of Adlai Stevenson II, although I am sure it is there, somewhere.)

One Saturday, however, I slipped away from the boxes and went into New York City to track down what I could find out about the life of Chester A. Arthur, Roscoe Conkling's collection man in the customs house who became president, just as Charles Guiteau had predicted when he shot James Garfield. Arthur had spent most of his life, aside from his one-term presidency, living and working in New York City. Aside from a statue that I knew in Madison Square Park, his life in the city, so far as I knew, was a blank slate.

I left from the Poughkeepsie railroad station—an old one—where I was surprised and pleased to find my last Looking for Lincoln plaque. Lincoln had stopped twice in Poughkeepsie, which is ninety minutes from New York City. The first stop was on February 19, 1861, so less than a week after he left Springfield. He said at the station:

> It is with your aid, as the people, that I think shall be able to preserve—not the country, for the country will preserve itself, but the institutions of the country; those institutions that have made us free, intelligent and happy—the most free, the most intelligent and the happiest people on the globe.

His next stop was on April 25, 1865, when his funeral train made a brief stop in Poughkeepsie, so that the president of Vassar College, Matthew Vassar, could place magnolia blossoms next to his coffin.

Instead of going alone in search of Arthur, however, I rounded up a group of my daughter's friends, and some of my own. The group dated to the time when my daughter, Laura, was a student at Barnard College, which is next door to Columbia University on the Upper West Side. When I would visit her from Switzerland, we got in the habit of visiting nearby historical sites. The first excursion was to Grant's tomb (behind Barnard on 122nd Street and Riverside Drive). Next we went to Alexander Hamilton's house in Harlem, the Grange. On another occasion, we went walking in Brooklyn Heights to see where Whitman and others had lived.

At first, the only ones on the tours were Laura and me. Then her roommate, Monet Eliastam, joined us, as did another Columbia friend, Anne-Louise Brittan. Into this mix then came Amy Weiss-Meyer (my sister's niece); sometimes her mother, Nancy (although not enough to get a passing grade); and my two friends, Tom Leonard and Allen Rhodes. Together this group began to describe itself as "the Seminar," and whenever I would visit New York City, I would send out an all-points bulletin that the plan was to visit Theodore

Roosevelt's childhood home (it's on East 20th Street, near Park Avenue) or perhaps the haunts of Boss Tweed (Tammany Hall, for example, at Union Square). Pretty soon the Seminar had picked up a language of its own, and for an easy laugh, someone could write in an e-mail "forgive me for pointing" (which was a phrase used by the Roosevelt home guide about thirty times).

For the Arthur tour, this group of middle-aged men and recent college graduates (give or take) met at a diner near Arthur's New York home at 123 Lexington Avenue, which is between 28th and 29th streets. After eggs, bagels, and coffee, we walked over to the Arthur residence, which by rights should be as opulent as Spiegel Grove, Rutherford Hayes's house, or Benjamin Harrison's house in Indianapolis. All it has, however, is a dated plaque indicating that Arthur had lived there. Otherwise, it's an apartment building, although the ground floor has an Indian deli, which sells a variety of Asian spices. (In honor of Arthur, I bought some curry.) Occasionally the *New York Times* will run a story about distant plans to turn Arthur's house into a museum and a memorial, but the tone of the writing makes the house sound a bit like Buffalo's Central Terminal, with a nonprofit corporation and eager volunteers.

Not everyone in the Seminar made it downtown to see where Arthur had practiced law (not far from City Hall). By the time we got to Madison Square Park, where there is not only an Arthur statue but one of Roscoe Conkling as well, only Laura and Amy were among—how shall I put it?—the Stalwarts. Clearly Arthurism has its limits, even for my gifted friends. Later that day, when I went to the Strand bookstore and bought a copy of Zachary Karabell's *Chester Alan Arthur,* I was alone.

New York City:
Roscoe Conkling Plays Hardball

For anyone sympathetic to James Garfield, Chet Arthur is a sinister figure, a man in black sitting with Roscoe Conkling at the Fifth Avenue Hotel, dividing the proceeds of the customs house or plotting against the man from Mentor. Even without loyalty to Garfield, Arthur gets deservedly low marks for the company he kept in a political career of deal making and opportunism, although he and William Seward frequently agreed on the large issues.

Arthur was also something of a Thurlow Weed man, which in terms of political genealogy puts him closer to Abraham Lincoln. In the election of 1860, Lincoln was a "hurrah candidate," and the one leading his "hurrahs" was Weed.

The pleasure of Karabell's book is that, while short, it gets to an essence of Arthur that defies the stereotype of party hack. About Arthur's early years, the book is terse. He was born in Vermont, where his father was a schoolteacher. (Arthur's father emigrated from northern Ireland, where there is an Arthur Cottage in honor of the presidential family and the hint that perhaps Chester A. Arthur was born in Canada.) Chester did his undergraduate study at Union College, as did Seward, although in a later class, that of 1845. He was an early enthusiast of the Whig Party, as was Lincoln. Arthur taught school for a while, and then read the law, being admitted to the bar in 1854 and later joining a firm in New York City.

Come the Civil War, Arthur had the chance to move to the sound of the guns, but his genius was as a quartermaster in New York, and he kept the troops fed and clothed as they came through the city. At one point he was given the rank of brigadier general, within the supply administration, and he held onto his posts—half military, half political, and probably all patronage—until 1863, when a newly elected Democratic governor cleaned house of Republican placemen.

Happily or not, Arthur went back to his law offices, and in the years after the war, he was a machine man in the Republican party, rubbing shoulders with Seward and Weed when he could. Closer in temperament to him was Roscoe Conkling, the Utica congressman, although at the time Arthur was under the wing of Thomas Murphy, whom Ulysses Grant appointed to the New York customs house.

When Murphy was forced out, Arthur became the collector. It was a plum job, and on it Arthur had many plums. Nor were the conditions of the job particularly onerous. Karabell writes:

> Until he became president, Chester Arthur used the Fifth Avenue Hotel and Delmonico's as his offices. They were where he met with the Astors and the Goulds, the Morgans and the Conklings, the patrons and the robber barons. They were where promises were exchanged; where donors pledged money; where candidates were selected. They were where power was.

Karabell describes the compensation system at the customs house as follows:

> This "moiety" process made it possible for even a low-level official to double or triple his income. Arthur's salary as collector was twelve thousand dollars a year, but his actual income exceeded fifty thousand dollars because of the moiety system, which was many times more than the average salary in the United States at the time.

Although Congress would repeal the "moiety" system (the kinship world of patronage and bossism) and put Arthur on $12,000 year, he still got some money back from those he employed, and some three thousand customs officials reported to Arthur. In the meantime, he also enjoyed the political support of Roscoe Conkling, to whom Grant was indebted. Karabell describes Conkling: "Dubbed 'Lord Roscoe' for his impressive hauteur, he also became known as 'the Apollo of the Senate,' and people often found themselves reaching for Greek and Roman mythology to describe his outsized personality."

It was Conkling's feud with Rutherford B. Hayes that cost Arthur his job as collector. Hayes needed to prove a point with Conkling—that he was president, not Roscoe—and the sacrificial lamb was Arthur. [21] In response, Conkling made a frontal assault on the legitimacy of the Hayes presidency, as Karabell writes:

> Lord Roscoe drew on a smorgasbord of tactics. He challenged the president's right to remove Arthur on the same grounds that had been used to impeach President

---

21: Hayes explained to William Dean Howells why he didn't want to be president again, saying of Congress: "They seemed to have no principles at all. They were like unruly cattle."

> Johnson ten years before, the Tenure of Office Act. Conkling claimed that Hayes had violated the cherished tradition of senatorial courtesy that demanded a president not take action against a political appointee unless the senators from that person's state concurred, and he marshaled the Senate to oppose Hayes. Almost as an afterthought, he also defended Chester Arthur as a man above rebuke.

Hayes held his ground until 1880, when he lacked support for the nomination, and Conkling managed to place the name of Chester Arthur on the ticket that James Garfield headed. Mostly he was there to do the bidding of Conkling, but Karabell also writes that Arthur had an inoffensive personality that grated on no one, which helped him rise through the political ranks. Karabell says this:

> While firmly identified with the Stalwarts, Arthur managed to remain friendly with just about everyone who mattered. His ego, unlike Conkling's and Blaine's, did not walk into a room before he did, and few people felt strongly enough about him to hate him. He was the Teflon candidate of his day, and in an era of dirty campaigning, he neither received nor threw much mud.

By 1880, Arthur was a professional politician, in all senses of the word professional, and he did not openly oppose Garfield while he was president. (Karabell writes: "His political career was not built on the passion of his ideals; it had been based on his loyalty, diligence, and effectiveness as an operator.") And keep in mind that the office of the vice presidency, in the nineteenth century, was thought to be a throwaway position, much less important than secretary of state, except when the president died in office.

Garfield did just that, in September 1881, and Arthur ascended to the presidency, without any principles for the job other than to check with Roscoe before making an appointment.

For reasons no one can explain, as Arthur grew on the job of president, he saw less need to curry favor with his overlord, Conkling, and he began to make a name for himself based on incremental changes. He undertook civil service reform, perhaps thinking it was to paper over the abuses of the era, but the Pendleton Act did bring order to an employment system that before functioned along the lines of draw poker. Regarding the surplus that Arthur inherited from Garfield, he favored lower tariff rates more than increased spending (the congressional solution), which was another difference that grew between the president and Congress.

It turned out that Arthur, the loyal party man when in the customs house, was less wedded to the machine when he became president. Karabell writes of this estrangement: "He had no pressing vision for the country that consumed his ambition, and the party that he had dedicated the past thirty years to was turning away from him. He had not inherited Conkling's mantle and could not even claim to lead the Stalwarts."

As a result, Arthur was a lonely man in the White House. Karabell continues: "In fact, Chester Alan Arthur may have the distinction of being the president who derived the least amount of pleasure from being president. And that is saying a lot, because in his five decades of life before that happened, he took about as much pleasure from life as any of us ever do." He would not have minded the nomination of his party in 1884, but he had few supporters among the rank and file, and lost to James G. Blaine at the convention.

Among the admirers that Arthur earned as president was Mark Twain, who said: "I am but one in 55,000,000; still, in the opinion of this one-fifty-five-millionth of the country's population, it would be hard to better President Arthur's administration. But don't decide till you hear from the rest."

Arthur lived only a year after his presidency, and much of that in failing health. He died in 1886, unloved by many, especially within his own party. Karabell, however, sums up his life well, writing: "In short, throughout his public life, Arthur conducted himself with honor at a time when politics was venal and petty."

Long Branch, New Jersey: Grantism Goes on Vacation

ALL TRIPS HAVE TO END, and mine did—this time, anyway—on the Jersey Shore. I had a late flight home to Europe, and beforehand I wanted to get in a bike ride with my friend Lee Harris. He and I had met some years before at a radio conference in Barcelona, and since then we have many times mixed together the pleasures that we get from biking and history around New York City. Often our friend Mark Gibson joins us for the rides, although on this day he did not.

Over the years on the bikes, Lee and I have explored the battles of Harlem Heights and Fort Lee, old railroad terminals in the South Bronx, Greek neighborhoods in Queens, the effects of Hurricane Sandy in Breezy Point, and where the ruins of Pennsylvania Station were dumped in the Meadowlands. As a radio news broadcaster, Lee has an encyclopedic knowledge of New York history, which over the years has allowed us to find where Mayor Ed Koch grew up in the Bronx and where the Yankees doped-star Alex Rodriguez was born (under the George Washington Bridge). Lee's tour around the Bayonne oil refineries is rich in the aromas of high test, and he knows all the radio transmitters on City Island.

For this Jersey Shore ride, Lee and I met at the Red Bank station of New Jersey Transit, which we often use to get back to Manhattan after a ride has ended in Newark or Edison, New Jersey.

Although for our rides we are dressed in Tour de France regalia, neither of us goes too fast, and the tempo of the excursions is like that of guys playing golf—there are some serious moments, but mostly banter and chatter.

On this ride, we started toward the shore on some back roads, cutting across inlets around Monmouth Park Racetrack, until we got to Broadway, where Lee started hunting for a church that, he claimed, had a stained glass window of Ulysses S. Grant. We circled around several churches along the rundown avenue until we found St. Luke's United Methodist Church and, on the front of the church, a stained glass image of the general.

In the depiction, General Grant has assumed the role of St. Luke (James Garfield would understand) and the angel Gabriel is descending to crown him with a laurel wreath, the Roman symbol of war. We both decided it was possible that Grant had used this church for devotional services during the time the Jersey Shore was his summer retreat (between 1869 and 1877, exactly when he was president). However, it looked too modern for that era, and I always had read that Grant (while nominally a Methodist) had not spent too many Sundays on his knees. As well, he was friends with Mark Twain, who liked to say that "man is kind enough when he is not excited by religion."

The one thing certain about our bike rides is that both of us are prone to digressions, of either a conversational or cycling kind. Here in the parking lot of Our Savior of St. Ulysses Victory Church, I delivered a Sunday homily on whether Grant had written his own memoirs. (I think he did write them.) The speculation comes up often that Mark Twain actually wrote them, which accounts for the excellence of the writing. For a while I had believed in such superstition myself, until I roused myself from sloth and ignorance and bought a copy of Mark Perry's *Twain and Grant: The Story of an American Friendship*, which makes it clear that the general did his own writing.

Before the trip, I had finished reading the book, which allowed me to hold forth with some confidence in my parking lot sermon.[22] Although the book has aspects of parallel biographies—one each of Twain and Grant—Perry does write at length about the improbable friendship between the voluble Twain (and what his family called "Sammy's long talk") and the taciturn Grant (whose idea of a full conversation was to whittle a stick in front of a campfire and brood).

Perry makes the point that both were self-made men from the West who grew up near great rivers. (The Ohio is eight miles from Georgetown.) They met briefly in 1866 just after the war, when Twain, a newspaperman, shook Grant's hand, although they did not speak.

During Grant's first time as president, Twain—by then the celebrated author of *The Innocents Abroad*—was brought to meet him in the White House, and all he could muster was the blushing sentence, "Mr. President, I am embarrassed. Are you?" Ten years passed before they met again, as speakers on the same platform in Chicago. This time, they were again introduced to each other as if they were strangers, which in effect they were, although Grant took Twain by the hand and said, "I am not embarrassed. Are you?"

22: Sometimes on our rides, facts are allowed to slide, as happened when we found the house in Hopewell, New Jersey, where the Lindbergh baby was kidnapped, and we charged Bruno Hauptmann with the crime, when a later reading of the case makes him only guilty of hiding the ransom money in his floorboards. The real kidnappers had died or vanished.

By the 1880s, Perry writes, "Twain was 'a Grant-intoxicated man,' to be sure, but he was now also much more: He was a close confidant and admirer, a moral support, and a man whom Grant himself admired." Grant biographer Jean Edward Smith tells the story of Grant, in need of money, as always, consulting Twain on the terms of a book contract he was offered. Smith writes:

> The general read the Century contract aloud to him. "I didn't know whether to laugh or cry," Clemens wrote later. The magazine was offering Grant the same royalty "which they would have offered to any unknown Comanche Indian whose book they thought might sell 3,000 or 4,000 copies."

Instead of taking the manuscript in hand, Twain offered his services at the general's publisher, a business he knew well, and the collaboration was a success, with Grant earning some $400,000 for his family with the book, which was published after his death.

Perry makes it clear that Twain only saw Grant here and there when Grant was writing his memoirs, and certainly did not spend enough time with him to rewrite any drafts. Besides, Grant's style was clear and effective, and worked well for a military account.

Anyone who has read Twain's *Autobiography* and read Grant's *Personal Memoirs* knows, instinctively, that they do not share the same author. Grant writes in simple, declarative sentences, almost like Hemingway. ("I have always regretted that the last assault at Cold Harbor was ever made.") Twain's sentences, by contrast, build toward a punch line. ("The oil was not discovered until about 1895.

I wish I owned a couple of acres of the land now, in which case I would not be writing autobiographies for a living.")

My copies of *Personal Memoirs* came from my wife's grandfather. They are all that I have from his estate, and few gifts please me more. I read the two volumes in spring 1979, when I was home from work with a weeklong flu. At the time, I had only been to a few Civil War battlefields—to Gettysburg during college, and to Antietam with the young Earl McElfresh. So much of Grant's *Memoirs*—about the Mexican War, Vicksburg, and Chattanooga—was lost on me. I read the books as I would after-action reports, but did not think then, nor do I now, that they compare favorably with Caesar's *Commentaries* or Tolstoy's *War and Peace*. Nor does *Personal Memoirs* get close to Grant's political maneuverings under Andrew Johnson or during his own presidency. Think of watching *Romeo and Juliet* without the balcony scene.

Perry disagrees with my assessment (which, by the way, is the word Chester Arthur used to describe political contributions). He believes Grant has written the great American history, saying:

> If Twain, as Hemingway supposes, wrote the quintessential American novel, then Grant, his friend, wrote the single most important work of nonfiction in our literature: It ranks with *Walden* as a symbol of the American character. Grant's book is not simply a profound narrative written with "dynamic force"; it is, as Twain rightly described it, "a literary masterpiece." Grant attempted to tell *our* story to *us*—and he succeeded.

To me that's a little rich (the literary equivalent of an angel bringing down a laurel wreath to Grant's desk), but I did like Perry's analysis that Twain's friendship with Grant, in the mid-1880s, allowed Twain to finish *Huckleberry Finn* and to understand that it was a river book about freedom.

Perry describes Twain's writing at the time this way:

> Mark Twain wrote sixteen chapters of *Adventures of Huckleberry Finn* during the summer of 1876, and then he stopped. . . . At the end of August, Twain finished writing the end of chapter 16, looked it over for a time, then wrapped it up and put it away. He returned to it only in 1884, when, in the midst of his friendship with Ulysses S. Grant, he finally realized what *Huck Finn* was really all about.

Although it sounds a little like literary criticism on the greatness of Mark Twain (or the book Tom Leonard gave me, *Huck Finn Among the Critics*), I do take Perry's point that in the friendship between Grant and Twain, the Mississippi River was part of their bond, and maybe Twain needed the proximity to Grant to return to the Study at Quarry Farm and finish the novel. Perry writes:

> Clearing the Mississippi of rebels and Grant's capture of Vicksburg had been a key to the Union victory. It occurred to Twain that the Mississippi had served as much as a highway of freedom for Union troops as it had for the young Samuel Clemens. . . . That Grant looked at the Mississippi in the same way Huck did—and that Sam Clemens and Jim did—is so true as to be clichéd, but there are a number of remarkable similarities between Grant's descent of the Mississippi to capture Vicksburg and Huck's descent of the river to free Jim.
>
> Grant's journey was intended to free the slaves, Huck's to free *a* slave.

Asbury Park: The Boss on the Beach

From the town of Long Branch, we cut down to Asbury Park (summer home of Boss Springsteen and the E Street Band), to find the small house on Bond Street where Warren Harding's lawyers had stashed Nan Britton and her love child. Lee knew the story from the TV series *Boardwalk Empire,* while I had the version from *The Shadow of Blooming Grove.* Nevertheless, the accounts matched.

Nan Britton grew up in Marion, not far from the Harding's house, and as a young schoolgirl, she had plastered her walls with Harding posters and campaign literature, as though he were a rock star. As a child, she would watch him pass on the sidewalks, and when in her late teens, she wrote to the senator, asking him for help in finding a job.

Harding did remember Nan Britton and her infatuation, and he found her both a job as a secretary in a friend's company and one as his mistress. (By then, he was winding down with Carrie Philips, although he had other distractions around Washington.) In the season of his presidential nomination and election, he was often meeting Britton in the course of his travels, sending her money for train tickets, and checking them into hotels as husband and wife. At one hotel in Chicago, according to Francis Russell, "the sardonic desk clerk remarked under his breath that if Harding could prove he was really married to the young lady, he could have the room for nothing!" Harding even had a somewhat public rendezvous with Britton just after he received the Republican nomination, if Russell is to be believed. (In our age of social media, it's hard to imagine a newly minted married candidate checking in to a convention hotel with someone other than his or her spouse.)

When Britton became pregnant before the election, Harding's handlers packed her off first to the Hotel Monmouth (assuming it to be long gone, we didn't look for it on our ride) and then to the drab house on Bond Street. According to Britton, Harding never saw his child, although he did pay her money until he died, after which the Harding family denied the paternity allegation. They said Harding was sterile from mumps as a child, and pointed to his childless marriage with Florence. Maybe Grover Cleveland helped out with the defense?

In 1931 Britton even lost a libel case against an author who called her a "degenerate" and mocked her claims. That said, anyone who has seen a photograph of the young Elizabeth Ann Britton Harding Blaesing can see that she was a dead ringer for her presidential father.

Nan Britton died in 1991, in Oregon, never having salvaged her reputation, which was that of a self-confessed presidential paramour. Even the otherwise sympathetic Dorothy Parker, in reviewing Britton's book for the *New Yorker* in 1927, took sideswipes at the starstruck young woman's book, writing that "it is the story of the affair between Nan Britton and Warren Gamaliel Harding; Miss Britton takes you through the romance in a glass-bottomed boat, as it were." She goes on:

> Surely this story of so bare and shabby a love, of those meetings held in hotels recommended by taxi drivers, and, sometime after the man had been made President of

> the United States, of that tryst in a clothes closet, should be a pathetic thing. But so smug is Miss Britton's style, so sure of himself does she make Harding appear, that one can look upon this affair only as a comic, and a slightly horrid, matter. There was no wistfulness in either the practical young lady or her pompous lover.

In perhaps her greatest understatement, Britton wrote of her former lover: "Harding, as a juggler of irreconcilables, had always done his best not to face issues squarely."

Britton's daughter, Elizabeth Ann, died in 2005, never having known if she was related to the president. From her mother, she assumed she was, but avoided the limelight or perhaps the lowlight that attracted her mother. Only in 2015 was proof of paternity found, after DNA testing of Elizabeth Ann's descendants and Harding's. The Harding Home issued a press released that began: "Nan Britton, the woman who penned the controversial book, *The President's Daughter,* in 1927, has been vindicated." Too bad, by then, *Boardwalk Empire* was off the air.

Elberon: Seven Presidents on Bended Knee

Our Jersey Shore ride ended in Long Branch, first, at a church in the Elberon neighborhood called the Church of the Seven Presidents, and then on the boardwalk overlooking the Atlantic Ocean.

The chapel in Elberon (not St. Luke's back in town) is where the vacationing presidents went to church, and in all, seven presidents—Ulysses S. Grant, Rutherford B. Hayes, James Garfield, Chester Arthur, Benjamin Harrison, William McKinley, and Woodrow Wilson—worshipped here.

The chapel has been undergoing renovations for the past ten years, since falling into disrepair, and we saw the new roof and other improvements that will allow the church to reopen as a presidential museum. Near the church, we found the marker that shows the spot on which James Garfield died. A volunteer connected with the Elberon chapel said that when his train brought the dying president to the seashore in late summer 1881, residents pitched in to help lay track from the nearby Long Branch station to the cottage where Garfield would try to recover. They didn't want him suffering any more than he had since July.

Why were all these presidents in Long Branch, which today looks like many such towns along the Jersey Shore? I think credit belongs to Mary Todd Lincoln, who was happy to get away from catty Washington, DC. She never fit in with the local society ("she tried too hard" is how many describe the situation). To get away from the nasty gossip, Mrs. Lincoln would go shopping in New York (which scandalized her neighbors and had Abe regretting the bills) and come down to Long Branch for the sea air.

Lincoln himself never came here—his idea of a vacation was a cottage on the grounds of the Soldiers' Home in Washington, DC. But in 1869 Grant did, proclaiming it the summer capital of the United States. And as Grant went, so went most of his successors, except Cleveland and Teddy Roosevelt.

Mark Perry has this passage about Long Branch in *Twain and Grant*:

> Long Branch was popular, but Grant made it famous. (Other presidents followed his example: President Rutherford B. Hayes spent nearly every summer at Long Branch, President James A. Garfield died of his wounds there (in 1881), and, later, Presidents Benjamin Harrison and William McKinley were often seen riding the Long Branch streetcar to the beach. But it was Ulysses and Julia Grant who first gave Long Branch its national reputation.

Not surprisingly, the summer tradition ended when Warren Harding became president, perhaps because Nan Britton's Asbury Park is next door. Clearly his admiration for Grant and McKinley had its limits.

On the boardwalk, just north of the Elberon community, Lee and I found the small semicircle of presidential markers that face the beach and the ocean. Out of season, the presidential strip of the boardwalk has a deserted feel. Garfield is the only one in the group with a statue. (He looks like a top-coated lifeguard in bronze.) The rest just get markers, which note briefly where they stayed here. For example,

Grant "vacationed for 12 years at 991 Ocean Avenue which was known as "The Summer Capitol." Hayes stayed at the Elberon Hotel, as did McKinley. Arthur had a cottage on Park Avenue. Only Wilson was away from the beach, preferring a mansion called Shadow Lawn on what is now the campus of Monmouth University. Much of the 1916 presidential reelection campaign ("He kept us out of war") was run from Long Branch, where in 1916 for the first time Wilson brought his newlywed bride, Edith Bolling Galt, whom he had married in December 1915 (the first Mrs. Wilson died in August 1914).[23]

23: Theirs was a whirlwind courtship in 1915, such that a popular joke in Washington that year became: Q: What did Mrs. Galt do when President Wilson proposed to her? A: She fell out of bed. Then in Washington, and not fans of the Wilsons, the Hardings were known to enjoy this story.

Homeward Bound

LEAVING THE BOARDWALK, we biked back to Red Bank, ate a sandwich from a nearby deli, and went our separate ways—Lee to Manhattan, and me, after picking up my bags, home to Europe.

At the airport, I had to pay a fee for extra luggage, such was the pile of papers, maps, and books that I wanted to bring back. I didn't have much in the way of souvenirs—of the physical kind, anyway. I might have liked a bust of Mark Twain or Adlai Stevenson, but bicycles don't lend themselves to souvenir hunting, so I had to make do with my pictures, which, as I looked back through them, seemed weighted toward Grantism.

Like any traveler, I left with some regrets—especially that I had missed the inside of the houses that belonged to Ernest Hemingway, Eugene Debs, and Ernie Pyle. I felt silly that I had not given myself more time in St. Louis and gone to see Grant's Hardscrabble Farm. In Indianapolis, I could have done a better job, had it not been dark and close to midnight, exploring the neighborhood where Robert Kennedy gave his eulogy for the slain Martin Luther King Jr. And I was still angry that Amtrak had backed up my plans in Buffalo to take stock of Fillmoreism.

Left in Buffalo with more time, I would have found some better books about Grover Cleveland or maybe seen the fireplace from the Twain house that is on display at the Buffalo Public Library. Finally, I would not have taken the bus to Newburgh but the train to Utica to see Roscoe Conkling's house, even though it is little more than a shell. Conkling is a common denominator in many of the lives I had crossed, and an unpleasant one at that. Karabell has this sentence: "Former President Hayes, in an interview with the *New York Herald*, said that Conkling was 'a monomaniac on the subject of his own importance.'" Such a man should have been worth a detour.

Normally on a trip such as this one, I would have ended up at the Princeton house of my parents, where over a week's visit, my father would have grilled me about everything I saw. We would have had many conversations long into the night about Garfield's performance at Chickamauga, Lincoln's debate in Quincy, his friend Bob Koch's grave in Barrington, the poor condition of the Central Terminal in Buffalo, or what I had learned about Dana, Indiana, Ernie Pyle, and the battle of Okinawa. He liked it when my travel stories had the details of a military debriefing, although one laced with humor.

But my parents had been dead for several years when I took the Poughkeepsie train into Grand Central Terminal or rode on my bike along the Jersey Shore. So I missed having them as a captive audience for my stories about the Cleveland waterfront ("unchanged since 1965") or St. Louis, where I went with my father on the train from Cincinnati in summer 1962 ("no, Dad, I am not sure exactly where Grant was selling his firewood"). But I do think they were connected to the story.

Maybe like Dreiser on the road to Indiana or Twain back along the Mississippi, I, too, had been looking for home? I had liked Twain's phrase about his travels that he "went home to dream and was not disappointed." But none of these travels had, directly, involved going home. I had not been to Sands Point, on Long Island, or Princeton, or any of the schools I had attended growing up. Instead, the closest that I got to home were the memories of my parents and sisters that I stirred on roads that, earlier in life, we had traveled together.

Growing up, I had been often to the Midwest with my father, and on the family summer cruise around the Great Lakes, we had seen Buffalo and Cleveland. So while this time I had come close to rekindling some home fires—spending time with Rob Koch in Chicago or riding in the darkness for the train in Cleveland—maybe I had never set them alight? At least, to use Lincoln's phrase, I had stretched the mystic chords of memory in the right direction, which lessened—as he said at the Great Western depot in Springfield—the "feeling of sadness at this parting."

About the Author

Matthew Stevenson was born in New York City and grew up on Long Island, attending Buckley Country Day School and Friends Academy. His university degrees are from Bucknell and Columbia universities, and he spent a year abroad with the Institute of European Studies in London and Vienna. He moved to Geneva, Switzerland, in 1991. He is a contributing editor to *Harper's Magazine* and has worked professionally in finance and investing. His essays and reporting have been published in many magazines, including, most recently, in *CounterPunch*. He is married to Constance Fogler, and they have four children: Helen, Laura, Henry, and Charles; and a grandson, Raymond Stevenson.

matthewstevenson@sunrise.ch
www.odysseusbooks.com
www.matthewstevenson.com